PRAISE FOR *THE BOY KINGS OF TEXAS*

"With *The Boy Kings of Texas*, a new and important truth about those Rio Grande Valley border towns like Brownsville and McAllen has finally emerged, one that takes into account the brainy boys of the barrio who read Cyrano de Bergerac between waiting tables at the Olive Garden, and play hooky at the Holiday Inn in order to discuss foreign films. Sure, there have always been stories about smart kids who want to leave town or risk going nowhere in life. In the Valley, where there is also a high chance of succumbing to border violence, Martinez unveils the lives of smart kids who feel they need to leave town or else simply die of boredom."

—*DALLAS NEWS*

"*The Boy Kings of Texas* is a spirited confession in the tradition of smart, self-deprecating comedies about young manhood like Robert Graves's *Good-Bye to All That* and early Philip Roth. Martinez weaves artful comic asides with anecdotes about poverty so crushing that it leads to the death of his friends."

—*TEXAS OBSERVER*

"This compelling, often heartwarming book explores how Martinez and his family tried to find their place in Brownsville.... *The Boy Kings of Texas* alternates between serious, often violent stories, such as the uncle who beats up Martinez in a cocaine-fueled rage, and humorous stories showing his family's softer, loving side. Often, the most moving chapters combine humor with a dark undertone. For example, Martinez writes about how his sisters dealt with their own feelings of inferiority by creating two blonde, Anglo alter-egos."

—*SAN ANTONIO EXPRESS-NEWS*

"There is no easy resolution to this personal journey told through a series of anecdotes that range from hilarious to heartbreaking. Martinez simply splays out the different chapters of his life with a raw honesty that dispels the myth of the big happy Hispanic family and critiques the codes of machismo that lead to reckless choices. An incredibly engaging read and full of colorful characters that keep the writing vibrant...."

—*EL PASO TIMES*

"Martinez's story is heartrending and uncomfortable, but he maintains a surprising sense of humor that keeps his reader cringing and rooting for him. A starkly honest memoir of growing up on the Texas-Mexican border in the 1970s and '80s, with a wry twist."

—*SHELF AWARENESS*

"...offers experiences that readers will find informative and emotionally engaging."

—*ALA BOOKLIST*

My Heart Is a Drunken Compass

BY THE SAME AUTHOR

The Boy Kings of Texas

My Heart Is a Drunken Compass

A Memoir

Domingo Martinez

LYONS PRESS
Guilford, Connecticut
Helena, Montana
An imprint of Rowman & Littlefield

Lyons Press is an imprint of Rowman & Littlefield

Distributed by NATIONAL BOOK NETWORK

Copyright © 2014 by Domingo Martinez

British Library Cataloguing-in-Publication Information available

Library of Congress Cataloging-in-Publication Data available

ISBN 978-1-4930-0140-8 (hardcover)

∞™ The paper used in this publication meets the minimum requirements of American National Standard for Information Sciences—Permanence of Paper for Printed Library Materials, ANSI/ NISO Z39.48-1992.

This book is a combination of both memoir and creative nonfiction where the privacy of some of the characters needed protecting. It reflects the author's recollections of his experiences over several years; certain names, locations, and identifying characteristics have been changed or modified to remain as true to the form as possible while telling the larger story within the approximation of memory. Dialogue has been re-created from memory and, in some cases, has been compressed to convey the substance of what was said or what occurred through what was remembered.

For Sarah, with love everlasting

Even in our sleep, pain that cannot forget, falls drop by drop upon the heart, and in our own despite, against our will, comes wisdom to us by the awful grace of God.

—Aeschylus, *Agamemnon*

In the middle of the journey of our life I found myself within a dark woods where the straight way was lost.

—Dante Alighieri, *Inferno*

CONTENTS

Prologue

I.

Sarah is holding me by the elbow as I'm trudging slowly to the busier part of my neighborhood, an intersection of Asian-fusion restaurants and the hangover hook-up bar that seems to be in constant operation. She's convinced me to wrap my neck in a scarf, put my coat over my decaying cashmere sweater, which I've been wearing for three days now, and encouraged me to leave my apartment for the first time in five days. I listen to Sarah, and do all this with a sense of catatonic disengagement.

It's the longest I've been away from the hospital. Well, the longest I've been away from the ninth floor at Harborview, where Steph is in a coma, sitting upright with a tiny silver spike sticking out of her forehead, an image of a medical unicorn, the spike measuring her cranial pressure. I've kept guard at her bedside and in the waiting room with her family for over three months now, sometimes defending her even against her family, as an intruder or interloper into their family's pain, because I am no longer Steph's intended, had no connection to her when she'd driven her Jeep over the side of an overpass except for "recent ex-boyfriend." And yet, I couldn't bring myself to leave her side, couldn't walk away just yet, not like this. But it was tearing me apart to stay.

I'd been in another hospital myself three days earlier, after ripping one of my arms to shreds in a psychotic break at 3:00 a.m., alone in my own bathroom. A combination of Xanax, some SSRI that had kept me awake for four days, and a steady intake of gin—gin to quiet the shouting in my head, gin to thicken my terror to a sludge, gin to drown out the crushing sense of guilt I felt the moment I awoke during those rare times I could actually get about twenty continuous minutes of sleep—gin, which turned the Xanax and the serotonin inhibitors into assassins, and I finally gave up, found an old-fashioned double-sided razor blade and went at my left wrist, working for the one deep cut that would end it, end all of this, in a bathtub, alone in darkest, wettest February, as I sucked down one last Pabst Blue Ribbon for courage, or self-pity.

It was Sarah who had found me at the emergency room that morning, told them she was my mother, and they let her through. Sarah is thirteen years older than me and should not be able to pass for my mother, but this is an emergency room in downtown Seattle in the middle of the night, so they're accustomed to odd family engagements, even the blatantly incestuous, as would have been our case.

"Can you do this?" she asks me now, as I'm stumbling along and beginning to breathe shallowly, quickly, in fear. More fear. People are going about their business, crossing the street against the light, drivers avoiding them and making abrupt turns, people meandering on an otherwise unexceptional February weekday, and my blood is pumping with cortisol, stress hormones, and anxiety, and I am feeling very much like I want to run again, and hide again, and get underground again, and pull the door shut behind me. Feeling that I don't belong here, and that they will all find that out at once, point at me and burn me out in a "scorched earth" policy, where the herd weeds out the weakest, the one who broke and gave up, and they all turn on that one, and offer him up for the survival of the whole.

"No," I say to Sarah. "I don't feel like I'm a part of this anymore." How do these people function, day to day? How do they step up onto a bus, ride a bike to work, shop for groceries when at any minute their foundation could be pulled out from under? They slip through life like people who have not experienced horror, move around like their closest loved one did not die horribly just a few days ago, like their children are not at the mercy of the closest maniac with a rifle and low self-esteem, like nature is not out to kill them and their families and they have many layers of protection between abject terror and their lattes.

"You feel 'other' to yourself," Sarah says, in the way that she has. Sarah can be both wholly sympathetic and the detached observer. I couldn't understand or trust this about her when we first started our twice-weekly walks around Greenlake, when we'd simply talk the whole length and blather on, like new mothers in the mother's ghetto that the three-mile park tends to be. It was a friendship like I had never before experienced. I'd met her at a time when Steph and I were having trouble, but there was no chemistry between Sarah and me, we told ourselves. I told myself.

We weren't age-appropriate; I didn't want to do that anymore. We'd both found the other incredibly interesting and talked ourselves into thinking it was only friendship. That was all.

Sarah was quoting a sentiment from Martin Heidegger, the German philosopher. She was a professor of philosophy at the Jesuit university here, in Seattle, and had become my one guiding star in this darkest night, an Archimedean point of truth, when all the craziness was swirling around it. She was the one thing I believed to be consistently right, and I'm not sure why, or why I was convinced of it. I needed someone to trust and she happened to be there, had been there a few times previously.

Sarah was also fond of repeating, "Everything changes in the instant," from Joan Didion's seminal work, *The Year of Magical Thinking*, which Didion wrote after she lost her husband and her daughter in the same year, and catalogued her recovery in a sort of autonomic function of writing. Everything had changed, for Steph and me, in the instant, and I was slow to understand how comprehensive that term *everything* really was. Sarah had purchased a copy of the book for me, a week after Steph's accident. I couldn't get past the first hundred pages, couldn't concentrate anymore, focus on words. I couldn't put three thoughts together. But Didion's pain had been akin to my pain: We had both suffered profoundly. Though Didion had not nicked at her soul, like I had. Didion had support, had people around her. Didion had not given up, acted out in desperation, decided she could take no more.

I did. And that's why Sarah found me that morning in the dark emergency unit, alone, sitting upright like Steph, with stitches in my wrist, a deadened feeling up through my left arm and into my heart, wondering how the hell I ended up there, with security guards standing outside my door.

II.

When they wake you, those early morning calls never really tell you they're about to change your life.

Cell phones have changed the late night phone call; it was once far more dramatic when your bedside telephone started clamoring for attention at 2:00 a.m. You were naturally alarmed, not simply because of the volume but because the decorum was different. Now, when your phone buzzes in the dead of night, it can be anything from an errant dial or a text message from someone who expects you to have your phone on silent, to your kid letting you know he or she will be late: Don't worry.

I've had two of these phone calls that changed my life.

"Flashbulb memories," they're called. What's interesting about both is that neither raised any particular alarm when I received them, when they made my cell phone glow blue in the dark of my bedroom. I was alone each time, the first at 4:25 a.m. on March 17, 2007, the night my younger brother, Derek, an ostensible student at the University of Texas at Austin, drank so much liquor he blacked out and collapsed backward, like a felled pine, and broke his fall with the back of his head.

The call came some hours later from Robert, my mother's second husband, his voice teeming with controlled hysteria as he drove my catatonic mother west from Houston at top speed. I began to comprehend, as I was coming awake, what he was telling me, as he yelled over the cell line as if he was declaring testimony in a courtroom, at 4:25 a.m. in Seattle, 6:25 a.m. in Texas.

"June, this is Robert," he said. "I'm calling for your mother, Velva. Derek had an accident in Austin. He's in the hospital there, and we're on our way now. I've called your sisters and Dan, and we're all going to meet at the hospital in Austin. He's still alive but they say it's serious and they want your mother there. He's going to have surgery in the next hour. That's all we know right now. We should be there in two hours."

I remember hearing his voice, him shouting over the sound of a stressed engine and calling me "June," my nickname within the family, and in my memory of this moment, I felt like I could hear the sound of the Texas wind roaring by, but that's likely false since there hasn't been an open automobile window in Texas since the late 1980s. But I do know that I didn't hear a word from my mother, who I imagined was in a collapsed bundle in the passenger seat, crying. I know my mother, and I know she was crying.

And so I didn't ask Robert anything. I didn't have a reaction, because what I was hearing was impossible.

It had never occurred to me that anyone in my family could die. Never. Or, not yet.

I know how that sounds, but until that moment, it was true. Certainly not the youngest, certainly not Derek. And it was that line, that tone in Robert's voice when he said, "He's still alive, but they say it's serious . . ." How that means so much more than what it says, even then.

I think my response to Robert was, "All right, call me when you know more." I shouted it over the cell phone, like tin cans attached with string over five states.

And then I was alone, in my apartment three thousand miles away, sitting on the edge of my bed, the light around me already changing and my mind going nova with the idea that I would never again speak to my lost little brother, who died without redemption.

III.

The second early morning phone call that changed my life came about two and a half years later, at 2:24 a.m. on a Saturday morning.

It's funny how you remember specifics: Your awareness opens up to twice its size to absorb detail when mortality is in the air. It was mid-December, 2009.

For this one, I was awake. I had developed a habit of playing fifteen or twenty minutes of Jim Dale reading one of the Harry Potter series every night before I went to sleep, and then also when I'd awaken during the night, which happened often, as I suffered from a severe case of apnea. Three minutes of Harry Potter and I'd be under with no problem, and it was helping me sleep. Better than anything over the counter.

I was awake for this call, though, with my iPhone in my hand as I was making my way back to bed after a groggy bathroom visit.

I'd become a fat man at this point, after I'd been dating and breaking up with a woman named Stephanie, who preferred "Steph," for over a year and had gained about twenty-five or thirty pounds, which made it hard to move around. Hence the apnea. That night, I'd had three slices of pizza and a six-pack of Miller Lite while watching a movie before I felt the food coma and went to bed, alone in my studio apartment near downtown Seattle.

Steph, as my . . . ex-girlfriend? Ex-fiancée? Girl I was having trouble with? She was busy, had been at work all night, as she was behind during her busiest time of year, and I was free to go to "zero." That's what I called it, when I had an evening free and I could spend it alone, doors and curtains closed, phone off, and I could idle watching films or documentaries or TV and have some beers and keep out all stimulation that would otherwise annoy me. We were, after all, child-free, and at this time, free of one another, while we figured out what we were going to do next, independent of one another.

And she was at work, safe: Even though we were split up, I was still concerned for her.

So it was a bit of a surprise that her father was calling me that morning, as I was setting the Jim Dale reading back to *Harry Potter and the Goblet of Fire*.

I remember smiling as I saw her father's name light up my iPhone, immediately concluding that he'd accidentally made what's affectionately called a "butt dial," or meant to ring up someone else at 5:24 out east, as Steph's family were Yankees, from New England. The sort of people who fought off the British way back.

"Hello, Harold," I said, upon answering. "What a pleasant surprise."

Harold and I were on good terms, in a sort of collusion that conspired around the idea that we both knew Steph was quite the handful. In a manner of speaking. When we met, or were around one another, Harold would give me looks on the sly when Steph had one of her "moments," like, "See? I told ya."

But this morning, I heard the panic in his voice as soon as he heard me answer my phone.

"Domingo, what the hell's going on?" he asked.

"Sorry?"

"I just had a call from the Washington State Highway Patrol. They said Steph was in an accident and she's downtown in a hospital."

My first response was that of betrayal, because this was an emergency, and Steph had never changed her emergency contact numbers. Meaning that she never trusted me enough to change her information. I made a mental note to bring this up, if we ever argued again about "trust."

My second response was, "What?" It was nearly 3:00 a.m.; what was she doing up that late?

"I'm not sure what you're saying here, Harold; I haven't heard anything . . ."

"The deputy said she's in . . . hold on a sec," and here, I heard Steph's mother shuffling papers and shouting to Harold, "Harborview Hospital," and this was where I came fully awake and frightened: Harborview is the shock trauma specialist on the West Coast.

This was really serious. Holy fuck.

I was dressed and waiting at the front desk, in the freezing cold, in less than thirty minutes.

Harborview Hospital is built into the side of First Hill, deep in the labyrinth of the downtown Seattle grid, possibly one of the only sections of the city that is laid out in right angles, a predicament endemic to most Pacific Northwest cities, due to all the damned nature.

There are lakes and hills and mountains to plan a city around, so logic took a hit with early urban planning. Harborview is one of the oldest hospitals in the city, and has been built upon with modern extensions added yearly like a half-hearted Lego project, byzantine. It takes a tour guide and the friendliness of the doctors and nurses who work there to guide you through the buildings, some of which are connected by an underground tunnel. It's possibly the most disorienting building I've ever seen, in the densest part of the city. But after this night, I would know it very well. Or rather, I was going to start knowing it very well.

***

The drive to Harborview that morning through the dark and empty streets felt ominous, with the radio off, felt like everything was about to change in an instant, and for the serious.

I drove my car straight to the front steps, parked right in the emergency zone, figuring no one would mind at 3:00 a.m.: I had no idea what I was doing, or where I was. A feeling of utter helplessness radiated down my limbs, and I'm sure, settled quite telegraphically on my features.

I parked the car and forced myself to stride purposefully to the front desk, careful not to betray that sense of powerlessness.

A homeless man sat in the chair opposite the one receptionist, stuttering out a perceived or fabricated ailment so he could spend the night indoors. Ten other homeless people waited behind him.

I gave him a full three minutes before I kept myself from physically lifting him out of the chair and shoving him aside, and when the receptionist could finally sense my mounting anxiety and eroding self-control, she acknowledged me and bade me forward, asked why I was there.

I elbowed the smelly little man to the side and started with what I knew—name, car accident, emergency call from the state patrol, her parents were back east . . . how big is this fucking hospital? How do you not keep track of the intake of people?

"Here she is," she said finally.

"She's headed to ICU on the ninth floor soon, but she's been kept in the emergency room."

"Why was she there so long? What's happened to her? No one's told me anything and the highway patrol called her parents, back east. They don't know anything, either," I said, in a panic.

"She was in some sort of single-vehicle accident," the receptionist replied. "There aren't any notes other than no one else was hurt, and that her car fell off an embankment. It says she was hypothermic because it took so long to cut her out of the vehicle. That's all it says here. You can see her in ICU in a little while. Just take the elevators to your right, down the hall. I'll call the social worker to meet with you and see if she can get any more information to her parents. Just calm down; it's going to be all right," she said.

So she's not dead, I thought to myself as I walked with mounting dread past all the freezing homeless people. *That's a start. And they're letting me see her, so that's probably a good sign, too.*

I started feeling something familiar and realized this was how I felt when Derek was in the hospital, that morning we found out he was in a coma. And I recognized that my mind once again started doing the same thing as it did then, praying but not praying, hoping but afraid to hope, bargaining and looking for clues, cues, or indications that things would be all right. Tea leaves, unintended meanings, divination—the mind becomes haruspicate in moments like these, and as the elevator door closed, I began to shake, a cold feeling carving its way up my spine from my center back, feeling like ginger ale bubbling up toward my medulla oblongata, on its heels the idea that I would never speak to Steph again, that she was no longer here, ferociously denying another idea that the conversation we had earlier that day would be the last time I ever spoke to her.

PART I

SONGS OF HIS PEOPLE

CHAPTER 1

The Oops! Baby

My parents had Derek when I was nearing fourteen years old, and he usurped my position of the youngest in my family, a station I was happy to see filled by someone else. Being "the baby" of a Mexican Catholic family was, to others, something to be venerated and enjoyed, like an office of leisure and grift, but I was always uncomfortable in it, felt diminished, suffocated.

Still today there remains speculation among my siblings that our parents had decided on the pregnancy in order to save a marriage crippled with rot, but I personally do not adhere to this conclusion because it would involve a degree of foresight and planning, stratagems that I knew neither parent to adequately possess, not at that time.

I'm still convinced Derek was an "Oops!" baby, but a welcomed one at that.

He was an adorable kid, and we all loved the shit out of him, both figuratively and literally, as everyone pitched in raising and caring for our fifth sibling, living in Brownsville, Texas, during the 1980s and '90s.

None of us really understood what we were doing to this poor boy, how we were affecting him, in his confusion of having a forum of seven parents, like he'd been raised in a hippie commune in Michigan. We all learned to feed him, change him, nurture him, coddle him when he cried, nurse his wounds when he fell, and surrounded him with the sort of love no individual one of us had ever experienced, growing up poor and stressed and in direct competition with four other siblings, all vying for the same resources and affections.

Certainly there were complications. In fact, one night, much later on in our lives, my older brother, Dan, was drunk and decided to tell me that when she first brought Derek home, Mom sat sentry by his crib side for the first few nights because she was concerned I would smother him as the envious, competitive sibling dislodged from my supposedly coveted position at the bottom of the totem, as "the baby." And because the old hens and men of the barrio thought that the position was something cherished, there was long-standing folklore and wisdoms about the potential for fratricide by the original youngest, an act almost biblical in its violence, culminating from envy and resentment, and this talk had frightened my mother.

More than hurt, I was disgusted and offended by this revelation when Dan finally confessed it to me, if it had been true. It beleaguered me that it could even be considered by my mother, that I'd somehow try to smother the new baby, and for *that* reason. How primal, animal, that response would have been, like a mother cat eating her kittens. Or Greek mythology, in the way the Titans ate their children, too.

"There's no way that happened," I said to Dan. I'd been drinking, too, but I was more clearheaded than my stupid older brother.

"Yes, it did! You ask her! Just go ahead and fuckin' ask her! She'll tell you, she was scared you were gonna kill him because you were the baby!" he yelled back.

Of course, I couldn't wait to ask her—and have her deny it.

Instead, when I was next able to gather both my mother and Dan in the same room and levy the charge, for a moment I caught a microexpression of shame and sadness cross her face, right before she vehemently denied the accusation. I wasn't sure which to believe—the betraying signal of guilt or the firm denial—and it confirmed for me, once more yet, that I would never be reconciled with this family, forever the outlier.

Dan had sense enough to be ashamed of what he'd said and then made some sort of awkward admonition, hid behind a Glomar response that neither confirmed nor denied his position in relaying that bit of information, and that toxic mix of shame sort of hung in the room for a few minutes after that, as uncomfortable family revelations tend to do.

That conversation has stayed with me all my days. Obviously.

Two of my sisters named our youngest brother, back in 1985. My sisters wielded a type of "will to power by fashion" over my mother, Velva, and she would do much of what they asked from her. Mom had been far too young when she married my father and started her family, and she had also felt isolated herself, during her adolescence, and as a mother found herself overly bonded to her daughters as they matured, as if they had all, in fact, been born as sisters in the same family.

So it wasn't exactly outrageous when the Mimis (as they liked to call themselves) came up with "Derek Allen," as another signal of their unrelenting and sublimated desire for assimilation and comprehensive need to shed every evidence of their indigenous Mexican origins, primarily by anglicizing the Christian name of the third generation; it wasn't entirely ridiculous or out of place that Margarita Martinez and Maria de los Angeles Martinez and Domingo Martinez had a brother named Derek Allen, in 1985, in Brownsville, Texas.

Last I heard, this was still 'Merica, buddy.

For a few years after Derek was born, we really enjoyed being a family. Things were good, it seemed. We were happy, and the photos from this time prove it. In fact, a photo of Derek at this time as a toddler holding an Easter bunny in his puffy little toddler hands is the only photo I carry with me, and when I dream of him, he's eternally this age, which is another indication of our idealization of the youngest brother.

There was this weird flicker of prosperity in my memory of this time, when everything seemed to be going right, and even Mom and Dad looked like they were going to cowboy through the tough times, like they always had before.

And yet, this is the point when all the older siblings struck out to make their fortunes, my sisters off to college and Dan and I moving west, to Seattle, and we left Derek and Mom alone in Brownsville, in that house on Oklahoma Avenue. Dad, meanwhile, was living the gypsy life of a long-distance trucker, and it was here that Mom had sprung her plan of independence, hit Dad with the divorce he never knew she had in her that would, in her later assessment of things, create a wound inside that perfect little boy that would never be healed or drowned out, not by all the drugs in Austin nor all the liquor in Texas.

While we were growing up in the '70s and '80s, my mother, Velva Jean, was a quiet, calculating—if entirely intimidated—force in her role as the mother to five children, born in a barrio system in South Texas. My father and she had married far too young—he was seventeen, freshly graduated, and had a big 1A target on his back for the draft, and Mom was sixteen, trying to escape a terrible life at home. They did as he knew and had a litter of children in a Mexican barrio on the Texas side of the Rio Grande, what his mother would have done, what was all around them at the time, and together they managed to graduate five kids through high school and into the state university system without ever having been to college themselves.

They suffered greatly, did terrible, questionable things to survive and keep the family from ruin, and Mom, for the most part, kept all the grim realities and harsh truths from my three older sisters, Sylvia, Marge, and Mary. My sisters were never exposed to Dad's ferocity and feral, male Mexican nature: all the inappropriate, oversexualized commentary he shared with me and Dan, the inexplicable anger that could go off with no warning, the whippings, the unpaid, long labor hours spent either idling in fields or doing horrific manual labor—my sisters endured none of this. My mother shielded them from that life, took them shopping, or at worst, had them doing regular, normal "girl" chores, like dishes and sorting laundry. Meanwhile, Dan and I were doing the sort of labor expected from convicts at medium-security prisons, or the illegal Mexican guys that hang out in front of Home Depot, hoping for ten dollars an hour, from age ten until we were in our late teens.

Velva Jean—again, strategically playing her long game—didn't take on this fight, didn't get between Dad and the damage he was doing to Dan and me, because she had her daughters, and this is how our family had been cleanly delineated: The girls were my mother's property and were safe, protected, guarded, and reassured. Dan and I were labor, treated like men as soon as we could drive, at age ten. Exposed, brutalized, used, and discarded, expected to continue the cycle as soon as we hit eighteen.

Mom had no choice but to accept this. But she had another strategy in mind, but I don't think she knew she had it in her until she started her education once again, and quietly, without any fuss, studied for and passed her GED one night, when no one was looking. From there, she began classes at the local community college and would, eventually, obtain a degree in business.

Dad, on the other hand, would give up on his local trucking business and begin that long-haul driving, and it was in that vacuum where the family really began showing the diaspora, the flight of the children—all of us headed north on our own adventures and progress—and Mom, keeping Derek as close as possible, was growing well beyond the control of her old-world obligations and Gramma's dominion. And Dad, now capable of misadventures much more to his liking, set loose upon the unsuspecting United States behind the large, overgrown wheel of an eighteen-wheeler and, staying away from home for three weeks out of every month, was content.

It was here that Velva created her chance for escape, filed for her freedom after twenty-five years and finally falling out of love with my father, who pushed it way too far, fell behind in his own development, and realized far too late that he had been married to a Titan all this time, who had been silently incubating like that Greek myth, eating some of her children so that others might spring from her forehead.

So when she asked for her divorce, taking eight-year-old Derek with her, it was interesting that her daughters, my sisters, out on their own paths, entirely successful and fulfilled as strong women in their own right, were thoroughly blindsided by Mom's decision, and were not shy about letting Velva know their displeasure.

There was a real sense of betrayal on both sides, primarily from my sisters, who had been kept from all of Mom and Dad's secrets growing up, and now, as adults, simply could not understand why Velva was leaving their father in his darkest, deepest time of need. And Dad played into this betrayal as well, offering up only a shrug of helplessness and bewildered innocence at Velva's decision to break up the family and rob Derek of growing up in the same stable, structured environment that the rest of us had supposedly experienced.

Mom bought this line of guilt wholesale and believed it thoroughly, felt despicable every time she'd come home to find Derek playing video games, miserably ensconced in his "urban" isolation away from Dad and Gramma, in a shitty two-bedroom apartment in a bad Brownsville neighborhood where he was exposed to an entirely different Brownsville than Dan and I had witnessed growing up, but never participated in. She wanted to keep Derek safely tucked away in his prelapsarian bliss.

Brownsville was very different, without the dirt of the farmyards under your feet.

CHAPTER 2

Mom Leaves Derek

As an outsider from my perch three thousand miles away, watching my mother's development during this period was fascinating, as if she was rooted temporally in both the shared timey-wimey, wibbly-wobbly fabric of time and space as the rest of us but also exploding forward in growth, so that every year she spent in school and working for herself after her divorce, it was also about five more years of experience for her, lurching forward through all her growth stages. She was like Doctor Who.

Her biggest sacrifice in this hyperdriven development was Derek, as the youngest kid still dependent upon her spare time and affection, both of which were now limited resources that he had to share with her ambitions and her social life. His standard of living had become destabilized, and he had become listless, bored, drawn to the dangerous, which, in Brownsville, Texas, can become incredibly dangerous incredibly quick.

Dad tried to keep involved with Derek, would pick him up when he was in town so Derek could spend time with him and Gramma, who was suddenly feeling lonely and left behind in that empty spread out on Oklahoma Avenue, where once lived her son's huge sprawling family. Gramma was like Moses, who brought his people to the Promised Land, but could not, himself, enter.

Dad went through a tremendous heartbreak when my mother left him, and he decided also to quit drinking, to get sober after thirty years of unabashed debauchery. In one of the most impressive displays of self-control, and one that I would never have previously imagined my father capable of, when he made the decision to get sober, he never looked back, never touched another drop, never relapsed, not even once.

And he'd spend days crying, missing Velva.

Years later, he would tell me about his sobriety and those first few months when Mom left him, left the house on Oklahoma empty, and he would spend his days at Gramma's house instead, crying in her bedroom, only to emerge and find Gramma standing there, looking at him in disgust, and she actually laughed at him, once, for being so weak.

It was my Uncle Richard who humiliated her into being a mother after she had laughed at Dad, and he had growled at Gramma and then enfolded my father in a stepbrotherly embrace, metabolizing his hurt at losing the family, like Richard had also experienced, some years before.

Dad told me these stories a few years later, things he had shared only in AA meetings, thinking his family wouldn't understand.

He couldn't have been more wrong.

So when he had a chance to see Derek, he'd bring the little kid back to the house on Oklahoma, and he'd do with him things he never did with Dan and me. He would take Derek on a jog through the geometry of farmlands, buy him fancy slingshots and air rifles, take him exploring through the expanding city dump, which was now just a couple miles from our former house. Dad would drive Derek out to Boca Chica beach, just to look around, and then when no one was looking or around, he'd say, "Let's go in," strip down to his Y-fronts and jump in the lukewarm beach, spend the afternoon swimming on the Texas Gulf Coast, with no towels or swimwear or preparation. This is how Dad did things.

Derek loved this time spent with his father, as weird as it sounds. The trips to the dump especially. I would do this on my own, when I was in my late teens and feeling listless sometimes, and I can report that it's quite fascinating being out there, like a postapocalyptic landscape of industrial abstraction. Once, I saw a huge unloaded field of doll heads, as far as the eye could see, every size and shape and hair color. I still have nightmares from that.

But back to Derek and Dad. Derek told me this story about one of their trips to the dump, and his new shiny slingshot. Out of nowhere, he said, this big fuckoff spider came out from under something and ran right at Dad.

"About the size of your hand," he told me. "Big and black and brown, just shoots out from under, like, a shoe, right at Dad, who screams and jumps and runs."

And not skipping a beat, Derek nailed the huge spider with his slingshot.

It was a wolf spider, we found out later, after a brief Internet search. He said he never felt more proud of himself after the way Dad was praising him and hugging him, saying, "Not even June was that good a shot!" which kind of pissed me off, since I was like Annie fucking Oakley when I was a kid, but I'll give him that.

When he wasn't with Dad back at the place on Oklahoma, it was a much harder time. It was no way for him to spend his adolescence, living with a single mother who wanted now what she had missed out on then, and she made a heartrending decision to have Derek live with our sister Mary and her husband, Mark, in Corpus Christi, and it was perhaps the best decision for everyone. Mare and Mark, in their incredible generosity, gave Derek the structure and home environment he was lacking throughout elementary school and into middle school, and they became a fantastically tight unit, with my mom's diametric gravities pulling her in opposite directions, leaving her with her heartbreak in the middle.

———

This is really where Derek became estranged, in a way. He felt disjointed, like an intruder into Mare and Mark's life, though they were as gracious and loving as anyone could ever be. Mark, as a coach at a tough Corpus Christi high school that was predominantly black and Hispanic, brought Derek into his orbit and Derek became a good athlete, played football on Mark's team and then tried competitive weightlifting, and Mare saw to his academics.

His first day at possibly the roughest school in Corpus Christi, a place called West Oso, Derek made his entrance as Mare's little brother dressed in wire-rim glasses, braces, and a cardigan thrown over his shoulders with the cuffs rolled into a ball at his chest while he shambled in on a pair of crutches, an injury sustained on the football field. The getup was, of course, Mare's doing, as a former Mimi, and Derek only succeeded in avoiding getting the shit beaten out of him because that day, inside the first ten minutes of him being there, there was a race riot in the cafeteria. A Mexican kid had stabbed a black kid in the side of the head with a pencil, and both sides erupted in a huge, police-involved brawl.

Eventually, Derek figured out how to dress so that he didn't look like a pretentious prick and wasn't targeted, excelled under Mark's tutelage in the sports program, and sonofabitch if that kid didn't graduate as valedictorian of his school, when the time came, and had a full ride to the School of Journalism at the University of Texas at Austin, choosing to take a career path like his older brother, June.

We were all very proud of him, very impressed. He was fulfilling his role in the idealized version of our family, like we all wanted.

Mom, of course, remained involved and carried her guilt as best as she could as she rebooted her vitality and libido, finished her own eight-year degree plan and kept her job at JC Penney, which was the closest thing to a social life as she'd ever had, and after a while none of us begrudged her anything: If anyone deserved a second act, it was Mom.

But still, her guilt over losing Derek permeated everything, and it would leave a mark.

--- ~ ---

He was a good kid, back then. I'm sure the burden of being the youngest of a sprawling, motivated family in the ascendency was crushing, with every one of his older siblings holding a degree of authority over him and exercising it in the vacuum of a family in partial disorder as our lives became untidy. And this time with Mark and Mare, this time being the perfect kid, after being shunted from our family home to a shit Brownsville apartment and then off to his sister's home, it spun him tight, and tighter still, and when he made it to college in Austin on that full scholarship, Derek spun out of control. It frightened and disappointed all of us, and I'm sure himself.

Personally, I had lost my ability to connect with him. I failed my younger brother as an older brother, I know. I carry some of that same guilt Mom feels, but in a different color.

Because I never spent more than a couple of days with him, as I had made my decision to live on the West Coast, I had no idea who he was, as a person, and treated him simply as a category, as the younger brother.

When he was a boy, I'd make my yearly hajj back home to report in and feel superior, reconnect with Dan and sometimes with Derek. I'd come home and I'd bring him gifts, give him some of my best T-shirts and comics and CDs, and Derek would devour these things, build his identity around most of it like an internalized shrine.

I'd show up wearing a cool T-shirt, looking thin and urban, and he'd look up to me in a sort of hero worship that I did nothing to discourage. I gave him his first "Yoda" T-shirt, something I'd bought from a street vendor who'd hand-made the shirt. Another of an M. C. Escher drawing that was all the rage at the time. And I brought back lots of music. Lots and lots of music. The latter moved him so much that once, for show-and-tell in his second-grade class, Derek did a one-man improvisation of a Beastie Boys song that had the teacher leaping over her chair in order to slam off the tape player because of all the cursing, which befuddled Derek because he didn't know these were "bad" words. Mostly just slang, he thought, as he rapped about getting "a girlie on his jimmy."

But this all ended when he arrived at university. I mean, he still did the hero worship, but his idea of college and independence meant that he could do drugs and booze and sleep all day without having a single sibling or parent expect anything from him, and academics kept slipping down the ranks of his obligations and priorities, and he began to drown in his genetics and compulsions toward addiction, took to alcoholism like the Sheen family took to movies about the Vietnam War.

This is where we started to miss him.

—◦—

Ironically, I was fascinated by my younger brother, in a way, and continued to crave the sort of hero worship from him that I had once bestowed on Dan, even though Derek had become incapable of returning calls, was basically unfunctional as a human being. Living in Seattle, it became my role to seek out and find new and cool things that he would never find in Texas (after all, that was why I was living in Seattle, no?), and in order to keep myself firmly ensconced in the position of guru of good culture, I would still supply him with steady access to great music and recommendations and mailed gifts, discs, shirts, and videos.

Which, in turn, would eventually lend themselves as a commodity in that shitheap of a college town, because it gave Derek a sort of social elevation, and people would then seek him out, want to "party" with him (possibly the most distasteful distortion of a verb in common usage) and ply him with booze, marijuana, and hardcore drugs, and Derek's walls were never so willing to erode, so willing to come down, like the defenses of Jericho under a million chemical trumpet blasts.

⎯ ⎯

Mom's guilt contributed tremendously. She'll be the first to admit it, so it's no shock if she reads it here. She was permissive and enabling and heartbroken, hoping his better angels would somehow rise from the ashes of the bridges he insisted on burning. Every semester, he'd beg the family for money to pay fees and fines to the university or the rubbish fraternity he was homesteading, just the minimums and just enough to squeak back in, and he'd beg for a reprieve, beg for that second chance, just $200 from this person, $800 from that family member, please please please: "I just need the chance," he'd say. "Please."

He'd wear us down, make my brother-in-law crack his checkbook from fatigue and disgust, saying, "It's not about the money, Derek. It's just this lying...."

"Please; it'll be different this time."

"You know what you're going to do, if you go back."

"No, I promise I won't. I need to finish this."

"Fine."

Once the check was signed, he'd disappear again for three or four months, communicating exclusively by text message, usually something garbled and nonsensical sent at 3:00 a.m.

It was so painful, so terribly painful, that time.

And I vacillated between a profound desire to beat him and six of his closest friends senseless, and to hold him down and just hug the broken homunculus inside him, and have him cry it all out, give him some sense of dignity and self-love, enough to say, "I'm better than this. This isn't what I want for myself."

But he never made it to that stage, under the weight of his addictions.

Which is incredibly hypocritical for me to say, as I was languishing within the first stages of alcoholism my own self, but hey, I would tell myself, *I'm holding down a job and my own place to live, taking care of myself otherwise. Mostly.*

I mean, at least my weaknesses aren't public, I'd say, when I met myself in the mirror.

I'm just a happy-go-lucky scamp.

Then, of course, I'd meet my friend, Dough, short for Dougherty. Dough was also single and isolated, lived in the same neighborhood, had a hole in his heart he liked to drown out with booze sometimes as well. We'd terrorize our neighborhood bars for a weekend, making complete dicks out of ourselves after never-ending pitchers of stout beer and martinis, laughing like maniacs around conversations and jokes and this mania of the broken artist—we undiscovered geniuses holding down regular jobs—and so we rubbed alcohol into our wounded egos and drowned our delights in fried foods and pudgy barmaids who never threw us out, just overserved us because the tip would correspond accordingly, and, to be perfectly fair, we were actually rather entertaining. It was a rare evening indeed that we caused any real trouble for anyone, made anyone uncomfortable.

We were just loud, funny drunks.

Why couldn't Derek do this, instead? Continue the tradition?

What Derek was doing, well, Derek was into pure destruction, gripped firmly by ghosts of unreasonable rage.

It made me terrifically sad that he and I were left unbonded, even in our addictions.

⸺◦⸺

He was eventually ejected from school and became one of those pathetic hang-about people who live near a campus just for the parties and the hepatitis. I'm not sure where he was living, or who he was living with. There are no records for this time in his life, like his life had been blasted over by a sandstorm of drugs and booze.

Every few weeks, my mother would get a gripping sense of doom and drive from her home in Houston to Austin and spend an afternoon looking for him, a sort of scavenger hunt to find her youngest son. Some of his "friends" were actually good kids and would take pity on Mom because, even for their lifestyle, they saw how far Derek would push things.

Eventually, Mom would find him holed up in some shanty UT rat hole and shake him awake, then pour him into her car and take him to a grocery store, buy him food, find his clothes and few meager possessions—most of which had been bought for him by my other sister, Marge, and her husband—and by this time Derek would be alert, fed, and ready to get Mom back on the road so he could trade some of his food for beer. That was who he was at this time.

Completely without *vergüenza*, the Mexican Catholic depiction of pride and shame that forced oneself to have a sense of dignity enough to do better for oneself, for those who loved you, for your family. Derek, somehow, because he wasn't raised on that farm in that barrio like the rest of us, had been raised with no sense of *vergüenza*; that genome had never kicked in and developed, or at least remained dormant at this time, and it was killing my mother, and the rest of us.

My sisters saw and understood what was happening, but they pulled back and established boundaries because they were building their own families, had their own lives to live. We were all deeply saddened by Derek, but none of us really knew what to do. We spoke of interventions, of hospitalization and rehab, but none of it ever took shape: It cost money, and Mom's insurance, which was still covering him at twenty-two, would not cover that.

We felt helpless, and could do nothing but watch, as his demons wrapped him in shrouds and took him away from us.

Everyone tried to reach him. My father would also travel to Austin, try to find him, but Derek knew that as a sober man with little income, Dad would prove wearisome and Jesufied, try to talk to Derek about AA, and would get little from the interaction, so Derek managed to avoid him most times, which wounded my father greatly.

Dan tried, too, driving from San Antonio to Austin to find him sometimes, and he'd take Derek out to dinner, buy him a few beers and try to talk sense to him, but at some point Dan would call an end to the evening and either head home or stay at a hotel, and Derek would launch, once again, and disappear. This was when our club was disbanded, and Dan and I were estranged, so Dan was chasing after that same frequency of communion, needing the familiarity of his brothers' warmth, was as lonely as I was, but not ready to talk to me.

And I could never reach Derek, on the phone, from Seattle, could never get a returned text. I deleted his number out of anger and frustration so often I eventually had it committed to memory because I'd feel shitty a day or two after writing him off, and then ask Mom for it once more. It was her number, actually, her bill, since he was on her family plan, and Mom refused to cancel the line because it was the one method of communication that he used.

I wanted to grab him by the ears and head-butt him, bring him to Seattle, kick his awkward, large Hank Hill Texas ass and just . . . I don't know. Dealing with addicts is a wormhole to nowhere.

I wanted to yell at him, "Why can't you be a functional drunk like me and Dan? Hold down a job, be miserable like the rest of us and stop worrying Mom?? Jesus, Derek! You're making it a choice between you and her, and I *will* kick your ass, Derek! I *will* fucking do it, and I'm not talking in metaphor, motherfucker: I will beat the shit out of you and all your fucking friends!" I actually did say that to him, and often. It's probably why he didn't like talking to me. But he always accepted my care packages, the swine.

———

In the end, it was following my lead that nearly killed him.

He did, finally, get a job, working as a stock boy at the Gap, or Old Navy. Either which.

He worked a little over two weeks, through the end of a February and into a March, and when he received his first paycheck, he took that money and went out with his friends—it was the most money he'd had in a very long time—and he drank far too many Bombay Sapphire martinis, which was my drink of choice at this time, but he drank them like beer, one right after the other to the point where he became a walking corpse, his cognitive processes drowned and his eyes gone out, and as he stood in a road by a bar in Austin, Texas, in some side neighborhood street during that dreadful SXSW convention, Derek blacked out while standing straight up, right in front of his Hungarian friend named Mogyorodi, and he fell backward, like an evergreen, and he cracked his skull on the sidewalk, his body finally giving up on his bad choices and desire for oblivion, drawn heavily to a conclusion.

And he broke every one of our hearts, finally.

CHAPTER 3

Drinking with Dad

It's in the moments that slip quietly by when we affect those closest to us most, moments unnoticed and unintended, when you think no one is looking: We leave the deepest marks when we least mean it.

Dan and I left a serious indentation on our youngest brother, Derek, without noticing or caring when we were growing up with him, in the way our father left the mark of Cain on both Dan and me when Dad was fully cognizant of what he was doing, what we were seeing, as his boys under his care.

More than common, it was expected for the men who worked for my father to start their drinking of the smaller, seven-ounce Budweiser pony bottles around 10:00 a.m., either at the sandpit or in the driveway where much of Dad's broken-down trucking equipment was parked throughout the '80s. Nothing was said to discourage it, and if the women disapproved, they weren't allowed to voice their disapproval or send covert glowers in the direction of any of the men, regardless of their status, because except for my Gramma, who ran the place, women weren't allowed near the trucking equipment or near the men, unless they were bringing food. Work was a boy's club, though the work just got in the way of the drinking.

But even among men, there were limits. Once in a while, someone would make a comment if someone started *too* early, allowed the beer to interfere with basic functionality, saying that so-and-so had awoken that morning "*con la mano hinchada,*" meaning "his hand was already swollen, holding a beer bottle."

He's a hard one for the drink, that one.

The men drank slowly all day so that it wouldn't interfere too badly with their driving of the large, barely operating 1950s- and '60s-era GMC and Chevrolet dump trucks, with squishy brakes and suspect steering that argued rather than answered. And yet somehow they managed to get through my entire childhood without murdering a single person or family in a vehicular collision. In fact, the only driver who very nearly killed a pedestrian was actually me, driving an eighteen-wheeler when I was about fifteen. And, for the record, perfectly sober. Might get to that story later.

Through their twenties and thirties, my father's neighbors and cousins drank with no sense of mortality or health or consequences, destroying kidney and family both while sharing their bewilderment over breakfast ponies, wondering why a wife had packed up the kids and vacated, or why they felt so depleted and weak so often. It wasn't denial: It was a deep, sincere cultural inability to understand the direct connection between alcoholism and their ongoing health and psychological issues. Beer, simply put, was the answer to all of life's problems; how could it ever be the source?

Their commitment and faith in alcohol was as absolute and religious as the Peruvian tribes have in the coca leaf: It's manna, it's relief, it's life sustaining and ego enhancing, though admittedly, for some reason it can also be a bit illegal.

And if it was so much good, how on earth could it be at all bad?

Once, I remember watching a conversation between my father and one of his closer cousins, Raul Medrano. Raul was a small, rail-thin man with dark, nearly red skin, made much more amber by his flushed face and his body's instant insulin reaction to alcohol, as the first and sometimes only thing he put down his throat every morning.

"*Mira, primo!*" he claimed in exasperation and alarm, as he spat out a dry, cottony spume, seemingly devoid of any moisture. "*Mira!*"

He'd eaten nothing for days and lived on Budweiser while he worked with Dad, but he'd become so broken down from alcoholism, his body had bloomed in huge, painful boils, and the minute he'd have his first beer, his liver would protest violently and he'd turn a hot crimson color with all the arteries in his neck and face dilating. He looked tortured that morning as he stood swaying in the glaring, primordial South Texas sun, standing there looking bewildered and uncertain as to what was happening to him, and no one had the presence of mind to say, "Jesus Christ, man, drink a glass of water and get some help with your drinking."

Instead, Dad would volunteer to drive him home, and Raul would smile around a huge lump in his cheek that should not have been there, and say, "No, no, that's fine. I can walk," and I'd watch as he stumbled down the dirt road toward his house a couple miles away in that blazing heat, and wonder at their inability to make the connection between the beer and the level of disease. He died in his mid-forties, left a widow and two boys with nothing but hospital bills, and that would have been my father's fate as well, if my mother had not left him.

Still, that didn't keep Dan and me from glorifying the whole culture of drink, in the world of men and their secret clubs.

We were boys constantly surrounded by drinking men and their war stories, watching them relish that delicious first beer as they drove out of the sandpit, overloaded with their first haul of the day and stopping at Mike's Korner Store at the crossroads of Boca Chica and Indiana, or Route 511, to gas up on the company credit line: an account kept in a notebook and verified by invoking my father's name. They'd buy that first eight-pack of ponies and a couple of bags of the dried Mexican shrimp with the lemon juice packet that I positively lived on at that time of my life, except I'd follow them down with tamarind-flavored soda instead of Budweiser.

It was mystical, religious, that first cold beer of the morning, for my father and his people. It changed everything, made them better drivers and rewrote their stories as womankillers, long-shanked fighters, and respected *machers* of these rural country roads.

And the more you drank, the more you could hold your beer, the tougher you were.

More macho.

And Dan and I wanted to be macho: We were told it was the most important thing we could be, for a man. So we swam in that water, believed in the same contradictions.

Being born nearly a generation later, Derek didn't see much of this. The trucking business was long gone, and with it went the secret club for men that met mysteriously under derelict dump trucks or at the back of backhoes, standing around saying nothing and knocking back beers while avoiding responsibilities and family, or telling stories of conquests in winding, euphemistic Spanish so that younger ears could not track the particulars, specificities, and details.

What Derek did see was much of Dan and me as teenagers, awkward and clumsy and lost in various transitions of youth; he saw Dan transform from an angry, puffy teenager to a cockstrong private in the army at seventeen, taking an early release from school in order to get the hell away from Dad as soon as he could. Dan played football and then followed it with a devotional fervor from season to season on television, taught Derek how to talk to other men of the meaningless, manufactured importance of franchises, following an athlete's career like men at betting tracks follow horses. And later on, when Dan moved in with my mother and Derek, after the divorce, it was Derek's job at eight years old to keep Dan's supply of beer replenished in his own swollen hand so that Dan didn't have to leave the couch or miss a single frame of football, and Derek would leap up and run to the refrigerator to keep Dan supplied. Later on, he began popping the beer bottles open himself, covertly, inside the refrigerator door, and he'd take a quick gulp before he delivered one to Dan, who didn't notice.

This education, this exposure, taught Derek how to blend in as a man in bars, to talk sports, a skill I never quite developed, and have no interest in doing so now.

And he saw me go from a lanky, scrawny adolescent with hair like Lyle Lovett to a lanky, scrawny teenager with hair like, well, Lyle Lovett with a haircut, and I taught him about music, and the usual moping, faux-artist adolescent agonizing in literature—the Salinger, the Camus, the James Joyce, and the soundtrack to wankerdom in The Cure, Joy Division, and The Smiths, peppered here and again with the punk energy of the '70s. I looked vaguely Semitic at this time in my life, more Ashkenazi than Mexican farmhand. I wore thin cotton tees with a single totemic image center mass, walked everywhere with a pair of earbuds hooked up to my Walkman, which was clipped to my backpack and played an eternal loop of mixed tapes I made at home.

In short, I was the prototype for today's college wanker, having created the style before Steve Jobs spoon-fed it to your children. Parents can blame me for that. And yet I was still a Texan and, therefore, had some rough edges; you can't live in Texas and become entirely artsy. You're bound to have the hide of some endangered beast on your wall, or longhorns on your Cadillac—if not physically, then somewhere in metaphor.

So this was the polarity in which Derek was raised, these were the two opposing thoughts held together in his young mind: Dan was the body, I was the heart.

And I was tortured, of course. I was the image of "burning heart Jesus," holding his heart in his palm, and I would take extraordinary pleasure in the exaltation that Derek and his friends accorded me, at this time the only audience I had, and I would also drink too much in front of the kid, regale him with stories of my misadventures and hearts left broken, mine among many. He'd listen and learn and take it all in, like I was his personal artsy swashbuckler, and I left my own dent, in his head.

Though it wasn't all terrible.

Here, I'd take the poor, terrified kid on these calamitous nap-of-the-earth drives at fifty and sixty miles per hour on dirt roads in my pimped-out 1982 Buick LeSabre, low to the ground and windows rolled all the way down with Gibby Haynes and the Butthole Surfers just blaring out of my speakers. Derek, his eyes wide with ecstasy and terror, biting down hard on a pacifier, would be simply buckled in at age four, because fuck, this is rural Texas, and we don't know about baby seats. We'd rocket by like low-flying aircraft, listening to "Who Was in My Room Last Night?," down the flat, chalk-dusted farm roads, and make our own dilemmas and distractions because there was nothing, no one else, and this was ours, only ours and all that we had, for now. It wasn't much, but it was there, and that was enough.

That was the Sunday morning drive to get *barbacoa* at the house of some family that supplemented their income by throwing open their garage door and cooking a series of calves' heads in a pit in their backyard on the Mexican holy days. That was the drive to get fresh tortillas from the other family that built their own tortilla maker in their living room. That was the drive to the corner store, five miles away if you went by the geometry of the grain fields, which we were forced to do because we lived in between two of them. That was the drive to the beach—not the beach itself, just the drive there, because the driving was the point, and the music, and scenery whipping past, because it felt like you were doing something, it felt like you were finally moving.

That's what I imprinted on Derek. Gave him a taste for the tragic and the terror and the need for oblivion, without realizing what I was doing.

The morning we heard of his accident, when he was in the ICU at a hospital in Austin after falling and crushing his head when he was blacked-out drunk, this was all I could think about, how both Dan and I managed to provoke or elicit Thanatos, the death drive, *l'appel du vide*, in our younger brother, sort of bleeding through our own damage and letting it spill unknowingly onto the poor, stupid beautiful beast of a boy, now twenty-four years old and intent upon flinging himself off the nearest chemical cliff.

Derek's addictions, not in the least bit limited to boozing, had become unmanageable, and he couldn't get close to anything resembling a cliff without wanting to jump off.

And now, though it started recreationally, it was ending rather medically, and much too publicly to remain a secret family curse. There was no coming back from this cliff, and it had taken Derek, the last boy in line, to illustrate quite clearly a definition of cultural cliffsides in both my older brother and myself, leading off into either horizon, and certainly into both our futures.

CHAPTER 4

Cain without Abel

The morning Derek was laid up in the hospital in a coma, I was reluctant to get on a plane and fly to Texas, and it wasn't simply because I was an underpaid magazine designer barely scratching a living in Seattle, though that was certainly a part of it. There were several complications to it, some that were sort of indiscernible until even now, as I'm writing about it.

There was Dan. I hadn't spoken to Dan for nearly three years at this point, after an estrangement that began from another one of our fights. I didn't think the family needed another drama to play out in that waiting room.

So I stayed in Seattle, alone, in isolation, and paced.

Ironically, the argument between my older brother and me that caused the deepest division, and the longest we went without speaking, never really happened.

Or, it happened, but he was having one argument, and I was having another.

I remember it clearly, and I also remember being a bit mystified that morning, but the momentum to separate—for clear individuation from my older brother, after all those years—was there, so I went for it, for both his sake and mine, but mostly because we had both become incredibly fatigued by each other at this point.

So this Sunday morning, Dan was planning a large barbecue, like he did when his damned Cowboys were playing, and he'd invited some friends over. I'd been out the night before with Dougherty and woke up terribly hungover, so I met Dough at that same hangover pick-up bar we'd been at the night previous and downed a couple Bloody Marys. Then I was off to Dan's.

One of his friends from the nursing home, Gabriel, was there early. He was from Central America and a devout evangelical, and I really didn't like Gabriel because he reminded me far too much of everything that I hated about South Texas, even if he was from El Salvador. I looked down my freshly minted Seattle nose at the simplistic platitudes of his faith, his misogyny, and his repulsive attitudes toward non-Latin races. It was one of the first times I'd ever seen the competition and striations of hierarchy between immigrants up close, and it offended me completely. Also, he would "date" white women—meaning he'd sleep with them and take advantage of their generosity when they'd pay for a night out—but he had no intention of ever settling down with one; instead, he planned on flying back to his village in El Salvador and finding a teenager to bring back to Seattle to serve as his wife. He was nearing fifty.

Gabriel and I were mistakenly left alone in Dan's living room while Dan was showering and preparing for his big day, and Gabriel began his pitch to get me to talk about "real things." "Real talk." Jesus talk. How Jesus could help with *my* things. *My* anger, my problems with Dan.

I could see by his preparations that my issues had been a topic of discussion previously.

So I opened a beer and became angrier. I could see the machinations in his head, twisting with minimum sophistication, grinding like heavy stone wheels: Bronze Age farming tools churning out some leavened Jesus biscuits.

"So, Domingo," he said, in the flat, proper Latin pronunciation, "tell me, what do you think is the best way to—"

"You do not want to be talking Jesus to me, Gabriel. I'm not like Dan: I do not suffer fools, and I don't know what he sees in you that he invites you to his house."

I was not afraid of Gabriel. He was tiny. Played soccer. Called it "football."

"Yes, but, tell me—"

"You need to be quiet now," I said. I felt like Hannibal Lecter. "You don't want to try and operate on my motivations and behavior with that blunt little Jesus scalpel. Do you really think you can make an incision into my mind with your faith? Compared to you, I'm a goddamned genius, you little—"

Which was as far as I went in my drunken declaration of superiority, because Dan erupted from his bedroom in an offensive, forward fighting posture, and I immediately turned and faced him, as the velocity of the flung door startled me into high alert.

I'm not sure what he thought he'd heard, but it wouldn't have been the first time he'd heard me lamely declare myself an undiscovered genius; I mean, I'd do it at least once a month after I'd successfully insert words or phrases like *obfuscate* and *erstwhile* or *insofar as* into a conversation.

But this was something different, I could tell. And I wasn't sure why. I was too drunk to understand what we were fighting about *now*.

Dan stood there, shoulders back and hands balled into fists at his sides, and he was breathing daggers and looking at me like he wanted to seriously injure me.

Now, this occurred a few months after his knee had been rebuilt from his destroying it in a fight. He had actual bolts and plates holding together his tibia, and he wasn't recovered by any stretch of medical theory. And he stood there, as if he was about to swing at me.

Over *Jesus*? This just didn't make sense to me.

His, girlfriend, Orlene, walked over and placed her hand on his shoulder and pulled him back gently.

The idea of fighting him in this state—Dan on a reconstructed knee, me in perfect health, if a bit hungover—it just made me shudder, so I very obviously dropped any and all defensive posturing, lowering my shoulders, softening my face, even settling my hands in my pockets and stepping back, then softening my tone.

I asked, "Why are you so mad, man?"

His eyes became wild, bewildered, and crazy.

"Are you fucking kidding me? You think it's a fucking joke? All these threats and goddamn times I've had to stitch you up and keep this all a secret from the rest of the family? Do you know how hard it's been on Mom and me and everyone, and you're just going to stand there and make light about it?"

Now, this had me a little confused because it could *certainly* be the case that Dan was upset about me declaring myself a genius, and how it inadvertently affected both him and the rest of the family that no one else had managed to appreciate it, how it caused problems in personal relationships, et cetera, but somehow it didn't feel quite right. I wasn't convinced that was why he was this upset. There had to be something else.

But I shrugged my shoulders and left anyway, made my way back to my apartment and figured either we'd clear it up later or it would resolve itself another way.

Dan had heard the bits about "the blunt scalpel" and "incisions" and immediately leapt to the conclusion that I had been telling Gabriel—of all people—about my impulse toward self-harm when I was younger and crazier, as a potential yet-to-be-diagnosed borderline personality, and saying it in such a way that he felt I was bragging.

Up until this time, only Dan had seen me in my worst moments, sitting on the floor in my apartment in the shadows, when I was in my darkest places, and using an X-Acto or a switchblade and tearing into the meat of my biceps or forearms, working for scarification. It wasn't exactly Thanatos, but perhaps a kissing cousin. Something French, like *l'appel du vide*. I never understood it, and it would come upon me when I felt my most frightened—losing a girlfriend, a job, my apartment—and then suddenly Dan, as primogeniture, would be there, yelling, "What the fuck are you doing? Jesus fucking Christ, look at all this blood! I'm going to have to take you to the psych ward!"

And I'd stare at him like I didn't know who he was, until the idea of "home" began surfacing once again and I'd come to, with him cleaning all the open cuts and stitching up the bad ones.

I have no explanation for it, except that it felt like some sort of blood sacrifice to a low saint, in a time of pain. Low economy of self. I was feeling something primitive and inexpressible, so it needed venting. No more wars to fight, horses to steal, or counting coup. Just a sense of aggression, unyielding rage, shame, and fear. Or maybe I was just checking that the trapdoor was still there.

That's what it felt like, back then, when it would surface. It doesn't anymore.

We didn't speak for months, and before I knew it, Dan had moved away from Seattle, deciding that he'd had enough and it was time to be closer to family in Texas. That drunken Sunday argument began the longest estrangement of our lives, which kept me from flying to Austin, to Derek's bedside while he lay intubated.

I never knew how difficult it was to be brothers, never understood how it would overwhelm and inform every other relationship in my life as an adult, or how I'd have to constantly reevaluate Dan every time I'd see him, how much more complicated he'd become as what was basically a life-partner relationship in which I had no choice but to participate. We had unknowingly become overbonded from our childhood, both hating and needing one another in a cyclic rotation rooted deeply in the sort of love only POWs who help one another through death marches and the building of Burmese railroads can fathom. And we had no idea about the commitment; we ripped one another to shreds constantly as kids—then knew we had to make a reparative effort after, because neither one was going anywhere.

It's the hardest club, and the only club, in which I've had membership, and perhaps the reason why I find artificial associations like unions or fraternal orders calling one another "brothers" distasteful, even offensive.

It is a marriage, from birth to death, and it takes years to figure it out, to stop hurting one another and say, "We have only a few years left, considering how we've been living, and I'm exhausted from fighting. Please, let's get along better and enjoy only the love."

You're not going to get that by "pledging" at a Greek house. You're not going to experience that by standing next to Bob at the plant for twenty years, working the swing shift, and sneaking off at 10:00 p.m. to slug down a six-pack of Milwaukee's Best in thirty minutes for lunch. You might get something very close to that in combat, as I've understood it, but it's still not biologically imperative, still not the common threading of DNA, still not family.

Brotherhood, at its most elemental, is a shared psychosis, a *folie à deux*, an intimate social obligation based on genetics, overlapping damage and testosterone, and you do not have a choice except to participate. Even running away is a participation, as I experienced.

And by the time I figured out how to be a brother to Dan, when we had figured out how to de-escalate arguments and opinions, knew how to step wide, stay out of the mud and let the other person spray and be an asshole, knowing he'd be back around in a bit, and we finally figured out how to navigate our club of two, then we had Derek to deal with, who knew none of the codes, had none of our neurological wiring, had nothing in the way of potential to join, except that Dad was his father (we were pretty sure) and Mom was his mother, and he knew most of the same people we did. Knew a really good corn tortilla from a microwaveable one, so to speak.

This might actually explain why I went through a period where instead of collecting father figures, I switched to collecting little brothers. I would meet them at work or from my neighborhood, or at my old karate school, and I would adopt them for a while, then feel uncomfortable and weird, and then just leave them, never to talk again.

I missed Dan and Derek so much sometimes that it ached, profoundly, in my core sense of self, sense of family.

We had some great stories, as brothers.

With Derek, I remember visiting him on a vacation from Seattle, after I'd started karate, and one perfect summer Saturday, three or four of his friends were visiting at our old house on Oklahoma Avenue and we had an improvisational karate riot, right there in the front yard. I was Hercules, if he had taken tae kwon do, and I was wrestling and kicking and taking down these five little fuckers to the grass, without ever hurting a single one of them, as I "kapowed" and "hiyahed!" and made every Bruce Li noise possible for like an hour, and they'd climb low-hanging branches and jump on my back, get mildly punched in the gut or head, and we were all laughing and sweating and yelling, like puppies at a puppy mill. It was fantastic, and he talked about it for years after.

Another time I taught him how to climb the tree outside Gramma's house in order to break in through the bathroom window, so he could look for any porn our previous Uncle Richard might have left behind, and I went through every single hiding place in that creepy, old house that Dan and I had figured out, and sure enough, there were still strong echoes of a 1970s porn habit, lingering in the darker little corners Gramma had yet to rumble.

As he grew older, I'd bring him up to Seattle, and it was here that he saw snow for the first time (a watershed moment in every South Texan's life), and he actually engaged and played with some kids from Montana one crisp spring morning when I drove him to Hurricane Ridge, and he took a photo with that family, who had built a slide into the hillside and were taking turns. Derek was a bit older than the kids, around fourteen, but he was no less enthusiastic and joyful. It was really sweet to see.

—✦—

With Dan, our bonding was a bit more complicated, as adults. Since we grew up together, there was little that we didn't know about the other, but still, we were able to surprise each other sometimes. For instance, one Friday night back in Dallas, Texas, after I'd accidently moved there (long story, and not interesting—I was back in Seattle after nine months), Dan had been staying with me while establishing himself as a nurse in a long-term care facility, and neither of us knew anyone among the Dallas population, so we decided to stay in and watch cable.

My apartment's interior design had a kind of midcentury feel, since most of my furniture had been donated by the crustier echelon of desk editors and reporters at the *Seattle Times*, thanks to an ex-girlfriend who worked there and had put out a call for donations.

Immediately, that generation of Seattleites who were putting their parents out on the proverbial ice floe and airing out their inherited properties, which now tripled in the booming real estate market, started offering up kitschy lamps and uselessly tiered coffee tables, rattan chairs and strange wall art and the like.

I didn't care: I took everything that was offered, packed it into a U-Haul, and drove it across the country to Dallas, Texas. Figured I'd pare it down when I arrived.

When I finished decorating my new apartment, it looked like a Boeing-era thrift store had vomited in my living room after a hard night of drinking bourgin.

I didn't care; it was "shabby chic," I thought.

Dan was taken aback when he first saw it, though; it didn't compute with his sense of interior design for a single guy. I could tell he was questioning my heterosexuality, and I was making no case for it.

Dan's idea of a single man's interior design, as illustrated by the one time I ever visited him and he lived alone, was a television sitting atop a hefty wooden table and a love seat directly across from it, with a shadeless lamp sitting on the floor next to it. And lots of beer cans. Lots and lots of beer cans.

So the look of consternation that flickered across his face when he saw my walls draped with Indian fabrics, dried grass stalks in mismatched standing vases, and two recliners sitting opposite a small television and separated by a tall reading lamp, well, Dan had to question what I'd been up to, and with whom, while he'd left me alone in Seattle for a couple years.

Nevertheless, there we were, two large Latin men that Friday night, sitting in midcentury recliners opposite my twenty-inch television (large enough to be allowed in Texas, but certainly not something to be proud of), looking like the very image of Edith and Archie Bunker, drinking Lone Star Beer, the National Beer of Texas.

And because this was my place, it was my discretion as to what we'd be watching for that evening's entertainment. After some considerable channel surfing, I had lit upon a small, independent Australian film called *Flirting*, by John Duigan.

To this day, it remains one of my favorite small films, and I forced Dan to endure it with me.

We sat, that night, watching this film on the Romance Channel, its logo popping up translucently every twenty minutes or so in the lower right-hand corner to remind us how nonmacho we were being by watching a "love movie" at 10:00 p.m. on a Friday night.

By midnight, and the final scene when our hero finally receives a letter from his beloved, who had survived the overthrow of Idi Amin. Dan and I were sobbing, both our faces wet with tears rolling down our puffy cheeks, and saying, "He loves her so much! And she loves him, too!"

It was one for the brotherly scrapbook, and one of my favorite memories of my brother Dan.

The big galoot.

Much later, there was one story that Dan liked to repeat about his drinking days with Derek, before Derek's accident in 2007. Some friends of Dan's from his time in Seattle had flown to San Antonio to visit him, and they spent an entire day on the River Walk, hopping bars and hotels from one end to the other and drinking, drinking, drinking.

Dan, of course, was responsible for Derek's tab because Derek was, as a false student, insolvent, and so when the final tally came to Dan the next day, he blearily counted up all his receipts and discovered he had spent just under $600 for a monumental drunk, worthy of a Kris Kristofferson song.

Very little was said about most of that day, except for a particular moment witnessed at closing time, when Derek was woozily standing at the end of a bar and was unexpectedly chatted up by a San Antonio cougar: big hair, large golden chains, shining nails, and lots of makeup. Derek, unburdened by standards or morals even on his best days, allowed himself to be chatted up thoroughly, thinking he might either have sex or a few free drinks. Such were my younger brother's priorities.

Dan witnessed this from the bar opposite and was immediately on high alert, for some reason, and decided to interfere on the older woman's interfering with his younger brother.

"Whattaya doing to my little brother?" he said, a bit too aggressively.

"Nothing!" replied the older woman, making a face full of disgust. "Have at him, if you're so damned protective."

Derek, at this point bewildered and confused, managed to follow Dan as Dan led him away and safely off to home.

Now, Dan liked to tell this story. And Dan liked to increase the age of the older woman every time he told the story.

By the time I heard it, she was in her eighties, in a wheelchair, and carried an oxygen tank while smoking a cigarette through a hole in her throat. She also said, "Dahr-wick," instead of "Derek." It was hysterical.

"Dahr-wick, come help me with my colostomy bag," Dan said, while pretending to inhale from a hole in his neck as he was driving and telling me the story for the first time.

"Shut up, she wasn't that old," said Derek, from the backseat.

"Dahr-wick, can you change my oxygen tank, Dahr-wick?" said Dan.

"Come on, man; stop being mean. You know she wasn't that bad."

"Dahr-wick, if you come back to my room at the home, you can meet my daughter on Sunday, when she visits. She's old enough to be your muddah."

"Jesus, Dan."

Personally, I was taken aback by Dan's routine. The years we spent apart, he'd been sharpening his material, it seemed. He was getting funnier. I was feeling a bit threatened, too: I was the Shecky Greene of the troupe. I was the Borscht Belt comedian. After thirty goddamned years, I was still competing for the same resources as my older brother, the bastard.

But I also noticed how Derek had taken to wincing when he was the butt of our jokes. Once he'd been very willing to be hazed, or initiated in the manner that brothers do with insensitive ribbing or outright humiliation, because any attention from us was in its own way nourishing to him—even the mean stuff—but in the years that I hadn't seen them, I was noticing that this sort of engagement had begun to leave an impression. And Dan either refused to notice or refused to care.

Derek was wincing, making faces when we said shitty things to him, or about him. He had hit a limit, but I wasn't there when it started. Our comments were unconsciously barbed now, surprisingly sharp and unintentionally demeaning, when they were once just brotherly teasing.

CHAPTER 5

Epiphanies

My father tells the story of the first time he realized he had a problem with drinking, and oddly enough he cites me as the vehicle of his clarity. Remarkably, I remember the exact same moment standing opposite him as a child, as it served for me as a lesson in the power of language and thinking your way out of a volatile situation, disengaging from the river of cortisol and adrenaline that would—sometimes—help me out of violent moments.

During the incident he talks about, my father was raging and spewing, spitting mad, caught in one of the endocrinal bursts of anxiety and impossible anger that would punctuate his youth, just explosive and unreasonable and, for some reason, directed at me that mythological morning. I do not remember what I might have said or failed to do in order to trigger it, but I was roughly eight or ten years old, and he was billowing around me like a bunker buster and I was standing in the vortex, his arms and curses and gesticulation flying around me like shrapnel.

But this particular morning, it was the sting emanating from his breath that really hurt me.

Jesus God, was it acute, piercing from alcohol, like needles in my nose and eyes, and I had to squeeze my own eyes shut and turn my face in a wince to get out of the immediate proximity. It was so bad that I was able to ignore the imminent physical violence of his anger and instead had to protect myself simply from his breath.

He'd been drinking through the entire night before, probably had a few more beers that morning, and there he was, trying to get to work and yelling at me for failing to be helpful.

And take it any longer I could not: I said, calmly, and in a manner unusual in that barrio, likely in English, "Dad, my nose hurts from your breath. It really stings."

And my father just stopped, as if I'd reached back and popped him square on the nose.

I remember the look on his face, too, and I'm not making that up from here.

It was pure astonishment. Out of the mouth of babes, and all that.

His frenzy came to an instantaneous halt, frozen as if in amber, and my remark did what nothing or no one else could do then and broke through my father's delirium, or addictive denial.

His drinking no longer a tertiary or passive issue. He couldn't even yell at his kid now without the fucking drinking getting in the way.

He was floored, he tells the other broken members of his AA meetings, when he repeats the anecdote about this revelation. And after twenty-odd years of sobriety, he was able to tell us, his family, about this crystallization, the first in a long series of realizations that would eventually line up and spell his sobriety, in something other than an unusual hieroglyph or a vague, abstract reading of tea leaves. It had spoken to him in a manner much clearer than an interpretation of raw eggs suspended in a glass of water, like he was accustomed to after a visit to his *curandera*.

That morning was the first point of a Latin character that would, in time, spell out "ENOUGH" for my father, perhaps in Latin or Spanish, but enough is enough in whatever language you think or feel in, and he credits me, as that boy, who started to draw the sounds for him. Gave him words to make that life-changing decision.

Of course, I took something different from that moment. Obviously, I did not realize that my father was having that moment of clarity through his addiction; for me it was more the idea that I could, using something other than reflected hysteria, step out of the torrent of emotion and, by using regulated tones, talk someone out of their fight, or their flight.

Step out of the way of the pain, using language.

But it's hardest to step out of the way of your own pain, step out of your own torrent. In my adolescence and youth, when I began noticing that my father had left that same impression, that same curse and same need to explode like a hand grenade in me, when I was drinking or not, I didn't have the resources or cultural cues to point me toward seeking help—mental, medical, or psychological—and I would instead simply point the nose of my stalled emotional engine right into the dive and plummet. I never even considered that I could turn out of the tailspin like Lincoln Beachey, the barnstormer who figured out that instead of going against the tailspin to restart your propeller, as the intuition of many dead pilots had previously told them to do, you should not fight it, but turn into the plummet and then restart the engine, and maybe once again regain control.

Instead, it was explosion after explosion. Casualty after casualty.

It was what I knew, though I knew better.

—◦—

In a fall from grace, you get to play both roles, the victim and the savior, the self-redeemer.

Derek hadn't figured out the second part before he fell, didn't get to turn into his stall and regain control. As a family, we were all well aware of Derek's secret corruptions. It was the most inexplicable, contradictory thing about him: When he was in front of you, when he was at family gatherings, when he had an internship or a job, when someone was in charge of him, he was the brightest, smartest, most agreeable person, the most competent employee, most enjoyable human in the room.

Turn your back, and he would be gone for weeks without checking in, drinking with dangerous people, doing illicit drugs or any sort of prescription medication that happened to be blooming in the subterranean culture in Austin at the moment, and Derek was always able to get a free line in there, always ready to be a party in a pair of trousers, because he was funny, smart, and charismatic, and people were naturally drawn to him, wanted him around.

For the first two years he was "going to college," I'd reach out to him and feel absolutely crushed when I received nothing in response, something that I didn't know Mom and Dan were experiencing as well. We never talked about it.

But then he'd surface, back in orbit with a text message, the electric dart in every parent's heart.

I just *hated* it when he'd pop back up and pretend everything was all right, that he hadn't squandered the full ride he'd won to the University of Texas, and tell us all he was still in school, just needed another $500 for this and $200 for that, maybe $600 for this other thing, and we'd all somehow allow ourselves to get bamboozled, and we'd work together as a family and generate what he needed, because that's what you do, even for addicts, when they're lying to you.

His lies and Mom's dedication to them were written on the back of her hands, sun damaged from driving in Texas, positioned at 11:00 and 2:00 on the steering wheel and baking in the hot equatorial sunlight as she drove monthly from Houston to Austin. She'd put another mortgage on her house, find another way to help him back into class and believe in him, in what she felt was unconditional love and not enabling. She'd take him shopping at the start of every semester, take him to the H-E-B (the Texas grocery chain) and load up on spicy ramen soups and sandwich fixings, then set him free and hope, eternally, for the best.

I had the chance to witness this once, when I happened to fly down to Austin on my own business. Watching the two of them together at the grocery store, their interactions and insinuated history as mother and son, it was clear to me that they'd never achieved their own individuation, never broken free as two complete organisms, two minds, two souls, two fully developed people.

Their communication was entrenched into years of backstory and inside knowledge, long-ago arguments and stunted grunts of information. No. Get *that*. Stop. Then a look: Yes, *that* one. Most of this went unspoken. They were the opposite of a married couple. They'd never separated, made it to mitosis. You see it sometimes, when people shift personalities in front of you, become completely different humans when they interact with their children.

That day, at H-E-B, readying Derek for another failed semester of druggie school, Mom was loading up her placenta with nutrients again, instead of stocking his nonexistent fraternity pantry, which is what she thought she was doing.

See, when he was born, Derek couldn't make it out of the birth canal because he'd had his umbilical cord wrapped around his neck and it would choke him when he tried to emerge. Eventually, he evacuated through a cesarean.

I walked behind them, watching as they shopped together, and thought to myself, "Jesus fuck. What a perfect metaphor."

Mom's umbilical, which started out choking this kid, was now stretched across half the state of Texas.

———

So here he was now, in intubation in this ICU in a hospital in Austin, post–brain surgery, barely surviving.

Because of his alcohol and drug problem.

Which demeaned the event. An unspoken Catholic response: He was being bad, therefore he should be punished. Or, he deserved this. He received what was coming to him.

Back in Seattle, I kept wondering: Should I fly down there, disrupt my routine, for this addict, who routinely lies, keeps from talking to his family and continues this lifestyle—does this SHAMEFUL moment need addressing?

My brother-in-law, Corwin, had more air miles than most countries have highway miles; the ticket would not have been an issue. But I felt a level of shame for Derek that I couldn't describe then. *Oh, no. Well, you've gone and done it. Cat's out of the bag now, mister. Everyone knows our little secret. Everyone knows we're drunks now. You had to go and fuck up. Had to fuck it up for all of us.*

There was that.

CHAPTER 6

Pygmalion, Texas

I made a number of terrible decisions around this time, my own self, searching for signals from the universe as to what steps I should take next, where I needed to be, what I could do after I found myself alone and isolated in Seattle, right before Derek's accident.

Growing up Mexican Catholic, and in particular with my old-world grandmother and father, I wound up tinged with an intricacy of superstitions, adapted to my neo-rebellious West Coast sensibilities. Combining that vulnerability with the advent of a burgeoning social media, it took Myspace to put me exactly in a position that I had not expected. That's when Elise broke through.

She was a girl I knew growing up in Brownsville, Texas, in high school, and had not thought of twice in twenty years. She had sought me out during the heyday of Myspace, and I took it as a sign that someone I knew from way back when was calling me back to Texas, like a raspy siren with a two-packs-a-day habit and a penchant for barbecue.

Not that she was a smoker, or a barbecuist. Or rather, she may have been, for all I knew: As I said, I hadn't thought of her since before I barely graduated high school. She wasn't that significant, just another target of written letters and mixed tapes back in high school, but really, that could have been any number of girls.

My heart was a drunken compass even then, before I was a drunk.

I remembered her as an awkward, lean girl with a laugh to make you reconsider your stream of jokes, if I'm to remain kind. Actually, that is a bit mean, since she was just a teenage kid, seemed a bit morose and a bad fit for South Texas, which is what I think drew me to her. And that she was a sort of echo of another girl with whom I was smitten, but too frightened to make it obvious. Bit of a placeholder, if that's not revisionist. So I gave her the full Pablo Neruda treatment with a daily letter and a few moody Mancunian tunes for a while, made no progress, and when it came time for me to leave high school and Brownsville, I genuinely never thought about her again.

Then she reached out, all these years later, when I was at my most vulnerable, transitioning chapters without Dan or a partner in Seattle, living entirely unto my own and eking out a living three thousand miles from a home that was no longer there, and, being who I was, I took it as a sign: *You'll do.*

She sent a photo, of course, and I was knocked back on my heels: She looked fantastic, like a Latin Winona Ryder, which isn't a stretch. Remember, this was the early days of the Internet, when social customs and etiquette had not yet been established and curiosity led you down some fairly dangerous catfish holes.

The mixed tapes I'd left behind like preverbal suggestions of romantic idealizations had left their marks, and here she was now, years later, wondering who I'd become, what I was doing, and most important to her, what I was listening to. This became clear after a few exchanges of e-mail, which immediately turned into full running daily electronic dialogues interrupted only by the two-hour time difference and picked up again later for six-hour telephone conversations that racked up $300 in cell phone bills, held nightly after I'd come home from work.

She'd taken to pursuing and obsessing on every band I'd left behind on the tapes I'd made for her, researching and indulging and spending her husband's money on rare pressings and taking pilgrimages to Manchester or stalking, when he toured America, Morrissey, of all people, to whom I'd introduced her years before on more than a few compilations, as he was one of my favorite artists back then. And I knew it was her husband's money only later, after weeks of talking, when she finally admitted she was married.

To anyone with an appreciation of absurdity, what was clearly unfolding here was a relationship long in the making, the sort of John Hughes fantasy story that drove the box office in the '90s. I thought, *Finally, here's the current that should be sweeping me along. I'll just let it take me where it wants to go.*

To indicate things further, it just so happened I'd scheduled a trip to Houston and Austin for later that month . . . *so what are you doing for dinner, say, on the 19th?* Everything seemed to be pointing toward the rightness of this, the universal correction in the vacuum of signifiers.

And it was with that idea that I traveled to Austin, Texas, that summer.

━━◦◦◦━━

Derek was there, at this time, and he was excited to see me.

I wasn't so excited to see him.

I had an idea of the sort of life he was living at UT, and I had become so cross with his decision to join a fraternity that I didn't even try to speak to him for over a year.

Dan described Derek as a chemical toilet. That's better than what I had come up with: a dust bin. Derek did anything anyone threw at him, and if excess went beyond, he did a bit more. There was simply no stopping how much he would drink, how much he'd snort or take: He could consume triple or quadruple what you thought was too much.

He had our Martinez peasant stamina, our crazy Mexican strength. He was Dumbo, made out of rubber. He still had our Gramma's strength in him, with his developed sense of the optimistic stupidity that made him love and trust everyone around him, who actually loved and liked him back, because he was nothing if not an incredibly likeable kid.

That was the problem: You combine this pastiche of personality with his penchant for addiction, and it points you toward the cliff edge.

And personally, because I loved the kid as much as I did, and I wanted always to impress him and for him to keep me firmly locked in as his hero, as his older brother and idol, I was always on the hunt for something that he'd find amusing, something that would keep me on the cusp of the most interesting and the finder of the coolest things.

I was Gryffindor; Derek was Hufflepuff. Hufflepuffs are good finders, and Derek always found drugs.

So all the things I would find for him to share in would inadvertently leverage him with a social currency that went well beyond anything his loose constellation of friends had previously been exposed to: I provided this credit of identity that proved incredibly lucrative in the lateral currency of "cool" in shit places like universities; by trying to win over my younger brother's affections, I was actually giving him the freedom to kill himself because his friends and peers and compatriots, who were all eager to learn more and more and more about what was cool and next and big and smart, were plying him with booze and blow and ecstasy and anything they had their hands on so that Derek could continue talking and talking and telling them about all that he knew, which is what I knew, and what Dan and I were giving him while he disappeared further into the miasma of addiction and a dither of definition and blurred boundaries and a declension to a level we never thought possible for one of our own family.

"Ashes to ashes, funk to funky," as David Bowie sang.

<hr/>

He was so happy to see me that afternoon I drove into Austin.

Derek ran out of the fraternity house and hugged me while I grabbed my bag, and I didn't hug him back, exiting our mother's car. A hot day, a shitty Texas campus, dicks in trucks, girls wearing excessively short shorts. I was pissed off. Turned on, of course, with the girls in shorts, but still pissed off.

He failed to notice my resistance; maybe he was high on something. But I wasn't relenting, and I was irritated that he was making me spend time in a fraternity house in Austin.

It wasn't as if he didn't know that both Dan and I had stood and fought a Hellenic "stand your ground" fight against an entire fraternity in Kingsville, Texas, ten years before, and that the whole idea of fraternities goes against my core principles, but he was lining up his friends like dwarves and hobbits in an adventure—Dimly, Wimly, Simpy, and so on—and attempting to introduce them to me like I was his own Yoda, and they all lined up, stupid and uninteresting and . . . well, dimwitted.

Or maybe I'm just his older brother, and I was being a complete dick about this.

But no; they were just younger kids and "friends" of my brother, helping him along in his unmonitored and unscheduled self-destruction. Encouraging, allowing, permitting, supplying his destructive tendencies—*can't you see what's happening here?*

Echoes of my own choices, and effects. Affects.

And Dan's. And Derek's helplessness.

And these fucks were resonating it back to Derek, in amplification, for their own fun.

And my mother, her umbilical throttling her hearing, chauffeuring him along.

I was angry at all of us, not just Derek.

———

The only night I was at the fraternity house, Derek paraded me around, and I was surrounded by these drinking children and maybe one or two glimmers of intelligence. The only kid I felt any sort of draw toward was Derek's best friend, oddly named Orlando, a tall, stringy Mexican-American kid with long straight hair and a keen sense in seeing the larger, more cosmic sensibility and the stupidity of this enterprise. He's from Del Rio, Texas, a border town similar to Brownsville, and a kooky family of artists, musicians, and cockfighters. The first time Derek visited Orlando's house, within minutes of parking, and the moment he entered, Orlando's dad appeared out of nowhere and grabbed Derek by his wrist, pulled him into a spare bedroom where Derek had a moment's pause and uncertainty, until the old man handed him a Bud Light and then produced a battered guitar upon which he began to pluck that one song Antonio Banderas sings in *Desperado*. That was his initiation to Orlando's family.

The second time Derek was at Orlando's home, he was awoken on Orlando's couch after an all-night drive from Austin to Del Rio to find an old man—Orlando's uncle—rubbing an ice-cold Budweiser on his neck, inviting him to sit for a drinking breakfast at 7:00 a.m. because the cockfights started around 9:00 or 10:00 that Saturday. They sat eating GBCs—tacos with carne guisada, beans, and cheese, which are such a staple in Del Rio, they're known by their initials—and the old man pulled out a magazine that displayed fighting roosters, and cooed and petted at the image of his favorite, which was way over his pay grade, and choked up with tears. Their house was on a hill that looked directly down onto the Rio Grande. Derek said it was like a Mexican version of Isabel Allende's *The House of the Spirits*, with the multigenerational family all minding their own quirkiness and the doors left always unlocked.

Orlando and Derek shared a room at the end of the hall in the fraternity, and it reminded me of a squat I lived in when I was roughly his age, but in Seattle. Mine was an unregistered and illegal karate school in an abandoned warehouse, but I saw the parallel. It was a square room, nothing exceptional; an elevated platform stood five feet off the ground with a plywood bunk supported by four-by-fours and bolted into the wall. On top of this rested a smelly, moldy futon. This was where Derek slept. It was unhygienic, disgusting. My billet, for the night.

Still, he tried to throw a party for me, show me what he did now, as if he were a grown-up.

He invited everyone he knew, and most of them were morons.

I couldn't move for having a throng of college students following me around, and a particularly large Southern brute took to following me, even into the men's room, when someone started passing around a pipe full of marijuana and I thought, *Yup, that's the end of the night,* and they became high and whatever conversation might have been longer had any possibility of being evinced. I crawled up to the futon and hid while the party continued throughout the frat house, and I was relegated to the back corner while emanations of scorn and unbridled resentment poured continuously from the older, professional frat guys up front.

And it built up to a moment when an Asian kid in a pressed pink collared shirt called down the hall to Derek and challenged him about his owed dues to the fraternity.

I heard how he was talking to my little brother, and I climbed down from the futon and came out into the hallway angry. I said, "I'm sorry, but who the fuck are you?" I stood up and expanded, chicken chested, elbows touching both hallways and my spine expanding about a foot.

"June, don't . . . don't; it won't help," said either Derek or Orlando, when these other dickhead yuppies in similar pastel collared shirts made some under-breath comments. I genuinely did not hear what they said, but I registered the scorn.

Derek and Orlando and their friends were, apparently, the punk fringe of the frat house. If there could be such a thing. They were months behind on dues, rent, et cetera, and way submerged beneath their academic minimums. They were now the fraternity equivalent of homesteaders, or homeless squatters, only there for the free booze and parties, seamless introductions to the sorority girls. And what I had walked into was the passive-aggressive hostility of their fraternity "supervisors," children pretending at social management and finding themselves lacking.

And I wanted to start a fight.

"June, please don't," repeated Derek.

I was brimming with self-righteous hostility. I knew this was ridiculous, and I knew Derek was an idiot for getting himself into this, but *who the fuck do you think you are, you mid-Texan fraternity nobody, to be judging my goddamned little brother?*

I was going to start some shit. I was pissed, and I was pissed.

I could take at least three of these fuckers, I thought. I'd done it before, and that was before I'd trained to fight. I didn't need Dan here. But Derek was trying to get me to stand down: Don't do this, don't start a fight here, and I said, "I'm not saying I'm not going to or that I am, but *motherfucker....*"

Then one of them started playing "Ghostbusters."

Not the movie, but the song, by Ray Parker Jr., loud, and in earnest. Coming out of his room from the front. Like he meant it. Like it was his "jams."

I stopped in the hallway, my aggression halted, bewildered.

"Is . . . is he Russian?" I asked. That was the only thing that could explain this.

Derek looked at me.

"How . . . yes; how did you know?" The kid was Hungarian, but Derek thought that was close enough.

"It's 'Ghostbusters,' Derek! Who else is going to listen to 'Ghostbusters' like it's a real song in 2007?"

And we burst out laughing, which neutralized the air that night.

That kid would be the one who would later save Derek's life. Mogy-orodi, with the very bad dress sense and bad taste in popular American music. Mogyorodi, who stood with Derek as Derek blacked out and fell, and who immediately called 911, had the ambulance there in minutes and saved Derek's life. For a year or two after, Derek carried a Polaroid photo of Mogyorodi in his jacket pocket, never explained to anyone who he was, or why he had a photo of a really hairy guy wearing a Nirvana *Nevermind* T-shirt tucked into tricolored sweatpants pulled up to his belly button, and holding a can of fortified lager and smiling at whomever was taking the photo.

The night I spent with Derek in his fraternity house, after picking up on some deeply sublimated homoeroticism and some horrible, horrible lapses of sanitation (Christ! What do they feed these boys? I had bowel envy, from the shared bathroom), I went back and hid in the rear corner of the house and decided I wouldn't cause trouble because I was seeing Elise the next evening, and this was Derek's choice now. These were his decisions.

Derek kept drinking, even after we had called it quits around 2:00 a.m. and I had elected to retire. He wandered off and left me alone in that foreign, horrible place, and I sat there, counting the minutes until daylight came and I could get a lift to my hotel, as I had planned.

Around 4:00 a.m. he finally wandered back, and I didn't recognize this boy.

He stood in the darkened room, holding a bag full of Taco Bell that he'd either pinched or had someone bring to him, and he stared out the window and made a horrible show of himself as I watched from atop the platform, hidden by the hepatitic futon, and he breathed slowly and deeply through his nose, like someone in scuba gear, and smooshed these terrible tacos into his mouth and chewed noisily, the food falling apart and smearing on his face. I could see his eyes in the reflection of the window glass, and it looked, to me, like he had no idea where he was, or who he was, at all.

There was no one home behind his glasses. His eyes were empty, his balance a slow orbit, his body a shell of the person that I was related to, the kid I helped to raise, but this wasn't him. I was witnessing firsthand what I had only heretofore suspected, that Derek drank into nonsense, into utter corruption of identity. It was almost like a possession, or maybe the opposite of a possession—a vacuity, an absence, an ejection of self. Derek was gone. This was just walking booze.

I'd never seen anything like it, not sure I'd ever been there myself, and believe me, I'd put on some pretty good drunks in my day. And I had met some other serious drunks, too, but nothing like this.

I was completely destroyed, looking at him like that, felt entirely at a loss, and helpless, hopeless.

This was my younger brother, and he was gone.

It took me most of the next day to recover from the shock of seeing Derek in that form, and he slept all day, reviving his strength so he could do a repeat performance of that same self-destruction the following night, as an encore. It amazed me that he managed to get that fucked up, that often, with no money. And yet, here he was, doing it daily.

My own bad choices kept pointing me into the ridiculous as well, kept collaborating with my drunken compass.

My friend Philippe monitored me at the time from his home in Los Angeles, questioning every decision I made on this trip and, I'm sure, telling his wife that I was having a midlife crisis at thirty-six.

It was the only thing it could look like, from without.

From within, it was a continuation of what the universal signal was telling me. If I pricked my ear just right, what should have happened fifteen years previously, in following these musical bread crumbs to Austin, Texas, where I was continuing my wooing of a girl I knew back in high school, could happen now. Perhaps I needed to follow Dan's example and move back to Texas, with a girl.

Anyhow, I had a date with destiny that following night. Or destiny's second cousin.

And destiny's second cousin showed up wearing about forty pounds more than her photo had indicated.

Now, I know this sounds like I'm being a judgmental asshole, but the reason I felt it was an indicator of something larger was simply because every photo she sent during our exchanges was, let's just say, a kinder, younger, gentler representation of her definitions and relationship with physicality, if not outright photoshopped. And I was very much of the *cinema verité* school of thought, sending her updated images of my own declension into middle age, with the thinning hair, the love handles lovingly cultured over hours of beer drinking, the slow deterioration of knees and lungs, and a forthright insistence that I was not, in the least, misrepresenting myself. I didn't have time for that. *We* didn't have time for that, now that we were in our late thirties: No time for love, Dr. Jones. It's time to make a choice, and I'm thinking my choice is you, if you're being honest and real.

So here is me, being real, is where I was.

And here she was, playing this game.

After all these hours of foreplay and flirting and exchanges, I arrived in Texas and she had presented a more, let's call it a "stylized," image of herself, and still, I thought, *I'm going to give this a shot.*

My passive sense, once again.

I heard Philippe's voice in my head, telling me to back out, call it quits, and get back home, *schnell, schnell,* or whatever the French is for *schnell.*

We would often talk about millenials and the sort of people who'd bewilder us, kids who live their entire lives on the Internet, develop their full range of emotional entanglements and nourishment through the fabrication of electronic relationships and then find themselves feeling hollow, emotionally desiccated because the relationships are all false, impressions or echoes of reality. They put up a good face, a good front as professionals, but when you really get them talking, get them open to the gooey middle, there's a land of tears, if they're programmed correctly.

And this is what Philippe was telling me I was headed into.

"No!" I said. "I'm taking the dive. I want to see where this goes," I told him.

"Domingo, this isn't you. This isn't healthy or smart. Obviously, there's something going on with this girl and she's projecting it out on you, and you're projecting it back."

———

Elise wasn't a successful producer in Los Angeles.

Elise was a false bottom.

I saw her as a trapdoor underneath my feet, and the answer I was looking for at the time.

She'd been a good-looking young girl, if perhaps a bit forlorn and melancholic, as she would eventually tell me.

From what I could gather, she'd married some palfrey accountant-type several years her senior and pretended to work at his office, much to the displeasure of the other actual employees. I was able to determine her "office" habits as our interaction developed, which changed considerably as our contact became more involved, with her getting online and on her e-mail earlier and earlier and working through a full business day, two-hour time zone adjustment included.

But then she would go completely quiet: the chief indicator of an affair, as I knew from a few before.

And we had a great time, flirting and writing and exchanging Internet media at the time, talking about bands and other things, her telling me about Austin, me telling her about Seattle, and the more we talked, the more clear it became that she did, really, nothing. She was a wife, I would eventually figure out, who visited her husband's office, and she only admitted she was married after about three weeks of concentrated flirting when I called her out on her circumstances: Either she was a trust fund baby or a married woman hiding a brace of children.

"Jesus, Domingo," said Philippe. "Her husband's going to come after you with a shotgun. It's Texas, remember. Look at what they did to JFK."

"That was Dallas! This is Austin. It's supposed to be a bit more worldly. I'll report back to you if it's true."

It wasn't.

———

I eventually made it to the hotel and met Elise, had my little "catfish" surprise, and went on with the evening nevertheless. She showed me her Austin, showed me her record store and her coffee shop and things she thought I might like, and was entirely too invested in showing off her car, some kind of Audi, and then I remembered that she grew up lower middle class, somewhat deprived of resources, and had a level of shame around her vehicle, as we had been taught to do in Brownsville. The car was a coup for her, bought entirely by her sexiness in snagging a duffer of a husband who bankrolled this leisurely lifestyle where she ostensibly did nothing, or very little indeed, except pursue whatever next whinging musical indication caught her fancy.

We drove to some storage facility where she had a box of memorabilia, and she found all the letters I'd written her, kept for these last twenty-odd years, along with the original cassette tapes. Clearly, I'd left a mark. I sat and giggled over what I'd written to her back in high school, noting the emerging sensibility and sensationalism, and felt a bit saddened for the kid who wrote them, asked if I could have them, but she said, no, the letters belonged to her, and I thought, *Fine. You keep them.* And we spent the whole night driving around and wandering the streets of Austin, which left nothing of an impression on me.

We continued driving and listening to music all night, and then when she dropped me off at my hotel and came up to say good night, I couldn't tell if she understood the signals that she was sending. Here it was, nearing 4:00 a.m., and she was in my hotel room, saying good night. Was it me?

"I'll come get you for breakfast," she said. "There's a place I'd like to take you."

"Sure; what time?" I asked, not sure what she was indicating.

"How does 7:00 sound?"

"That's in three hours. Why even go home?"

"I have to feed the dogs," she said.

Then we hugged, awkwardly, for two people who had spent the last two months opening up the way we had.

Three hours later, she returned to the hotel, and I was up, bleary eyed and ready for more, having convinced myself again that this was the right track, this was the right path, and I heard Philippe's voice in my head asking, "Christ, Domingo, what are you doing here? She's clearly deluding herself into something that you're actively refusing to acknowledge."

"Shaddup, Philippe!"

"What?" she asked.

"Oh, nothing," I replied. "These are fantastic tortillas."

"Yeah, this is my favorite breakfast spot. They play good music here," she said.

Also she kept saying, "What are you on about?" in full reproduction from some of my favorite British films, and it just didn't work with her, made me think, *Fuck; is THAT what I sound like? That's horrible.*

I was too tired and too weary from the trip to bring the Pygmalion in the room into focus, at this point, so I let it go for the moment.

Austin, in the morning, looked identical to how I remembered every other Texas town, with a bit more mesquite. I just didn't understand what people saw in it, couldn't wait to get some distance between me and this city.

My mother picked me up for the drive back to Houston from the hotel, and I introduced her briefly to Elise before we drove to the fraternity to resuscitate Derek to say good-bye. That was more for her sake, as I couldn't look at him the same way after the other night, needed to get away from the proximity of his self-destruction, so I could take it all in. In the meantime, I had two martinis with lunch because I needed the anesthetizing, and I once again tried to broach Derek's self-destruction, but Mom just shook her head and these nearly tangible emanations of fatigue and defeat cascaded off of her, and I just couldn't really press that point either.

I flew home the next day, feeling defeated and beaten, my own self, and like something was in the mail, following me home.

I called Philippe and uttered the sentence he enjoys hearing above all else: You were right, my friend.

You were right.

CHAPTER 7

Bread Thou Art

Back to March 17, 2007, with Derek in the ICU.

I think those few minutes on the phone that morning with my sister Mary changed the deepest chemistry in my mind and reintroduced me to my family in a way that therapy and thinking and years of distance could never reconcile, never clear the corrosion and adolescent convictions that protect the deep, deep traumas.

Sitting there, with Mare on the line, hearing her sniffle and absorb this new information about our younger brother's casualty, just holding on and saying nothing, sparked a regeneration of love, and a tethering back to my family that grew in that silence, in that need for her presence, and the presence of my other family at the moment when we, as a cognitive whole, took in the idea of our mortality with the possible loss of the youngest brother.

For years after my mother's divorce, we'd each traveled our own paths in a diaspora of personal enterprise and, at least for me, never once considered the idea that one of us could just, you know, actually *die*. We were like the lower animal kingdom, as cognitive psychologists and French poststructuralists accuse them of having no concept of their own mortality, allowing them to live without personal accounting, or too much ennui, experiencing only "the moment." And then suddenly we found ourselves here, the idea of death interrupting an ordinary Saturday morning in March, and all of us clutching to cell phones like crucifixes, the possibility of death now a very real thing.

All we could do was wait, and cling to our phones.

In my apartment, in Seattle, I began pacing.

I started walking to the window, then back to the bedroom, in a straight line, at first counting my footsteps in one direction (eight) and then back in the other (oddly, six; I think I took longer, more determined strides, like I was going home). Eventually, I learned I could stop the warfare in my head by counting steps, but I couldn't concentrate past the first hundred or so, and then I thought of saying the Lord's Prayer, the real one, without the Lutheran addendum, and the Hail Mary. These were the first passages I'd ever memorized as a good Catholic boy, so it was like UNIX or C++ programming and should have undermined all the shouting and racing geometry of images exploding in my head—images of a funeral, images of Derek gone, Derek missing, Derek erased, flashes of life-crushing guilt and Dan, and Mom, and Dad, and Mare—but it all became a sort of broken-up chant with a mishmashed word-gruel of early Catholic images and errant bits of Shakespeare. *Our Father/Wherefore Art Thou/Holy Mary Mother of God/Hallowed Be Thy Name/Give Us Thy Bread/ Forgive Us Our Fruit/Blessed Are You As It Is in Heaven/In Thy Orisons May All My Sins Be Remembered/Pray for Us Sinners.* I couldn't stop, couldn't even complete a single phrasing of prayer, because I kept losing the thread and couldn't concentrate, not until the phone would ring, and someone would reach out with an update. Nothing ever completely reassuring, in the way that updates are when you're not there at the hospital, in person, looking for signs, looking for behavior that's out of the ordinary for the people in the scrubs, waiting for the signals betraying their loss of control, betraying their panic, and listening to their chatter, eavesdropping on the nurses' phone calls and hoping, just hoping it comes out well, and wishing you had Jesus to cling to, or who could come around the waiting room and bring you an Americano and biscotti, saying, "I just heard; I'm so sorry; I'll text my dad and see what He can do," either that or that maybe he would send a priest to swing round, or, at the very least, you still had the knees and the depleted sense of irony that could once again handle prayer, if it didn't feel so goddamned dishonest.

CHAPTER 8

Bread Thou Shalt Remain

That first morning, at 4:30 a.m. in Seattle, sitting on the edge of my bed after Robert's phone call, the idea was growing in my head that my younger brother was dead.

My mind was lacerating my soul. Derek was dead. Dying. Hovering somewhere in between.

– No, came another voice. We don't know that yet.

– An unguarded moment, and he slips by.

– No, he hasn't. He hasn't slipped by.

– When was the last time you talked to him? Was that the last time you'll ever talk to him?

– No. Don't think like that.

– A gin-soaked boy. Dead on his feet.

– Stop it. Stop thinking like that.

– That poor kid. We did this to him. You, me, and Dan.

– No, he made his own choices. He would never listen to you or Dan. He was a pigheaded little prick after he went to college. You couldn't stop this. So stop this.

– Hardheaded. Hah. Hope that helped him.

– He's a Martinez boy. He can take more than most. Even him.

It was my reptile brain and my higher functions engaged in spiritual warfare, in a competition to make it somehow my fault, my responsibility that Derek was in the hospital with his brain pan crushed in. It was hand-to-hand combat, from the deepest Catholic catacombs and programming, and totally biological: Your basest impulses fighting their governors as two independent voices, in vicious disagreement, one determined to make you carry the guilt of the consequences of the actions of others, and the other trying to maintain your sanity, your social function.

These two forces slowly erupted into war, raging barbarically on one another like fighting, snarling dogs, as my mind tried its best to get wrapped around the idea of a world with my younger brother no longer in it. Two voices, two impulses who could each hold a disparate and contradicting idea and believe it wholly, at exactly the same time.

And my mind was never the same, after that.

Back in my apartment, and on the edge of that same bed, at 4:45 a.m., the explosions continued:

– Derek's soft. You know that. He's the third boy; they're usually weaker, effeminate.

– It's my job as his older brother to constantly check his toughness. It's what older brothers do.

– We did this to him. Me and you and Dan. We gave him this need, this idea to fuck himself up like this, fuck himself up to this point.

– How do you figure that?

– The nights you went down there, down to Texas, and played like you were some sort of guru? You did that, didn't you? When he was a kid? The way you and Dan drank in front of him? How Dan drank during the football games, and you'd come home and tell him about your life in Seattle, appealing to that hero-worship?

– Fuck you.

– How you told him that it took all of that one-hit wonder band from Seattle to replace you at the *Stranger*, after you quit? How was he not going to be amazed by that, and follow your lead, or feel entirely intimidated by his older brothers?

– Goddamn you, you bastard.

– Remember that night you were drunk and Dan passed out, and you drove Derek to the Whataburger, all the while in character, and then had a 3:00 a.m. picnic on the tennis courts of the apartment complex Mom was living in, and you and Derek sat there eating your Whataburgers with jalapeños, and he listened to you, enraptured, while you told him to follow his own impulses, his own ideas, because he was smarter than everyone here? You think he wasn't going to listen to you?

– Just fucking stop it.

– Do you remember later when you told him to rescind that first command and do what people were telling him, to get through school and get a degree, but it was kinda too late?

– Just fucking stop. Just stop. Now.

– Remember how he poured the soy sauce on the pad thai, when he was a kid?

– Fuck you.

– And you yelled at him?

– Fuck you. Please stop.

– He was just a kid.

– Stop.

– He was . . . what? Nine? Ten? In Seattle? Eating Thai food for the first time. No distinction in Texas, is there? It's all Chinese. He didn't know any better. So he did what he always did, with Chinese. Poured the soy sauce, ruined the noodles.

– Please.

– Poured the soy sauce, and you yelled at him. You fucking prick.

– Please.

– Now he's dead.

– Jesus. You fucker.

– And you put him there. All he ever wanted to do was to be a part of your little club, you and Dan, his bigger brothers' club. And now he's dead.

– Jesus.

– All he wanted was to impress you and Dan, and look at where that put him.

—◆—

It went on for hours, the razor blades flying through my head as I sat on the side of that bed, alone in my apartment while the sun rose outside and people began moving around, and it was a Saturday morning outside and life out there went on, while it stopped for me, that morning, waiting for news, waiting to know if he would live or die. And if he lived, in what way.

My sisters called, in rotation, exchanging information, the latest news, holding onto hope, trying to keep from thinking the worst. I sat on the phone that morning mostly with Mare, a new mother, and I could hear Mare sniffling, also recently awoken with the shock, and we just sat there for minutes at a time, not saying a word, just listening to each other's silence as we sat and processed what had happened to one of us, needing not so much to have anything to say or hear, but only to have the other person in immediate contact, nearby, just the warmth of familiar beasts, even if it was over a cell phone.

Every member of my family was making their way to Austin, to St. David's Hospital, from every compass point within Texas. (Texas has its own compass, as a part of its joining the Union.) Even my oldest sister, Sylvia, who disapproved wholesale of Derek's "lifestyle" in Austin, was driving there with her husband and youngest child, meaning it was no longer a secret. Our little brother's addictions had grown completely out of control, and a permissive mother could no longer hide the harm he was doing to himself, and he'd ended up here, in a hospital, in intubation, with everyone descending into Austin on an emergency Saturday morning.

Everyone, that is, except for me, in Seattle. I never made it there.

CHAPTER 9

Caramelization

The neurologist had to wait to perform the surgery because Derek's blood alcohol level—on its own—would have killed most people, he said.

My family was gathered in the waiting room and it was now morning there, and I received text messages every few minutes from everyone, but no news.

Someone was finally able to reach Dan, and he made the hour drive from San Antonio to the hospital, and even from the distance, I felt a little better because hospitals are what Dan does best; Dan and Marge together can translate indicators and shrugs and insinuations and the non-promises the doctors and nurses have down to . . . well . . . a science, and they're able to read the medical tea leaves better than anyone else. The family was serving its function. Except for me.

I don't remember the next few hours, or I didn't remember them, until I finally found a letter that I'd written to Derek that day. I don't remember writing it, and it wasn't because I was drinking or on any sort of drugs. I just don't remember writing it, because when I break, writing is what I seem to do. It's become my new home, my new place of security. Instead of praying, instead of asking for help in moments of crisis, I now write.

Here is the letter I wrote to Derek, edited for readability, and so that I don't piss off the *Virgens de Guadalupe* or *San Juan*. Or that other guy, Jesus, and his Dad.

You're unconscious right now, still. It's like, 10:00 a.m. there. 8:00 a.m. here. This is the same unconsciousness that took you since your fall earlier this morning. Lots of stories being told about how it happened, but who really knows what the truth will be, when it surfaces. And you just came out of surgery—brain surgery, Derek—where a neurologist removed a blood clot from the interior of your skull to relieve the pressure it was putting on your brain. And still you're unconscious, hopefully sleeping through this hell you've put us through.

It's a sort of revenge, isn't it? This is how you choose to tell us how severely you resent us. Because we tried to groom you to be the best of us. To hoist you on our shoulders too soon and be too smart and too strong and too much better than what we felt we were. You're making us pay because what we know to be "love" is instead toxic, and it poisons whoever we get in its crosshairs. Do you think we don't know that already?

You're unconscious as I'm writing this. In a way, I'm glad, because just outside your door is the congregation of the whole family Martinez, except for me, who has been sitting here in Seattle in a cringe since 4:30 this morning, unable to stand fully erect because I will vomit from the nerves and the anxiety I feel, and I'm thinking Syl might be the only one of us who might not be there, back in Corpus Christi. She's the only one whose whereabouts I have not heard. Even Dad and Gramma are driving up from Brownsville, Mare told me.

Mare called me at 4:45 a.m. 6:45 a.m. your time. You're still unconscious, alone in a hospital in Austin, TX. Mom and Robert can't find any flights out of Houston at this time; it's too early in the morning for the decent folk. I finally talk to Mom. She is crying, and I am crying. I am whimpering, because I feel I need to prepare myself to let you go. For you to die. To peel off the planet first. And I'm so sorry for you. And I love you so very much. The way I know you love me. How you would feel if you were getting the news that I had been killed, here in Seattle. And so we're crying and I hear Robert in the background talking to people and there's no one around, really, so they make a decision to drive from Houston to Austin instead.

I get up from my bed. In the bathroom, I turn the light on. I want to pray right now, but to do so, to earnestly make a petition to God, that would be totally dishonest. I resist. But I do, eventually.

I'm shaking, sitting on my couch, crying and trying not to cry, staring at the TV for an hour, not knowing what to do. I can't move. You're going to leave me today. It's 3:30 a.m. or so. Maybe 4:00 a.m. I have no sedatives, nothing to take to calm down. I start to sip on a beer. Mom and Robert will be in Austin soon. I turn the TV on to a PBS station and I can take in about 5 percent of the program, something about the Medicis and Florence, Italy, watching the camera explore the naked form of Michelangelo's David, and I'm trying not to think too negatively, hoping against hope that the phrase ". . . they want his family there" is because some decisions should not be left to punk college friends like your skinny little nothing friend Matt, whose wee little head I want to beat in at this point.

And that they weren't really indicating last rites. That's what I was thinking, Derek. That they needed Mom to decide whether to pull you off the respirator or not. You're unconscious. Not asleep, but unconscious. I'm sitting there on my couch, shaped like the top part of a question mark, unable to breathe, imagining the world without you in it anymore. Maybe you just need the peace of unconsciousness right now. I force myself to stop from thinking this line from Hamlet that's racing through my head: "And flights of angels sing thee to thy rest," but it's cycling through my head like a mantra. Instead I try the Our Father, but it doesn't help, because it leads into the Hail Mary, but that prayer to me has always been about accepting death, so I try to stop thinking in words, try to start thinking in images, in memories again.

How I loved you so, since you were born, and we waited in the hospital for you just like this, twenty-two years ago. I was thirteen. Nothing has changed in twenty-two years. We're still waiting on you.

This is going to be one of those nights, I start to recognize. The sort of night that separates your life into one of two categories: Before this night, and After this night. This is when I have to let you go. There are tears on the keyboard right now, on my hands and fingertips as I write this. I've been crying since 2:30 this morning. I don't think I've ever cried like this in my life.

I take four Benadryl at about 4:30 a.m. and force down another beer, play a loud epic movie just to have something to look at while I wait for sleep. It comes hard, slow, and painful because I don't want to wake up thinking about this, do not want that clarity of hypnologic sleep where your heart, your subconscious, and your superconscious all align and give you great symbols for a clear few minutes, and you look into the mirror of your soul, because I don't think I can handle that today you're going to leave us—so maybe it's better to simply stay awake?

I crawl pathetically back into my messed-up bed around 5:30 or so and I lie there, and try to send my mind to you, in your unconscious state, and I grip the bedclothes like I'm holding your hand, and try to guide your way back home. I really think I can do this. You're not ready to leave yet, Derek. I'm "dreaming," like the aboriginals in Australia. You're not done here. I imagine you in the darkness, and I'm grabbing your hand and I'm going to bring you home, Derek. You're not going yet. We're not ready. You're not ready. And I fall asleep with your hand in mine, and you're still unconscious in Texas.

I think I slept about an hour. From 6:00 a.m. to 7:00 a.m. Mom and Robert arrived at the hospital and talked to the doctor. He has CAT scans, and there's bleeding in your head, Derek. Your blood alcohol level is so high, they can't operate until you metabolize further. You're five times the legal limit in Texas, and the doctor scares the family by saying, ". . . He was two to three drinks from dying from alcohol poisoning." Which might be fair to a normal person, but you're a Martinez boy. That translates to another twelve-pack, probably. I don't know how to compare that with real statistics. Perhaps it's ten times in a nanny state like Washington, especially with what I imagine your tolerance is now. I'm sure I've been there, too, and often. But I never took a dive off a stage on my head, Derek. The most damage I think I ever did was call some ex-girlfriends and mope, hoping for sex in the future. Stupid things that didn't involve Mom graying further and your family thinking that you were going to die today. I've never done the stuff you do, have such disregard for yourself and the people who love you. Doctor says this isn't a life-threatening situation, but they'll have to go in and remove the clot, for fear you might stroke. They're getting a neurological team together to cut a hole in your head.

Marge calls. And they're preparing to travel to Austin. I call Mare and Mark, and they are there, sturdy, reliable. Traveling with a very cranky Madison, who's imitating everything Mare says to me from the backseat.

I can't sit upright. I can't stop crying. You remember my friend Camille. Even she calls finally from Chicago, having received my message, puts the wood under my feet: Remember, the doctor said it wasn't life threatening. They don't say that if they can't mean it, she says. Millions of people have brain surgery every year. I don't mean to downplay it, she says, because it is serious, but it's survivable. He's going to pull through. This phrase, I have heard twice already this morning. Once from Mom: "He has to pull through. He has to pull through," though in her tone I could hear she was making herself believe it, and then I heard it a second time from Amy, who strangely always knows what's going to happen, even when I insist I KNOW the outcome, whatever Amy says is usually the case (we call her "the Queen of Everything"), and she had said, at 5:00 that morning: "He's going to pull through. You Martinez boys are of hearty stock. Look at what happened to Dan's knee, how he's recovered. Plus Derek's really young. People are made out of rubber at that age. He's going to pull through. Stop killing yourself. Besides, he fell off the stage at a Public Enemy concert. That's not even a good story. Derek is better than that." I think I smiled a little through my tears. Because I didn't want to spend my life trying to kick the shit out of Flavor Flav and Dr. Dre. Though I really think I would have.

Derek, you're the bloom on the Martinez tree. I'm just bark. All bark.

I remember to call and cancel my ride to work this morning with Bob and use my "cool" voice. We had planned to work at 7:00 a.m. and do a full shift this Saturday because we're that far behind. But I'm a complete mess here. And it's what? 8:00 a.m. now. Been up since 2:30. No point in going to work. I can't concentrate. I can hardly write this now.

Please wake up, Derek.

Please wake up. We have so much to do still. We've got to get started. It's getting late for us.

I love you so very much.

june

PS

I left messages for Andy McCarty, for Philippe in Los Angeles, hoping they don't call back because it's pretty unsettling to cry in front of your male friends. But I'm thinking I need to talk to Philippe's wife, Christine, because she's a psychiatrist and I think I might be breaking down now, think that I might be undone, that I might now, really be crazy, that this was actually it, that I might need evaluation, need help, need to be kept from feeling what I'm feeling. That I won't be able to integrate further, or ever again.

When I woke up again earlier, at 6:00 a.m., I looked out the window and started writing you a letter in my mind—not this one, another one—letting you go. It began like this:

"It's not raining today, the day you died, Derek Allen Martinez. For some reason, I always thought it would be raining."

I couldn't get past that line.

Do you know that you're the one person—no, that's not true; one of two or three people—in my life that I always think about, to impress? That when I think something "smart" or do something extraordinary, that it's you that I'm working for? "Derek will like this." "Derek will get this." "Derek will think this is funny." "Derek will understand how tough I am if I do this." Do you understand that you're my unter-hero? Reverse hero?

Destruction is easy, Derek. It's too simple. Though you've done a great job of it.

Let's grow up now. Please. I'm really tired. And I want to go home. But I have to grow home first, and then I can get us there. No matter where I am, no matter how small my apartment, you can always be a part of it. You have a safe place to come home to.

CHAPTER 10

Toast

It was roughly 4:00 p.m. when the doctors decided that Derek would not die and that he could be brought out of the medically induced coma within a day. It was about this time I could breathe a sigh of relief and try to sleep.

We were all overjoyed, and it was interesting because it wasn't just Derek who had come back from the brink, but my old man, Mingo, who had been there with his mother throughout. He had put away all his hostility and macho bullshit when he walked into the waiting room and took Robert, my mother's new husband, a proud, strong African-American man, aside, and put his arm around Robert and thanked him for helping Mom and keeping our family together through this crisis. No one could believe what they were seeing, but I did, when people told me, because I started believing in these shifts in people, and here was Dad, our Mingo, being a man for the third time in his life, in front of his family, and growing as a human being.

Such wonderful news, from such a tragic start. We were becoming a family again.

But being up in Seattle, alone, I think I chugged a bottle of chardonnay before I fell asleep and dreamt of nothing.

I called the next day and Derek had been taken off intubation, something Marge and Dan sat through, as medical masochists, and Derek was prepped to stay for a couple of days, the rest of the family hovering and attempting to be useful, but there was no further news, nothing of any consequence.

Still, I was shaking, up here and alone.

The next day, it was the same—no news, still shaking, in Seattle and alone—and I had to be at work. I was working at a derelict publishing company in South Seattle, producing really crap trade magazines, and that Monday, I was in trouble.

Or, rather, everyone else was.

I don't know why I even showed up at work. In a matter of minutes, my boss, David, who was this huge, paternal Chicano from San Diego, saw I was in the shit and—given our nature—even though it started in a shouting match with both of us squaring off, chicken-chested and about to fight (and he would have killed me, because he's huge), it ended with his arm around me and me crying my eyes out and telling him the whole story, and him telling me how he'd lost his own brothers and one of his sons. Mexicans in crisis.

By noon, he told me to get home and take some time off, but I decided it was finally time to find help. I couldn't do this anymore.

I needed therapy.

Fuck that; I needed hospitalization. There are some doors you can't go through alone, and I'd already been through ten. Couldn't do the macho shit and endure on my own anymore.

I started seeing a therapist because she was in both my neighborhood and coverage, and I didn't realize until our third or fourth meeting that she specialized in "coming out," making the transition from a heterosexual to homosexual identity.

Fantastic, I thought. *Not only did the Derek thing happen, now I have to dress better.*

And that's where Steph came in.

PART II

THE UNWEDDED

CHAPTER 11

It Was Just One of Those Things

I met Steph during my recovery from sinus surgery, about a year after Derek's accident. Derek's accident had opened me up in a way that I had never considered possible, exposed a vein of fragility that was still open to the elements. He had recovered, physically, from the fall and the surgery, but he was still listless and undefined as a human being and refused to talk to anyone even more resolutely. Mom and Robert took him back to Houston to recover, and he spent three months sleeping all day and watching HBO all night until Robert finally had enough, said it was time to get to doing something: either return to school or get to work.

Derek, of course, tried to get back to school, against all of the family's wishes and sense of doom, and for a few months, he tried to insinuate himself back into the curriculum, but of course it never worked. For a while he was lost once again in the same lifestyle, but by then, even his "friends" were wary of him, afraid of his capacity for self-destruction. In the end, Derek wound up in San Antonio, living with Dan, working at a Starbucks and a liquor store, part-time. He was miserable, different.

He was suffering from an undiagnosed traumatic brain injury, but no one knew it then.

We all thought he was just terribly ashamed of himself, how far from grace he'd fallen.

And me, personally, being left out the way I was, being so far away in Seattle, I felt a heartbreak like I'd never known, my neurology half-fried and my ache to see and talk to my brothers like a naked wound.

It didn't help that I didn't sleep for a year, suffering from polyps and allergies that were finally diagnosed and, because I finally had the health insurance, slated for removal.

My mother and sister Marge insisted on coming up and taking care of me for the surgery, and initially I resisted—I'd gone this long doing things on my own; I would do this, as well, I figured, but no: They insisted on being here, and dear God were they correct. I was as weak as a new-born joey, that morning after the surgery. And the kindness and caring they gave me for two days, it really broke me open because I hadn't been around family for so long, and after the incident with Derek, I had no idea how much I had been missing it.

⸺⸺

So, a week later, after they'd left, there I was, bundled up on my couch in my apartment in Seattle and high on Vicodin and Percocet, and the Three Buck Chuck from Trader Joe's, answering ads online out of boredom on a borrowed computer and someone else's unsecured Wi-Fi. This had been a bad time, as I'd been living in Seattle for more than fifteen years, and it felt like one day I looked around and everyone had just gone. Normally never at a loss for friends or work comrades, I suddenly found myself having less and less in common with the people I worked with in the print publishing industry as a graphic designer. Although I had moved to Seattle to become a writer, I never developed enough courage to write for the many publications I designed. Eventually, publishing became polarized: Magazines and newspapers shrank into mudpools of rednecks and old-school blue-collar printers while electronic publishing scooped up all the young kids who were enthusiastic about learning Internet design, and I became stuck in the middle. My closest work associates were now unlikeable working detritus, geoplanarians tired and broken down and uninteresting—not exactly the sort of people you'd want to grab a pint with after work. I had loose networks of other friends, good friends, but no one I saw regularly, since we no longer worked together. So I was often alone, and I was becoming quite lonely when I met Steph, online.

We could never bring ourselves to admit it to anyone that we'd met online, that Craigslist had been our method of introduction, but it was.

Or at least I had sense enough to be ashamed about it; Steph never was. *Caveat emptor* should be Craigslist's coat of arms.

The problem with dating people online, at least as I had seen it, was the lack of context, like a dependent clause dropped in the middle of a sentence without punctuation. It's disruptive, creates nonsense. Where does it belong? It's going to mess everything up because it doesn't fit anywhere. You need the punctuation to set apart the dependency, tell you where it relates. You meet someone at work, or through mutual friends, and there's a decorum involved: You know the same people, so you have a level of social responsibility to both the person you're dating and the people you know in common. There's a framework within the social contract. It's John Locke.

Not so, when you meet someone on a dating site. There's no framework. So you can be the most terrible person in the world, and there are no consequences, except you never see that person again. Or, if they're a schmegegge, then they ask you out again.

That's what you get online, sometimes. I've heard the stories. Online, I would have to woo girls that I felt were beneath me, but who wouldn't give me the time of day. The first girl I met for a date came back to my apartment for a bottle of red wine after we had dinner at a nearby restaurant, and right in the middle of watching *The Exorcist*, she excused herself suddenly and left. At first, I thought, *Hmm. Perhaps not the best movie for a first date*, since it had happened right after the crucifix-in-the-vagina scene, but then I realized she had taken all my prescription medication from my bathroom. Case in point.

So Steph and I settled on an origin myth and stuck to it: We met over work, on a shared project. Like Jesus and Mary. So there.

I insisted on it, and she would always be annoyed with me when I did, felt like I was ashamed of her, because she did most of her shopping and flirting and living through Craigslist, while I knew it for the dangerous electronic flea market that it was, and has remained.

———

I suppose I should have run away when I heard her ringtone.

Our first date was postponed indefinitely when Steph stalled our electronic flirting with an e-mail telling me that it would never work, and that she preferred women anyway. I remember she phrased it like, "Your parents gave you a chromosome that I'm incompatible with."

Hunh, I thought. *Well, I can stop responding to* that *one*. I thought it was a disguised method of saying she wasn't fond of non-Europeans. Still, I had a thing for tomboys, then.

Three weeks later, I received an enthusiastic invitation to lunch one Saturday afternoon, no mention of or *mea culpa* about the prior e-mail, just a completely optimistic and brilliantly happy message asking me to lunch in downtown Seattle.

"Sure," I said. "I have very little going on that day." And it was true. In my isolation, I had taken to drinking far too much with Dougherty. But we didn't drink so much on Saturday mornings. Not yet, anyhow.

But the severity of Steph's shift should have been my biggest indication that I was headed into troubled waters; how quickly her mind had changed—and the extremity to which it had changed—was a clear indication of issues. I see that now. I see a lot of things now that I didn't before.

Still, I was oddly passive back then, told myself I just didn't have any preferences, which was a half-truth. I was still just a slice of bread, had not yet caramelized my sugars into toast, if you don't mind the metaphor. Hadn't reached my transfiguration, like Jesus.

She drove up in a huge green Jeep Grand Cherokee, a sort of SUV that has trouble with the claustrophobic Seattle streets. I have a clear image in my mind of that green behemoth turning a distant corner and doing a slow crawl to the front steps of my apartment block as I stood waiting that Saturday morning, dressed in pinstripe trousers and a T-shirt and light jacket, pacing while I awaited the consequences of my online decision making, embarrassed that my life had devolved to even this.

I was smoking a Gauloises, the French cigarette, but not inhaling, as I have asthma, and after a few serious attempts at developing a smoking habit, I had to settle for the cigarette as an accoutrement and nothing else. In fact, during this whole period, it was all about the smoking accoutrements: My friend Philippe had taken it upon himself to introduce me to the films of Jean-Pierre Melville and Alain Delon and they had left a stylistic impression. I loved the cigarette cases, the Zippo lighters, the

Gauloises cigarettes, but I was damned if I could smoke them. So I puffed on them for flavor and held them in affected sangfroid, just inches from my lips, feeling *tres, tres* cool.

Or, at least pretending to feel that cool. I was taking after my sisters from long ago and reinventing myself as a poseur.

And then Steph rolled to a stop. Her window came down. And a redheaded pixie with bright blue eyes was at the wheel, hair pinned to the side with a barrette, a snaggletooth pressing down on her lower lip as she smiled coquettishly.

Oh, shit, I thought. *This is her.* That was the trap. The slim-hipped gentile promised to every son of an immigrant family as per the American Dream—Lois Lane for Superman. Diane Keaton for Michael Corleone and Woody Allen. Mary Jane for Spider-Man. Betty for the Hulk.

I needed to be careful.

The interior of her Jeep looked like she lived in it half the time, and I felt uncomfortable clearing a space in the passenger seat but eventually managed to carve an area large enough for me to sit, in the middle of bills, old makeup compacts, cereal bar wrappers, and the discarded indications of a serious coffee habit. When I finally settled in, I navigated her downtown and near a sculpture park she was interested in seeing by the revitalized waterfront, and she found parking. She lived north of the city, and I lived right downtown, so I knew the confounding intricacies of the downtown streets better than she did. As I emerged from the truck, I noticed an old sock in the street and I was unsure whether it belonged there or if it had once lived in the Jeep—such was the nature of her backseat—and argued with myself as to whether I should mention it. Perhaps a second sock existed, inside, equally caked with dirt and soot and pebbles. Maybe I was creating a sock tragedy by not mentioning it. I just didn't know.

I decided it would go unmentioned, and as we walked away from the Jeep, she received a call on her cell phone, and in a few simple notes, I recognized her ringtone: "Miss Otis Regrets." I stopped dead in my tracks and stared at her while she silenced the phone and plunged it back into her voluminous handbag, uncertain if that was her idea of a test, or a joke.

"That's 'Miss Otis Regrets,' isn't it? You know that song? Cole Porter?" I asked her.

"Of course I know what it is," she replied.

"You . . . you do know what that song is about, don't you?" I asked, hesitantly.

She gave me another of her big snaggletoothed smiles and thrust her arm through my crooked elbow, my hands deep in the pockets of my coat, and she pulled me along, laughing, with me unsure as to whether I was headed toward my execution, or just a friendly lunch with a bisexual second-wave feminist suffragette, like you sometimes did on the West Coast.

The sculpture park was relatively new at this point, and the groundskeeping reflected this, left quite a bit to be desired. Still, it was a waterfront installation, a part of the revitalization and renewal project for an area of downtown Seattle that had been previously left unused, a no-man's-land between a rail line and the Puget Sound shore, left derelict and un-touristed.

It was an easy walk from my neighborhood, but, being an ex-pat Texan, I hardly walked anywhere without reason, unless there was booze at the end of it. Certainly not for exercise. Today was no different, and we wandered about the place, which felt half-completed, partially abandoned, or simply badly designed as an urban project, and meandered about in full audition for the other.

She was a secret smoker, as she worked for a medical research firm and felt her boss, whom she held in the highest estimation, would be terribly disappointed in her if she found out her habit, so my smelling like a French gangster bothered her very little.

That afternoon, that audition, was very gentle, witty like a Noel Coward one-act, as we playfully teased each other and tried to sound out each other's definitions, boundaries, and issues, the usual kittenness of a first date, and something to which I wasn't much accustomed.

I'd never really "dated," I began to realize about myself around this time.

My romantic intrusions were usually a result of drunken workplace fumblings, out for drinks with a group of people and hey, here's an empty room . . . why not? Terribly inelegant, sure, but lots of fun when you're twenty-five.

Otherwise, my long-term relationships had evolved out of preservation and planning: I like you, you're a poor artist/musician/craftsperson/ painter like me, let's move in together and see how long we can stand each other. I think the term is *bohemian*, when the herpes stays within a certain element of the artsy part of a city. So to speak.

Anyhow, here, with Steph, was one of the first times in my life I was making a choice to "date" someone, to meet that person for a ritualized meal, one on one, and flirt and engage and see where it would lead, over coffee or drinks or the soup du jour, because I was finally independent, stable, and secure enough to make a choice, and not have the choice made for me by circumstance or poverty.

That first afternoon, we were both on our best behavior and we were both quite adorable if nervous, and we eventually strolled downtown and had lunch at a cliffside tavern (there are some steep embankments in Seattle), and then, again, in the middle of our conversation I had another indication that maybe things were not quite what they seemed, when I realized that Steph was checking out the waitress.

"Are you . . . are you checking out the waitress?" I asked her.

"What? No, of course not. But she looks great in that A-line skirt and peasant blouse."

I thought she looked like a sack of blond potatoes, but maybe that spoke to her European root vegetable/famine genetics, the way a good salsa spoke to mine.

Things were quiet for a minute, and I heard Steph mutter, "pink and tan," under her breath, and I thought she was going to order a drink.

"Great," I said, "I'll have a black and tan. What's in a pink and tan?" I asked, a bit loudly, and Steph hid her face in her menu and I looked over her shoulder to see a tourist that had seen far too much of the inside of a tanning booth, looking leathery and hard-ridden, with Day-Glo pink lipstick to match her tube top, and she gave me a hard look. The man sitting next to her also gave me a hard stare, in case my comment stepped in the way of his possibility for sex because I'd inadvertently wandered into the minefield of his date's insecurities.

I hid behind my own menu and began giggling, and we had our first true bonding moment, over someone else's pain.

A minute later, I ordered that beer anyway, the black and tan, because it seemed to be a knock-off Irish public house that we were in, and I sensed the atmosphere chill considerably. Steph ordered a chai tea for herself, and I had my "beer cocktail," named after the British occupation of Ireland, as goes one of its origin myths. While I calmed down a bit on the first date, she became quiet and uncomfortable, as the drink order somehow triggered something for her.

<hr>

We continued to see each other. We developed an odd chemistry that could ignite only between two misanthropes, two outsiders.

We loved e-mailing and texting every bit of cleverness back and forth so that working became a distraction, and I think for a little while there, we were able to break free of the Craigslist curse, the sense of "You'll do," and move into the "Wow, I'm really happy I met you" phase, though Steph was unusually secretive about some really strange things in her life.

She considered herself a writer, was rather impressed with my tenacity and dedication in that I kept writing on my own, quietly and in secret, while I continued working as a graphic designer. She ran a writers' group, she said, and asked if I would be interested in joining.

"Oh, no," I said. "I tried that once. It's not for me."

"Why not?" she asked, genuinely curious. "It helps a lot of people to have a deadline or a goal, some kind of obligation that keeps them writing."

"I'm not on any kind of schedule, really," I said. "And the writing is kind of compulsive for me. The stories are just there and I have to get them down in order to quiet the narrative in my head. That's why I do it at work, or at night. It's like a humming or a buzzing that doesn't go away until I ground it."

"And you can't share it with others?"

"I don't really trust or take anyone else's critiques as useful. I mean,

I listen to what they have to say about my writing, and then I read their own writing, and if it's inferior to mine, I don't feel they have the authority to comment. And the wounded egos are just tiresome."

"You don't play well with other children," she said, smiling.

"And I have to reserve my humiliation for these," I said, and pulled open a drawer to show her a stack of rejection slips. I'd taken to sending a few, disjointed chapters and writing samples to agencies in New York, addresses culled from the Internet because that's what I had seen on television and in movies as the first step in publishing, but what I was sending out was irregular and haphazard: I deserved the rejection notices. Still, Steph was duly impressed that I had taken that step, had pushed it even that far.

And while she was a consistent journal writer, would spend an afternoon writing a thousand words about something she'd seen or experienced that day, she didn't have a single project she was working on, would do her monthly writing group as an exercise, rather than for productivity.

The more time we spent together, the more our differences began to emerge, and we tried valiantly to overcome them because we liked each other as much as we did.

For our third date, she picked me up at work one Friday afternoon and we drove to a ferry and sat in line in the rain, while she pulled out a plate with a pork chop and asparagus and some mashed potatoes from a dinner party she had thrown the evening before. It felt odd to sit there, in the Jeep, and pick at the food while her dog, a weird, sometimes quite stupid lab mix she called Cleopatra, or Cleo for short, stared over my shoulder and drooled. I made as if to eat, was politely grateful, but then said I wasn't very hungry.

"Not a problem," Steph said, and then absentmindedly handed the plate over to Cleo, who clamped down on it like a prisoner of war, licking the plate clean in a matter of seconds.

We took the ferry over to the peninsula, drove into the old-growth forest, and rented a cabin for the weekend. On Saturday morning when I woke up, I couldn't find her, had a moment of extreme panic because I thought she'd left, but then discovered her asleep in the Jeep. She had spent the night in the back with Cleo because I had been snoring far too loudly for her taste.

I felt ashamed, but she was playful about it.

"I'm a loud sleeper," I said.

"We'll have to get that fixed," she said, as she took the dog out for the morning ritual.

That night, we sat in front of the fireplace and charted her family tree, her origins and relations, and then we did mine, and she listened to me as I told her about my own histories, my own family, how I'd started writing a book about it, mostly because I wanted to understand it myself. We sat down at a table and did a Venn diagram of my family, then hers, and we asked questions about one another and told stories about each member of our immediate families. While I was comfortable and open and transparent, I felt there was a lot that Steph was not saying, was leaving for the reader to imagine instead of trusting the author, so to speak, in much the same manner of the authors she loved best, who demurred and dithered and shifted with language and never told you outright what the truth of the moment might be, sort of the opposite of poetry.

But that was Steph, I was beginning to understand, and I decided I really liked her. She was a bad fit for the world, in much the same manner that I felt I'd been, and she was this tidy little combination of Sinead O'Connor's commitment to her beliefs cross-pollinated with Wolverine's ferocity. Sort of a modern-day Patricia Highsmith, before the mental illness.

It worked well for us, I thought, because once, before his event, Derek had told me I was a lot like the Hulk. "Except, maybe angrier," he added, on second thought.

And I admired her, as a person: She would work only for companies that had a cause, nonprofits. Would take a much lower wage than she could draw, if she felt committed to the larger cause. Currently, she said, she was tackling breast cancer.

That impressed me, as someone who couldn't think past my next paycheck.

I found out she also loved camping, was very much into the rural Henry David Thoreau self-independence thing that Yankees actually take seriously, since she hailed from the land of H. P. Lovecraft. I knew she loved reading, I knew she wasn't a fan of movies or television, and I knew she would go on mystic urban walkabouts with Cleo. I knew, eventually, that she'd been involved in a ten-year relationship with another woman and was now swinging back around to boys. I knew she wasn't big on food or drinks or drinking, so that was going to be a mark against her, because I'd become quite the urban hipster, not a foodie exactly, but I'd dated a foodie, just enough to know how to navigate in that world, and I enjoyed it.

I knew she began seeing me as the sort of eroticized "other," because I was Mexican American, from Texas. And I felt the same, as she was the slim-hipped gentile goal of every immigrant story, as I've mentioned before.

———

We ended the summer by driving a bit north to one of the many beachside parks that dot some of the water-view neighborhoods overlooking Puget Sound. Since it was a nice Saturday afternoon, it was fairly busy, so we took off our shoes and meandered in the hard, wet sand, walked along the shore and looked at all the beach art left behind by kids and hippies and the artistically inclined, using water-logged detritus as media.

We stopped by an embedded labyrinth of shells, laid out large in a swirling conch pattern, and entered at the open end; we made it halfway around before I stopped and said, "I can't go on; I'm afraid I'll never make it back out," and Steph laughed and thought I was speaking metaphorically about our relationship, and something flickered for a minute, and then vanished and was gone.

Her phone chimed the Cole Porter song and it was her mother, calling from Steph's hometown, and she decided to answer it. She sat on a log and made a kind of radio theater of her own with that conversation because she knew I was listening, and she helped paint a portrait of Rockwellian rhapsody, flared the phone out so I could hear her mother going on and on about how she and the other doyenne of their small town had banded together to keep a large "box store" out of the town square, and how happy they were in keeping the provincial integrity of the town. It was Arcadian, hearing them engage like that, and lit up every point on my compass; I wanted to be in, wanted to be a part of this bucolic idealization of Americana. It was something I thought I really wanted, back then.

"What do they have against boxes?" I asked.

"Not that kind of store," Steph said, laughing, and if there had been the thin bat squeak of something big brewing earlier on, it was an all-out foghorn in that goofy grin she gave me, when she wrapped her arm over my neck and kissed me on the cheek, and we wandered back through the beach to her Jeep.

CHAPTER 12

Stephanie of a Thousand Lives

It had taken a month for Stephanie to come clean and tell me what drove her west, what drove her to put so much distance between herself and her family, in the way I had done with mine. We were on another of the long, woodsy walks she loved to take with her dog, and I started telling her about Derek, and the wound that event had left on all of my family.

She was quiet for a while, and then somewhere in there she decided to tell me about her own reasons for moving to Seattle, her reasons for putting a whole country between her future and her past, but not until we were back at her house and in the safety of her basement bedroom, curled up in her huge sleigh bed.

She was twenty-two, she said, and she'd been driving a small car, a compact two-door Mazda, with someone she'd been dating in the front seat and her younger brother in the backseat, when she was home for a weekend from college.

An old man with a brain tumor, confused, in a large car, entered the highway going the opposite direction, came right at them, just on the opposite side of a rise in the road.

"He was just there, out of nowhere," she told me as we were lying quietly in bed.

"Jesus, Steph; I'm so sorry."

"My little brother was killed, from the backseat. I wasn't expected to survive. The other person wasn't even bruised. Funny how car wrecks are."

I remained quiet, unsure what to say.

"My skull was cracked in the impact. That's why I call it 'my dented head' sometimes. I heard my little brother dying, in the wreck. I kept telling him to hang on, but he was already too far gone. I have epilepsy now, as a result. And a plate in my head. That's why you can see that scar, going around."

I pulled her hair back a bit and noticed a small, thin line circling her scalp, like she said. I studied her face a little closer and saw that it was structurally unsound, like a Picasso painting.

"You poor thing," I said, not sure what else to do.

"I take medication to control the epilepsy, but sometimes it makes my thinking too fuzzy."

I was concerned more for the plate in her head. How do you protect yourself from that?

"And the plate, in your head, what's that like?"

"I can't feel it," she said. "It's just there."

"Hunh."

Run away, I thought to myself. *I can't help here. This is much bigger than me.*

Still, I was drawn to her, for some reason. Drawn to the anguish, the brokenness, and more than anything else, the intelligence, and the misfit quality.

She's like me, I thought. *And if there's redemption for her, there's redemption for me.*

We'll do it together.

—◦—

I began to suspect something was seriously wrong with her on the way back from our drive to eastern Washington, after I'd had an interview with a small company, specializing in bilingual marketing, that intended on growing into a media firm. Currently the owners were responsible for products that were travesties to printed publication, at least in English, as they claimed their Spanish was sublime, but I wasn't a good judge of that; I write in Spanish the way Irvine Welsh writes in English. I'd read about them in a business journal, seen an opportunity and leapt for it, offering to clean up their product and raise their profile so they could compete in larger, more sophisticated urban markets.

Great, they'd said; come out to the eastern part of the state and let's see if we can come to terms. *Fantastic*, I thought: This was the opportunity

I'd been looking for, within my skill set and at my leisure. I could work from home, off a laptop. Freedom at last.

So I rented a car and invited Steph, thought we could do with a stretch of the legs for a Saturday afternoon, since we were still getting to know one another.

I had a meeting with the business owners, two families of second-generation Mexican-American heritage, who grew up in the agricultural stratums of eastern Washington, their parents pickers before them, and now, this generation of children graduated from state colleges and set to illuminate the world, or at least their corner of the state, with the power of the Hispanic dollar and the megachurch. But first, they needed a spell checker, an upgrade to their literacy, and corporate identity in their literature, which was currently being produced by two high school seniors on Photoshop. It was shockingly bad.

———

Off we went, and the four-hour drive was not without its weirdness, as we had both made playlists for the trip. I began to notice that Steph was taking the lyrical insinuations from the songs I'd picked with just a bit too much sincerity, far too literally, and much too personally, to the point where she was becoming visibly upset at particular songs, which, to me, were an enduring liturgy of wordplay and the weary exhaustion of dying relationships—but certainly not a reflection on what was going on in that car, at that time. They were just good songs.

But Steph felt I was telling her something, through the music, and she was getting angry.

"Is that what you're trying to tell me? That this relationship is not realistic?"

"Steph, this is weird. It's just a song. The lyrics are fantastic; I thought you'd like it because you like words so much. This writing is some of the best I've heard in the last ten years."

"Why does it have to be so cynical?"

It was true, I began to notice: Everything she was playing was bordering on the coy, the optimistically naive and bubbly. Everything I was playing was *musica verité*, the deep complications and sharp-edged intricacies of relationships. I had none of her optimism, which, in all candor, I felt was put on and insincere. There was a sense of the forced, with her optimism, a desperation that I felt undermined any sense of calm or meditative guarantee of a positive outcome.

The tension in that rental car exploded into an actual argument about an hour from our destination, when I played a song by Evan Dando, which was actually a song about, well, negotiating the hairpin turns in a relationship, and she lost her temper, from the passenger seat.

"What does that mean? That I'm abusive?"

"It's just a song! I just like it! It's not a message to you from him or me! What the hell, Steph?? Are we supposed to listen to your granola shit for an eight-hour drive and I can't play what I like? I thought you'd like this, since he's from your part of the world. Jesus fuck."

Pause. Quiet in the car for three minutes.

"You know I have a job interview for something I've worked really hard to get in roughly an hour, right? And this is not going to help me interview?"

Quiet, for ten more minutes. Then we were unexpectedly closer to the destination than we had anticipated, and I was at the strip mall offices of the "media company," and I had to switch into interview mode with this tension hanging over me.

They were in the parking lot, awaiting my arrival. Before I could change into more presentable clothing, I was put in front of both families, the four investors who owned the company, in my traveling clothes (shorts, nondescript T, and sandals). Behind me, Steph peeled out in the rental, making the introductions a bit awkward. I began my presentation, trying to block out the weirdness of the drive from Seattle with Steph and attempting to ignore the worry as to whether she'd already decided to drive back home in a huff.

My presentation was spectacular. I was genuine, relaxed, and competent and showed everyone present how I could raise the image of their company with a few changes and uniformity and standardization of logos, branding, and, well, literacy, and with all this, I could get them in front of the big players, instead of the mom-and-pop bullshit they were currently stuck with. Then I pulled out reworkings I had done on their "newspaper" and brochures, whatever I could find online, materials I had rebuilt to standard.

It went over like gangbusters.

It helped that they reminded me entirely of the families and businesspeople of South Texas, spoke identically in that lilting bifurcation of Spanish and English of educated second-generation Mexican Americans, and yet, I felt very much that we were not cut from the same cloth. I was way too punk, and they were way too drunk on the blood of Christ, and not just the wine cooler/low-alcohol content of the Catholic Church, mind you. These were the sort of Christians who burned the Harry Potter books, I could tell right away. Still, their money spent.

I was invited to lunch, and I demurred because I was tired from the performance and wanted to leave things on an "up" note, wasn't certain in what mood I'd find Steph or whether I would encounter her again that afternoon. So I made some excuses and wondered if I was stuck in Kennewick for the weekend, when I was finally able to reach Steph on her phone, and she said she'd be right over.

She was a different person than the one who had peeled off two hours before.

She was bright and gushy and came around the vehicle and was introduced to the owners, who made an awkward, very un-white insistence on "welcoming everyone like family," and I was nervous at what Steph's reaction was going to be. And instead of embarrassing me, she was entirely likeable and receptive, though a bit too anthropological. But I could forgive her for that, because God knows if the situation had been reversed, I'd have broken out my pad and pencil and started sketching her Yankee family and their habitat as well, but it still left me feeling unsettled and uncertain.

What really set me on edge, as we headed back to Seattle, was that Steph insisted on playing only my playlist, and had memorized every song that had upset her before, and sang them without hesitation at full volume in a chirpy, optimistic enthusiasm that gave me the creeps for the full drive home.

"Those people were nice," she said.

"Yeah, they totally remind me of the Mexican Americans of South Texas. Like my sisters used to be, which is weird," I said.

"Yes, them, too. But the people I met at the mall, they were nice as well," she said.

"You mingled at the mall? How very small-town of you. Whatever inspired you to do that?" This didn't seem like her, for some reason.

"Oh, they came up to the car to check up on me," she said.

"Hunh," I said. Tingle, tingle. "Was there, did something happen?"

"I just had my head against the window and they came up and knocked to see if I was all right," she said, and then continued singing.

Holy shit, I thought. *This doesn't feel right.*

What was she not saying?

As I learned more about her, and upon reflection, it's clear now that she was on the verge of some kind of episode in the hour leading up to the destination in Kennewick. Her anger and hostility at imagined slights was an indication of her traumatic brain injury, which very likely led to an epileptic fit, in the parking lot of the mall, when she was alone, and she wouldn't tell me it happened, couldn't allow herself to be considered "damaged goods," so she hid it, tried to keep it under control.

I was offered the job a week later, and Steph wanted to camp as a celebration. I can't imagine why I would have agreed to this; I must have been thinking about something else and trying to assuage her when I said yes. It had to have been, because before I knew it, we were driving her Jeep to her favorite camping destination, a place called Bacon Creek that you could only find on those geosurvey maps. But I tried to get into the spirit, even went to a general store in a dodgy part of Seattle and bought "his and hers" machetes for thirty dollars.

She'd been there before, she told me, many times, and it was perfectly safe. Just a few hours northeast of Seattle.

"That's fine," I probably said, when I meant, "Absolutely not, I hate camping."

Camping, as someone I trust implicitly once told me, is at its best definition an agreement to be uncomfortable.

I was no longer willing to make that agreement, with anyone or any-thing, and yet, somehow, I found myself driving north and then east with Steph and her dog, Cleo, on a four-hour trip into the Cascade Mountains. Perhaps in my youth I'd have been much more engaged in this trip, in this destination of raw, untamed wilderness off switchbacks and log-ging roads, last traveled by men with huge fuckoff moustaches and sore bottoms, their knee-high leather boots squeaking from moisture. But I wasn't that guy anymore, no longer into Indiana Jones–style adventures and risk taking. I wanted gravel paths and stepped ascenders and at least the insinuation of a fence between me and a plummet: I wanted assur-ances and rough-hewn guarantees, placards telling me about the pioneers and conservationists responsible for this lovely meadow view onto Puget Sound. But watch your step, in case of soil erosion.

Lovely. Now, when's drinks? I'd ask, in my best P. G. Wodehouse. *Shall we repair to someplace warm? Capital.*

That was my renewed idea of camping; at worst, it was a motel room rented from a redneck.

But for Steph, it was the unrefined, untamed wildness of the North-west land that drew her, brought her closer to communion, called to her wild rumpus, fed her Max in *Where the Wild Things Are.*

It was a Friday night, after we'd finished work, and her truck was loaded with the camping kit. We'd made it out through I-5 and the North Cascades Highway when Steph turned off after a bridge she knew well and started driving through these rustic, nearly reassumed logging roads. The battered old Jeep's headlights were hardly better than a pair of weak flashlights, illuminating very close to nothing. She navigated this behe-moth through some frightening isolated spots for an hour, drawing us deeper and deeper into the natural brush, and my anxieties and primal sense of de-escalation of the predatory ladder grew with each slipping minute.

I really wanted a handgun, or at least a large-caliber rifle.

Instead, I had Cleo, who was going apeshit with all the smells of deer and bear when she put her nose through the back window of the Jeep. I can only imagine what she was experiencing and what frightened her. What she knew.

Steph arrived at the road's terminus, and a path continued, so in the dark we shouldered our gear a half mile farther into the woods and found a clearing, made a fire, and set up a camp in the near pitch dark. I lay awake all night, wondering if a bear would be so kind as to eat the damned dog first, to give me time to persuade Steph to make it to the Jeep, and fell asleep about the time the sun was breaking over the mountains. When I awoke, it was to one of the most magnificent landscapes I'd ever seen, like a raised level cliffside surrounded by evergreens, protected on one side by a steeper cliff, with paths leading off in two directions, one to a raw, wildly dangerous waterfall gushing with primal ferocity from the thawing mountain snow, and the other to a wadi of a sort, with huge uprooted trees and pristine volcanic boulders worn smooth from all the winters and springs they'd seen, so that they were like buildings laid down on this riverbed on their sides, at the bottom of the waterfall.

It was precarious and sublime. I'd never seen anything like it, in all my years of living in the Northwest, never taken a journey like this into the breathtaking wilderness.

———

Still, I was starting a new job in a day, so I was kind of put off, I realized. If we stuck to this plan, I'd return to Seattle late Sunday night and begin my new job Monday morning, after traveling four more hours back to the western part of the state.

I started unpacking our breakfasts and such, tied a bottle of warm chardonnay with a rope and immersed it in the runoff at the bottom of the waterfall, which was still icy and frigid from the melting snow from higher elevations, and then went back to tending the fire as Steph wandered off with the dog.

A bit later, we took a hike through an adjacent logging trail and wound up bewilderingly lost in the most unrefined, oldest-growth forest, which I imagined was really Lewis and Clark–type shit, real monkey brain forest growth, for the planet, where we felt like large, ripe organic treats to either mammal or insect. Seriously, it was like a badger would have found us within its dinner purview. Or a beaver. Hell, never mind a bear, black or brown (I had no idea what neighborhood we were in, or if throwing gang signs would have helped).

Sometime after noon, after we'd been trapped in another riverbed and had been hunted by the grandmother of all wasps, bigger than any I'd ever seen, we finally found a parallel logging road and were able to make our way back to camp. I broached the subject of leaving that night, when we made it back to camp, because, you see, I was kind of a passive dope and hadn't realized that Steph intended on spending both nights out there, and I needed to rest before the big start of the new job.

"So is that all right? Steph?" I asked.

She didn't let on what she was thinking as we reentered camp, and the dog was running this way and that, her nose in overload with information.

I fetched the chardonnay from the waterfall and opened it, taking a swig directly from the bottle with our lunch as I built up the fire. Steph walked out of the tent, accepted the offered bottle, and took a heavy swipe from it, wiped her mouth with the back of her hand, and then took another, handing it back to me.

I was impressed. Half of the wine was gone. I tried chugging from it but couldn't compete. Hesitated. Bit into my cheese and summer sausage, then took another draught. Handed it back. Steph ate some of her lunch, then knocked back the rest of the bottle in two big, open-throated gulps and announced, "I'm going swimming."

"I'll stay and mind the camp," I said, unsure of her declaration.

Bugs were everywhere, I began to realize. Little zippy black fuckers, getting all over. Sunlight, bright and crisp—different from the density and saturation value of the South Texas sun that I'm accustomed to—was hanging about, making things smell. I smelled the green, and the wet, and the bugs. Everything was completely still and quiet. I sat on a log, my ass bones aching. Was this camping? I built a bigger fire, tried to kill time by splitting logs with my blunted axe.

An hour slipped by. Maybe half of another one before I decided, fuck this, and started packing up.

I had packed up the whole camp and pointed the Jeep out by the time Steph returned, damp and bitten and itchy, her shoes in her hand, with the dog panting and soaked.

"Thought it was time to call it quits," I said, hoping for a response.

I hadn't realized she'd become so drunk from chugging the wine like she did, and she was angry. And she was even more furious when she returned and saw that I'd packed up the campsite.

So she unloaded on me. Really let me have it for leading her on, telling her I was a camping sort of fella, that I'd want to willingly place myself in this situation with her on weekends.

"Well, sure," I said, "there was a time when I actually wanted to do this, but I see this less and less as recreation rather than a willing submission to potential threats and harm, never mind the discomfort."

She remained quiet, intense.

"But it's not that, exactly, it's just that I hadn't considered that I'd be tired for my first day at a new job, Steph. Come on; you can appreciate that, right?"

No response from her, just passive seething.

"I thought we'd just be out here for the day, but I can't spend another night out here without sleep and then get back to my apartment and fall dead asleep for a few hours, then begin a new job the next day."

"You said you would!" she yelled. "You said you'd do this, and now you're changing your mind!"

"Yes," I said. "I really have no idea why I would have agreed to this, knowing what was coming. I really don't have an explanation, but I can apologize; I'm sorry."

———

She cleaned up a little and then climbed into the passenger side, packed the dog in her position, and I drove us out of there since she was still pretty drunk.

She ranted for half an hour more from the passenger seat, and I tried to remain calm and disengaged because I was losing my temper, until finally I did lose it altogether and instead of yelling, I just went quiet. Totally quiet.

I didn't speak to her for the entire four-hour trip back to my apartment. I drove straight to my building downtown, stopped outside my front door, exited as the Jeep kept running, and said, "You can keep all my camping shit," then entered through my front door, ensuring that it clicked shut behind me. I went inside, turned off my phone, had a hot shower, and climbed into bed, trying to suppress the bad feeling I had in my heart and convince myself this girl was not for me; she was just not for me, so for both our sakes, just bugger off now. For both of us.

This can't end well, so let it end now.

CHAPTER 13

Cannibal Hymns

Steph insisted on calling me over and over again, and sending these dramatic, sad photos of her that really punched me in the heart. She had taken to curling up in her bed and playing the ringtone repeatedly that indicated a text message from me, she said, because she missed me so much. Missed us together.

I had no capacity to reign in my compassion at the time, still felt raw and open from losing so many people in my life, and she had this power—no, I should own this: I had no way to move through my compassion and get to the other side of it, see that it was just sadness and that sadness ends.

I was addicted to being sad, and sad was my new home—and there was a lot of sadness with Steph.

Besides, I told myself, sadness generates good art. Sad is happy, for deep people, as Sally Sparrow said on *Doctor Who*.

So we gave it another shot. I gave it another go.

———

After I passively allowed Steph to inveigle herself back in my life, we oddly surged forward after another month or two of dating, deciding that I'd move into her shithole rental in North Seattle, right on the county line, in some terrible neighborhood called Lake City. She'd been having issues with her roommates (all of them, again, Craigslist finds: the pattern now clear), and in order to solve her roommate issues, like men do, I said, "Fuck it; let's move in together."

If the cultural and neurotic obstacles weren't insurmountable enough, moving in with Steph after only a few months of dating was probably the arsenic in our daily gruel.

I had moved west and to a "posh" city to learn how to swim in an urban environment, how to dress like the kids on television, and which fork to use when. No, really: It wasn't as if we read from Emily Post growing up the way I did in South Texas, squatting like *caballeros* around a fire at the end of the day, cooking slabs of personally slaughtered beef on homemade grills made from disused truck parts. Not much use for a teaspoon or a doily there. I was still trying to be a modern Frank Sinatra, didn't wear denim, carried a cigarette case and a Zippo, and had been particular about my distressed metal cutlery and Fiestaware; I wasn't quite up to the IKEA standards that Chuck Palahniuk describes in chapter five of *Fight Club*, mostly because I couldn't afford it, but I was close, with the throw rugs, votives, and a wingback chair in my hardwood studio apartment in downtown Seattle. I was still in the process of reinventing myself, curious to see who I'd become.

Steph, however, put little stock in her style, and her literature read accordingly. She simply refused to dress in a manner that was becoming or flattering, in retaliation to the possibility that she might draw unwanted male attention. Or signal to other lesbians that she was femme.

She dressed in jeans and flannel, was utterly disinterested in television and popular film. Nothing annoyed her more than when I made references to films or television, would assume some posture of superiority because I had a sense of what was popular in the spectrum of televised entertainment, as if I was somehow personally responsible for the erosion of language and literature because I'd rented a DVD.

She wrote and read in the abstract, was drawn to abstruse cadences and vague language and irregular constructions. I was the complete opposite: I wanted sharp, crisp, complicated sentences that painted a specific word picture, then did it again. I didn't want pointillism in my language: I wanted a yarn, told well, with wordplay and methodology, nuanced structure that informed the construction of the narrative through skillful punctuation. Actually, the only place we really agreed was in our mutual hatred for Ayn Rand, not just her social theories but her pathetic writing style.

"And she can't even spell her name correctly," I'd say. But still, we disagreed on almost everything else lit'ry. She wanted dithering, diffused colors and Rothko. I wanted blood spatter and Vermeer. "Tell me a story and tell it well," I kept arguing, because it felt right. "That's not what language is for," she'd say. "It's more for the insinuation of the story and letting the reader create the story in her mind— that's the connection between the writer and the reader," she argued back.

"That's just cowardice," I said, being an asshole, like I could be. "I agree with Stoppard when he said that Virginia Woolf's greatest contribution to the English language was her suicide." I felt clever, and mean, and she slammed shut her book and grabbed the dog, who by this time knew that raised voices meant Steph was going to get mad soon and they'd be on a walk if she just waited a minute.

What was interesting was that after we argued, we each agreed to read the other's favorite authors, and then realized we weren't so fond of our heroes anymore. We were left more impressed by the other person's favorites than we had been willing to acknowledge and were then able to laugh about it after.

Maybe we just needed to argue first, like foreplay.

We liked arguing with each other, would push one another to the verge of temper, then back down. We boxed, verbally, and sometimes one of us would be out of the other's weight class, especially when the smell of blood was in the word water, and it would hurt.

CHAPTER 14

The War of the Rats

Literature wasn't the only place we disagreed.

Steph aspired to gardening and was wretched at it, but it would never stop her from trying.

I despised any sort of yard work, and for obvious colloquial reasons. It wasn't meditative for me, being in the sun and mowing lawns. It meant something entirely different for someone with my background to clear brush, pull weeds, clip through bracken.

I preferred to spend Saturday afternoons sitting on a lawn chair, drinking light beer and shooting dandelions with my air pistol in the huge backyard. I found it intensely satisfying when I'd hit the bulb and the seeds would explode out, then get carried off in the wind. I was like John Milius in Los Angeles, shooting at actors.

Steph would struggle valiantly in that earth, carve out a small, coffin-like rectangle and attempt to coax life from seeds and sprouts, but I think it was more for the practice than the product, like dirt yoga.

She would use our dishes, too. More important, she would use *my* dishes, after I asked her repeatedly to desist from doing so. It made me uncomfortable, no matter how often or thoroughly I washed my Fiesta-ware bowls, to eat something out of them after I'd seen her blend her homemade compost with the store-bought nutrient-rich soil and use my dishes to stir it all up, blend it together, right out there on the back porch.

So long, middle class. I guess I'm a Yankee redneck now.

We even had a blue tarp, over the compost heap.

And the compost heap, well, that drew the rats.

At first, those rats kept to themselves, but when the winter came, they invaded the downstairs. When she ran the place like a boardinghouse, Steph had moved downstairs because it was the biggest area in the house, and she paid the majority of the rent for the privilege. But the downstairs was cut into the side of a hill, so it remained at an average temperature of about fifty-five degrees during the summer and ground frost during the winter, which I didn't mind. What bothered me about the space was that it was forever stuck in 1973, and not the cool, Los Angeles pornography and cocaine 1973 but the Paducah, Kentucky, 1973 (sorry, Paducah) with the Formica tabletops and mostly matching green vinyl stool chairs, the wallpaper with the forest—you get the idea. It was dingy and mean and dank down there, and there were some monstrous rats that could not be bothered with our human refusal for things that once carried the bubonic plague.

They could give a shit; they were cold. They wanted in.

And in they came.

I laid down traps to kill them, finally, instead of trying to keep them out. I had been reluctant to do this because I was afraid of the dog hurting herself. She wasn't the smartest dog in the world, wagging her tail so vigorously at times she'd leave blood spatter on the doorframes, so sticking her nose into the cheese blocks on a rattrap was not beyond the imaginable, when it came to Cleo.

But the rats left us no choice. They were colonizing our shitty rental, and so we had to do something.

The first morning after the traps were in place, I found a huge rat caught dead in one of the more obvious traps, and it was a strange moment, looking at it lying there, like I was seeing a ghost, or a mythological creature, and then I noticed movement coming from another corner and saw that another rat hadn't been so lucky.

Just as large as the first one, this one had half of its head crushed, along with a shoulder and forearm. It was spinning in a circle with its back legs, trying to escape the wooden mauling, with severe neurological trauma beset upon him or her.

I began panicking, looking for something to help ease its passage, having lived in Seattle far too long to take in the suffering of an animal of any kind, even the plague-carrying sort. I scampered about for an edged weapon, a blunt force instrument—anything, really—but there was nothing in the laundry room except a bucket and a mop.

And my axe! cried the badly timed Gimli in my head. (I had read that joke on the Internet, but it was appropriate here.)

It'll have to do, I thought, so I managed to get the door open and the rat and trap out the door, onto the back porch, and for some reason, I freed it from the trap and it began to flop around, every twitch and reflex muscle in its body in full fear and flight mode, but it couldn't see straight, couldn't work its broken body, so it just flopped around. I finally had my shoe on it and tried to maneuver the axe so that I could just end this horror, and I brought it down hard—the damned thing was as dull as a spoon—and I managed to sever the rat's head, partially, and I swear, it looked at me, looked me right in the eye, and I could see it cursing me, could *feel* it cursing me, as I sensed real anger and hatred emanating from this animal as it looked at me and finally stilled. A halo of blood began to form behind its head, right out of a movie, and, again, I swear I could hear its little voice in my head, telegraphing that last moment, *Fuck you, you bastard. I curse you, I curse you to hurt as much as I just did.*

Something in me believed it.

CHAPTER 15

Cleopatra

The one thing I couldn't reconcile, ever, about Steph, and still can't, after all this time, was her dog.

Cleopatra wasn't really stupid, but I liked to pretend she was. She was a rescue, an odd mix of Labrador and Labrador poop. Maybe that's not fair. She was just a weird dog that I believe had never been socialized among other dogs, so she was a bad fit in the canine world, much like Steph and I were in the human.

She had strange habits, like orienting herself in a north/south direction when she needed to poo, and she wouldn't go if you were looking at her, from shame. But the north/south thing worked for me because it meant she usually pooped in a matrix, so it was easy to clean up in the backyard.

She was actually quite well trained for the walk and would immediately understand that her leash would tangle if she walked around, say, a signpost, and with a brief pluck of the line, she'd know to stop what she was doing and turn about, and walk around the obstacle.

I was impressed. Quite impressed, when I first saw this.

I had owned dogs that would have pulled and yanked forward and choked themselves to death without understanding the physics of the collar and line, easily, especially if there was a *SQUIRREL!* at the end of their prey focus. And I considered them to be smart dogs.

When we first started dating, Cleo saw me as a contender to her place in the pack order, and would, when all three of us were walking in a park or on a beach, swing around and try to place herself between Steph and me. She would run up at a clip and stick her nose through our denimed legs and push me to one side, make sure she was next in line to Steph. Fucking brilliant, I thought.

"And she's so damned quiet," I said to Steph.

"Yep," Steph agreed.

"Was she like this always?" I asked.

"Nope," said Steph.

"Hunh," I said. "And you trained her to be this quiet. I'm impressed."

"Yep," she said, and smiled.

Later, she revealed how: electroshock therapy. Or rather, the shock collar, and my estimation of Steph dropped to near unredeemable levels. *That's fucked up*, I thought.

That's just abuse.

And the dog looked at me, with a smile, from the couch, and her tail started to thump.

Can we go for a walk? I need to poop. Which way's north?

Later on, after living together and having a few spats, I could see the look in Steph's eyes and I swear to God, she was measuring my neck for a shock collar.

I wouldn't do what she wanted, and we argued.

"No!" she kept saying. "You're not doing it right!"

And after I considered it, I decided that no, I wouldn't wear her collar. I wouldn't wear anyone's collar, thus far. Why start with a shock collar?

"No," I would answer her. "It's you that's doing it incorrectly."

❦

At any rate, after a few more months of living together, Steph arrived home one evening in an uncharacteristic desperation and said, quite timidly and with an expression nearing on vulnerability, "All right. Will you marry me?" She hadn't even dropped her handbag or her cardigan, keys still in her hand. I had been working on my first book that night, I think. (Or skimming through porn. Either which; it's the same thing, when you get down to it.) But I looked at her, saw how much she meant it, and said, "Finally. Yes; I've been telling you for weeks that we should."

Not your traditional proposal, sure, but it was how she and I did things.

—◆—

After I'd met Steph, our relationship had been hurried, on a timetable of desperation: We were both in our late thirties, feeling an unspoken, nearly conscious pressure to marry and "settle down." Maybe even just "settle." Settle down or up, but just settle. And things fell apart, as they were certain to do. Boy, did they ever.

For two days after her proposal, I couldn't look at her, not in the eye. I would study her when she was looking away, trying to imagine a future with both of us in it, five, ten, fifteen years from now. What we'd look like, how we'd be together, and I never managed the read. I never saw it. And when she turned back around and looked at me, I became bashful and shy, and smiled big. We were like two home-schooled Christian teenagers left alone in a hayloft. We were in love, and totally awkward.

Because we were engaged.

Because we were going to be married.

And that's when things really started to break down.

CHAPTER 16

Beating Up Lesbians

After being with Steph for a year, I realized I had let myself go a bit too much this time, as I passed age thirty-nine with a size 38 waist and wanted to regain the slenderness of my youth, but my habits and debilitating laziness were proving an obstacle. It was with some reluctance that I turned to the only place and exercise that I had ever truly enjoyed, that had ever truly moved me to conviction, and that was karate, but not just any karate, a particular karate school that had been, when I was attending, the coolest and toughest LGBT-friendly school operating in the gay-friendly neighborhood that happened to be on the same block as the start-up alternative newspaper I was helping produce at the time.

But then again, I was young and slim and strong and stupid: perfect genotype for a karate geek, in my mid-twenties.

At thirty-nine, I was thick through the middle. Roomy. I'd taken the Andrew Sullivan path, went from a slender twink to a bear, if my affections were that way bent. (Mind the British pun.)

So I started back at my old karate school, which had moved a few times and was in the throes of its own Cheyne-Stokes death knell, as most independently owned karate schools always seemed to be, underfinanced and undernourished.

When I returned, most of the original magic seemed to be gone, but I was still quite keen on coming back, and I called the owner and patched things up because we had left things on a weird note when I didn't return after an incredibly difficult green belt test, my first. I wouldn't break, back then. I was petulant and not ready to submit to anyone, not even for a karate instructor I exalted.

It didn't seem right. Wasn't American.

———

Kinesis back then was a show. Kinesis was exceptional. Kinesis was theater. Kinesis was the answer, and Kinesis was a question you never wanted asked. Kinesis was physicality. Kinesis was an education in domination and learned submission—and by God, were you ever submitting, slowly, with each class, with every strained muscle, every call and every answer—and you didn't even know you were doing it when you started, but the physical regimen (the fire hydrants, the push-ups, the diamond push-ups, the tricep push-ups, the crunches and crossovers and the constant leg overs) broke you down into a perfect receptacle, put you in a place where you could begin to see who you were, what your body could do, if you were perfect.

If you were willing to see yourself how you wanted to be.

Kinesis could put you into that range, within distance. Within sight of your own personal perfection.

But the deception was that you'd never get there. You just kept coming back for more, seeing your perfection shift, once again, just out of focus.

The school drew students who contributed their own magic, their own charismatic energies, and together the experience and the workouts were electrifying. And finally, our instructor, Brenda Brown, was simply mesmerizing, absolutely gorgeous, epicene and hard. Androgynous and better than a goddamned Jedi, an actual living superhero. Many of the students were there just to be around her.

When I first started, Kinesis was two blocks west of the *Stranger*, the alternative paper where I began my life in Seattle and where I was working as a graphic artist, and barely scraping by. Even so, I decided I could afford seventy dollars a month at this fancy place down the street. I don't remember much about Brenda from the first time I attended Kinesis, as she wasn't in my orbit and I had my own early dramas unfolding. I recognized her from photos at the time, just a belt rank or two ahead of me, a pudgy lesbian girl from the Midwest, Indiana, I think, who would turn into the hardest, fastest, strongest, most attractive woman this side of cinema imaginable, when I would return to the school fourteen years and forty pounds later.

I had fallen in love with karate that first time, because of that school, and my whole social orbit centered directly over it, right up until I was asked to submit my will at the green belt test, and I just couldn't do it, couldn't wear the shock collar, so to speak, and so I quit, and regretted that decision ever since. It was exactly what happened with college: I couldn't submit to doing what I didn't want to do.

So, here we were, fourteen years later, and I was willing to try again.

It never really worked, because I was more in love with my slovenly lifestyle and watching movies than getting fit. So I didn't drop too much weight, but I did regain my balance, did recover some core strength, did eventually grow stronger and into better shape—more pineapple than pear, if you will—and the best thing about the place, really, was the new friends I had made.

In particular, I had met someone exceptional, the sort of person you don't really ever know exists until you meet them and think, *Hunh; I didn't think people like you ever really existed,* and that was Sarah, one of the blue belts and the mother of one of the younger wunderkinds in the kids' curriculum.

Sarah taught ethics and German and Greek philosophy to undergraduates at the Jesuit school here in Seattle, and she had a wicked sense of humor to boot. I was naturally drawn to her intelligence, of course, and would chat her up at every opportunity, catch her attention over group e-mails after I volunteered to help with the administration of the school, which needed all the help it could get.

On the days we weren't participating in classes at the school, we'd eventually take to walking a three-mile park a bit north from downtown called Greenlake, which is a central part of any true Seattleite's city living experience. We became good friends and I don't believe either of us had any flirtatious intentions; we just enjoyed our incredibly sprawling conversations about everything either one of us knew.

We never ran out of conversation, never reached the end of any topic, and after she returned from a three-month summer stay in Spain, we had even more to talk about.

"Did you eat a lot of chorizo growing up?" she asked.

"Why is it that food is always the entry point of any conversation when someone wants to ask me about my heritage? It's as if I'm a food critic." There was a pause. Then I said, "I do actually own a *molcajete*. But I hardly use it."

"Probably because it's more polite to ask you about food than it is to wonder aloud how deeply you identify with your ethnicity," she said, after a moment of thinking about it.

"Hunh. Was there a lot of chorizo in Madrid? We mostly had it for breakfast, with eggs, growing up in South Texas. But it's an elastic term; like 'sausage.'"

"We didn't go to northern Spain; we stuck primarily to the south, around Andaluthia," she said.

"Are you lithping for a reason or did you pick that up unconsciously?"

"It's how it's pronounced. The King of Spain had a lisp, so instead of having him live his life feeling embarrassed, the population adopted a lisp."

"Hunh. Another reason why colonialism would never last in the New World. We would have pointed at him and laughed."

"Are you guys stinkpots?"

"Well, in South Texas, we would have made fun of his lisp openly, as Texans or Tejanos. We're as unruly as the Irish. You know why the doors in Ireland are so brightly painted? During the colonialism of the British, some overseeing royalty died, and the colonies were told to paint their doors black, in mourning. Instead, the Irish went with blues, reds, yellows, and greens. Ornery."

"Where did you read that?"

"Probably on the Internets, but it makes sense," I said. "That sounds like something we'd do in Brownsville."

That's how most of our conversations went. And while I considered the possibility that things might be "flirtish," I quieted that desire, because at my age, I decided I wouldn't pursue that impulse every time it surfaced, and Sarah never really put that forward, as close as we were becoming. I respected that and knew that if we moved into romance, it would abbreviate the relationship quickly, and I liked her far too much to sleep with her, I decided.

Besides, I was with Steph, even if the chemistry there was inert. I had made a commitment, and I was going to abide by it. Love is more than sex, I told myself.

Further, I wasn't attracted to Sarah, I kept repeating to myself. Sarah dressed in a manner to deflect male attention when it was unnecessary, which corresponded well with the karate suits, or "do-backs," as they're known in some Asian languages and martial arts schools.

Finally, Sarah was thirteen years older than I was, and I wasn't into another May-December romance, I told myself. I'd already had those. *We're just really good friends who enjoy the shit out of talking to one another, and that's that.*

Another time, Sarah asked what I was reading. I told her I was reading the maritime serial about the Napoleonic wars, by Patrick O'Brian.

"You like that Russell Crowe movie?" she asked, smiling.

"I like Peter Weir, yes. And Russell Crowe. But I absolutely love the books by O'Brian. They're a marvel of language, because while it's in English, it makes absolutely no sense whatsoever because of all the nautical terms, so I find myself skimming along, reading at speed, and my retention and comprehension actually increase if I don't stop and try to figure out what a 'foc's'cle' or 'mizzen mast' is, or where a quarterdeck is. It's like Anthony Burgess and *A Clockwork Orange*, and the made-up crypto-Russo language. If you just continue reading, you get the larger narrative by the context. It's really quite something else."

"Hunh."

"Yeah, and the most surprising thing is how funny he is. He has a great sense of humor. There's this one scene where the older, saltier seadogs feed grog to a ten-year-old kid, who mouths off to Captain Aubrey, calls him 'Goldilocks.' It's hysterical. Then they have to tie him to his hammock overnight while he sobers up. I chortled."

"And the . . . you know . . . buggering? Does he address that?"

"He does, actually, and said that while it did happen, it wasn't as rampant as people made it out to be. It's a total misnomer; the kids drew a wage and were expected to pull their own weight, so to speak. They usually had a chaperone in one of the officers. The British seamen weren't the buggering maniacs that Churchill made them out to be, in that speech, with the rum, sodomy, and the lash thing. They weren't child fuckers, like the Greeks."

"That's a misnomer, too."

"Really? None of that 'bashing the shuttlecock from the feathered end,' as Wodehouse put it?"

"The Greeks weren't homosexual in the same sense, in the contemporary way we think of homosexuality. Older, bearded men had younger men under their care, for education and advancement, but there was no penetration. The Greeks had no concept of homosexuality; in fact, that term wasn't invented until the nineteenth century."

"Hunh. So all the imagery and jokes about anal sex are wrong?"

"Well, they had sex, they just didn't carve their sexual identity into 'homo' or 'hetero.' The older men did this thing called 'intercrural sex,' where they would rub their dicks into the younger men's thighs, using olive oil, and get off. There was no penetration, which they would have felt to be diminishing. And when the younger men had their beards grow in, then it was their turn to be the top. They had sex for different reasons, like bonding with a fellow soldier, and then they went home and had sex with their wives, to continue their family dynasty. It's all in *Phaedrus*, about the 'lover' and the 'beloved.' Though it's been toned down in the translation. In fact, there are whole volumes of Greek wisdom that were lost because the translators felt their nature was too immodest, so they just destroyed whole passages that didn't appeal to their virtuous standards."

"That's just fascinating."

"Does that surprise you? That it would be edited by white, Christian men like that?"

"I suppose it shouldn't, but it still upsets me to consider all that was lost."

That was the nature of our conversations. They would go on and on and would stop only when we each had to return home to our obligations.

———

Of course, Steph was immediately jealous of my friendship with Sarah when I told her about it.

She was always really strange about sexuality and flirting. Once, when her mother sent her a couple of presents for her birthday, Steph opened the boxes and threw them across the room in disgust, as they housed a shawl of sorts and some bad hippie jewelry, very much in contradiction to how Steph dressed.

I tried to assuage things by joking with her, and then wrapped the colorful, gypsy-style shawl over my head and did a *Fiddler on the Roof*-type shimmy, worthy of Topol.

This gleam came into her eye, as if she was turned on, and I caught a glimpse of myself in the mirror, and I looked like Harvey Fierstein, without makeup. How could this turn her on? But it did, and we ended up having lots of gins and tonic and we messed around dancing to music from our youth—New Order, Joy Division, Sinead O'Connor, and the like—and she really let go that night, really let herself loose and danced and became incredibly attractive and fun and charming, and I thought, *Finally, here you are. Thanks for coming up to the surface and playing,* as we swirled around and giggled and danced and fell sprawling on my bed, which collapsed under us. It started a golden few weeks of intimacy and reminded me why we were together, and why the trouble was worth it, in the end.

Or so I told myself. Passively.

After four months of training at Kinesis, I invited my mother to Seattle for my green belt test.

What made it a bit pathetic was that the green belt was, as a friend of mine back then called it, a "rank amateur" standing. We weren't friends very long after that.

Mostly, it was an excuse for my mother to fly up to Seattle and meet Steph, since we'd become engaged, so I asked my mother to come up and witness the test, as a way of passively giving me her blessing. "Just take a few days, meet my betrothed, and see what I'm doing, how I'm living. It's important to me," I think I said.

And miraculously, Mom took some time off work to visit me, and not while I was laid up in a hospital or in a psych ward. It was touching.

There was a deep, sincere part of me that needed the validation from my mother, after all this time. The test was nothing, really, except the only sort of accomplishment I'd reached in the last ten years, with my "career" as a designer taking the swirly path down-sewer, and I remembered how phenomenally good it had felt way back when to do these tests, to mark your progress as a martial artist, and have your friends and family come to cheer you on, and watch as you plied yourself valiantly through exhaustion and had your face kicked in once in a while by an overzealous dickhead who didn't understand this wasn't really combat.

—————

So it was set, and I had been really earnest in my preparations for this test, remembering how it had been fourteen years ago when I was twenty-five or so, and how badly reductive it had been to me, both physically and emotionally, and had actually broken my fascination with karate and all martial arts: I knew, after that test, that this wasn't for me. Going past green belt, in this system, required a level of subservience and compliance I was still incapable of giving anyone. And I will credit my instructor then with seeing that quite clearly, ten years ago, and how uncomfortable that test became to everyone watching because I wouldn't break, and she wouldn't stop trying to break me, barking commands at me like I was a proud recruit in a boot camp, or a dog in dire need of an alpha, or a shock collar.

A month later, I'd quit, had given up that school, and I wandered around for a few years starting other systems, but never committing fully, like a series of karate one-night stands. I was a karate slut and hated all the schools I slept with after that. They just weren't Kinesis.

Kinesis was a magical place, back then. It was the Island of Broken Toys, from the *Rudolph the Red-Nosed Reindeer* Claymation film. The deeper, more committed the student, the more broken the toy, if you get the metaphor. Seriously. But there was real magic there, because of or in spite of it.

I returned to Kinesis because I'd never again been so fully committed to anything, after.

Not a person, not a career (except my haphazard conviction to writing), not a single thing, and certainly not a routine or a workout.

Early John Irving, from *The Hotel New Hampshire*, would shout at me in my head (*You have to get obsessed and stay obsessed!*), but I could find nothing that would compel me into a reasonable argument for obsession.

(Later John Irving would also shout at me, *Why aren't you picking my blueberries?! You can't go to the same school as my kids if your combined household income is under $750K!!* I'm kidding, of course. But just a bit.)

Taking the same test again at thirty-nine certainly flashed me back to taking it at twenty-five, and this time I was far more able to concentrate on the parts that displeased me, far more capable of reining in my body language and visible displeasure and disagreement with the bits of the test I felt were onanistic and idiotic, useless in the larger language of weaponless combat. By this point in my life, I had been in enough fistfights to know what was useful and what was television. I was in a graduate studies program with violence, actually felt peace when my amygdala switched to "flood" and my blood turned into a river of cortisol. My eyes no longer dilated, my breathing went deeper, my shoulders automatically squared, and I had a full 360-degree awareness of a room, all in less than a second, as soon as I felt threatened.

I had every marker of a combat veteran, of PTSD, after being in so many stupid fights growing up, or waiting to get hit by my dad, or someone else.

So the mat, in karate, felt like home. There was peace in it.

But there were other exercises in karate, the katas and the one-steps, and I had to get through those. Take orders, respond with compliance, bow my head to suggest my place.

So I did. Or so I tried.

―✦―

When I came back to the school, it needed help. Lots and lots of help. Within a couple of months I was a part of the administration, and then I found myself trying to get it advertised and mediated and mentioned out of my own shallow pockets. I did everything but show up to class more than once a week. I seeped capital to get it healthier, but like anyone who's tried to help a slipping 501(c)(3), I was completely disappointed when it was simply not coming out of the death spiral it had been in, when I had first been reintroduced.

Which was difficult to watch, but also satisfying, in a schadenfreude sort of way, if I can be fully transparent and confessional.

Continuing with the metaphor of the lover, when I rejoined the karate school, it had been uncomfortable, awkward, an experience like meeting an ex-lover in a coffee shop and being incapable of acknowledging an odd sense of competition, like, "Aha! I've been thriving since we split and you've been dwindling! I win!" And, admittedly, because I have such deep rivulets of abandonment and pettiness, there was indeed that moment, which turned quickly to shame, in accordance with my Catholic programming, and so instead I set about helping and building it back up as much as I could.

But to very little avail. Sadly, karate schools really aren't worth much more than the sweat and the blood left on their mats.

At any rate, this had been my near-obsession for my thirty-ninth winter, and Steph had been very supportive. I didn't slim down like I had hoped, made it nowhere near slipping back into my size 34 pinstripe trousers that I'd been wearing when we'd met, because try as I may have, I never did quite give up the drinking. So I remained fat, and as the deadline to the test drew closer, I tried dieting and jogging and wishing and praying. I was still a big fat man in a white karate suit, and I looked ridiculous.

But still, I persevered, as I kept hearing John Irving's voice yelling in my head.

You have to get obsessed and stay obsessed! Or maybe that was Garp.

—•—

I could sense that Steph was nervous, teeming with a weird anxiety about meeting my mother for the first time. I told her, "No, no, you don't understand my mother. She's not like your mother, what you've described." Still, I could sense that Steph was preparing herself for a fight.

"Mom's an incredibly on-the-level and kind woman, and she's dealt with a lot in her life. She's not in the least bit judgmental or hostile, to anyone. Mom's . . . I dunno. Full of love, I think is the only way to put it," I said to Steph.

"I mean, really. I've yelled and screamed and been a complete shit to her for a very long time, and she's never given up on me, and I've swung back around and now I'm her little Elvis. That's why I sometimes call her, 'Momma,' like Elvis did with his mom. You don't need to be *en garde* for passive judgments or double entendres," I said.

En garde she was, though, from the very beginning, from the moment we picked up Mom from the airport until we drove her all the way north to that rambling rental in that shithole neighborhood. Mom was exactly as I'd described her and entirely sincere and genuine in her affection in seeing us both, seeing us, at the time, happy, and she even loved the damned stupid dog, Cleo.

— — —

But Steph was on edge, uncomfortable, even after she realized who my mother was and had calmed down, on the second or third day. I'd taken us all to lunch at our favorite Thai restaurant, and we were talking about the upcoming test, and Steph said something to the effect of, "Domingo really likes sweating with all those boys; I wish he'd like sweating like that with me more often."

I gave her a look that said, "Are you fucking serious? You're talking about this in front of my mother?"

To be perfectly honest, I'd been far more brutal and vulgar in front of Mom, back when I was much more bitter, but I immediately became defensive, standing guard over her, thinking, *What the fuck, Steph? Seriously? I treated your parents with respect.*

But Momma, in her divine innocence, heard nothing of what Steph had indicated, and the moment passed. Still, I was unnerved and annoyed.

The day of the test, I had to leave them alone for the day while I did martial artsy things, and they spent hours downtown, at Pike Place Market, which is Mom's favorite destination in Seattle because of all the flowers. She loves the flowers and takes pictures of the window boxes downtown to send back home to Texas. It's actually quite adorable.

But I was nervous that Steph's neuroses would prevail and she'd take something Mom said badly, and the situation would implode, or explode.

So it was with some sense of doom that I awaited their arrival at the karate school for the test, see how their interaction went.

When they walked in the door, I could immediately discern that my worry was without foundation; Steph was beaming, and my mother was carrying flowers. My mother's simple sincerity and genuine personality had penetrated all of Steph's defenses and laid them to rest, and Steph, who was expecting the sort of interactions she'd had with her own mother—slights mostly imagined on her part—was now perfectly at home with my Momma, the way I was, too.

It's healthy to love your momma, when you're past thirty-five.

For the test itself, I was able to make it through the first part with the katas and the barked commands and the compliance of will with very little to report.

It was the sparring that was concerning me, which occurred at the end.

Sparring for green belt, in this style, was the gateway into the upper belts and the geometrically more complicated strikes and arm bars and kicks, so your green belt test was a way of really testing your commitment, testing your mettle and your ability to survive a full-on ass-kicking.

This was why, at twenty-five, it was the brick wall that I hit, stopping my advancement into the upper echelons, the more whimsical and insubstantial of martial flourish. And also because I felt anything beyond there was utter, useless bullshit in a fighting style: Most fights never get beyond a few thrown punches and a sprawling pindown or submission hold; I just couldn't get past that, internally, and it showed, externally.

And if there's something indisputable about sparring, it's that your fatigue will show your true spirit, will drop your pants and show your soul to anyone watching.

In sparring veritas.

And so, about two-thirds into my test, when I began revealing the first signs of fatigue, I also began getting sloppy and lowering my guard, dropping my head forward and encouraging my opponent to get fancy so I could throw a fat, slow lead right down the center at his or her throat, lazily, like a howitzer, retreating into my comfort zone of a heavyweight boxer just come out of retirement for a huge Las Vegas payout, the way George Foreman beat the fight out of Michael Moorer.

On the mat, when you're sparring, it's a number of conversations, of nonverbal discourses. You can have the most violent, damaging exchanges with someone you adore and trust, and it's out of a shared, mutual admiration of one another's gifts and athleticism. Complete nonverbal bonding, through affectionate pummeling. I've engaged in this many, many times.

Other times, it's a polite exchange with someone you loathe, mostly because the last thing you want to do is exchange perspiration and let that person know how much you genuinely disapprove of them.

And the more tired you become, the less you're able to disguise this.

So at the two-thirds mark the day of the test, one of the more ambitious members of the school started in on my reduction, started pushing me into that part of despair that truly tells a man, and I wasn't handling it well.

Earlier, it had been grand: I'd sparred with the house giant, who was my friend and remarkably agile for a man of his size, about 280 pounds, and could kick and punch with surprising frequency and acuity, utterly unexpected from a guy who was shaped like a Klondike grizzly. He'd actually bloodied my nose, when I had leaned away from him and thought I was out of reach from an extended kick, and sonofabitch if his foot didn't come right up at me when I was turned totally in the opposite direction.

BOOM. Right away, my nose sprayed red, mingled my biota onto both his karate suit and the mat. (Some part of me felt completed at this moment, seeing that my blood had mingled with the school, ritualistically, like I was no longer an outlier, but included in the symbiotic whole, just another pair of hands helping tow a nautical rope in a Patrick O'Brian story.)

He and I stopped right then—and I'll always love the big guy for this—and he grabbed my face in his mitted paws, tilted my head back, and looked up into my nose and said, "Yeah, you'll be all right. Come over here," and then someone handed him the medic kit, in which he found a tampon and a pair of scissors; he cut the tampon in half and stuck it up my nose, with the string coming out of my right nostril.

I never felt so goddamned tough in my life as at that moment, with half a tampon sticking out of my nostril.

And back at it we went.

Two big, heavy fuckers going at it like George Foreman.

It was great. That's love.

⎯ ⎯

A bit later, exhausted and stripped of my ability to hide my better self, my fresh opponent stepped in front of me to really test my control.

And *BAM:* Off we went, and he immediately started targeting my nose.

I should mention here that besides my mother and Steph, two of my closer friends, Andy and Kim, were in attendance, shouting their support from the sidelines. Dimly, I could hear them from their seats just off the mat.

I was a bit off in a corner, and they were behind me and to my left, so they couldn't really see what was happening as my new opponent kept tagging me with popcorn-like agility on the nose. I was depleted at this point, exhausted and somewhat incapable of stifling or blocking his little, insubstantial Orville Redenbacher–type *pop-pop* jabs going right at my bloody nose. I heard my mother from the sidelines saying, "He just had that sinus surgery a year ago!" and I said, I think for the fourth or fifth time, "Sir, please watch the nose," because it was, in all sincerity, a very good nose, large and Aztec and a pretty easy target, but finally I just lost it entirely and I grabbed him by the do-back after he hit me again, and I lifted him up off the ground and slammed him on his back, into the ground, and stopped myself before I hit him square in the face, on the ground.

(Again, point made about the higher flourishes of karate.)

⎯ ⎯

Right at that moment, Brenda Brown, who had magically appeared immediately to my left, called the round because she'd been monitoring me. I was aghast at my loss of control and helped pick up my opponent off the floor with apologies, and he brushed himself off in a persnickety sort of way and walked off in a huff. I sheepishly made my way to the next station in the circuit, utterly ashamed that my mother and friends had seen that and feeling quite horrible, and then things really went bad.

Again, I should mention, this is what this test is designed to do—reduce you to your baser impulses so that you meet yourself, know yourself in such a way that you're able to understand your limits and triggers, in the hopes that in the future, when you're able to beat someone to a pulp, you're also able to keep from doing it.

And at this next part, I met someone I didn't know, not just in myself. She was standing at the final station.

She was an older, gray-haired lesbian, wearing a red belt in the Kinesis style—from this school!—and patches from a series of other women's karate schools in Seattle.

A red belt, which was two belts higher than—no, scratch that, three belts higher, since I was just high yellow at this point, testing for green—me.

And I'd never seen her before.

After all the fucking money and time and promotion and SHIT that I'd put into this school's survival, this ostensible "student" showed up to the test, which is considered the "cream" of the student experience, to enjoy the sparring, to show her karate plumage to an audience.

To "test" the testees, if you don't mind the double entendre.

Something switched over in me.

And I heard Brenda behind me shout, "GO!"

⌒⌒

Right away, it was George Foreman and Michael Moorer.

I started thudding her—*thump thump!*—with big-mitted left jabs right at her face, keeping her from gauging where I was and then bringing the big right straight down the middle and hitting her square in the mouth, to get the conversation started on the right foot. So to speak.

BAM.

She responded with nothing in return.

Now, I should emphasize, this is all *perfectly* acceptable and legal on the mat, in this "conversation" with a student of her status as a red belt and as an opponent of mine at high yellow: I was doing *nothing* wrong here.

Duck, dodge right, and a low right hook to her ribs.

Step back and wait for her to recover her breath.

Shift stance, lead with two right jabs—*fump fump*—and a left hook to the head, and the support I had been hearing from my mother and Andy and Kim went totally quiet, off to my right.

I didn't care, at this point. I was too exhausted for higher functions, like sympathy.

I was locked in, like a terrier who's noticed a squirrel scampering up a tree.

And still, there was this thought in my head: *This is all perfectly legal. This is the fight game. She's a red belt.*

She kicked, responded with a "fancy" quick turn, and I saw it coming and moved just off to her left, where I would be just out of reach, and I dug the ball of my right toe just under her ribs. And I followed it with another combination to her face that went right through unanswered.

I started pummeling this sixty-year-old woman at about 10 percent more than I should have. Maybe 12 percent. Here and again, a 15 per-center would slip out. And this was all taking place not ten feet from my mother, my girlfriend, and my two best friends.

And I didn't care.

I was telling her, nonverbally, *You're a fraud. Stop pretending.*

Then I'd hit her again.

I was asking her, nonverbally, *Where the fuck have you been, in helping this school? You wear this school's red belt, and this is the first time I meet you, in five months? How do you like your patches?*

Some more hits.

———

It went on for about two more minutes.

I was a real asshole.

And that's why I never made it past green belt.

I just couldn't play at that level.

My mother never really looked at me the same way again, after seeing me for who I really was.

I realized I was much more like my brother Dan than I admitted to myself, had been trying to deny, and that I only liked a good boxing match where I was winning. I saw that, at a fundamental level, I was competitive and unyielding, unwilling to compromise when it meant something to the other person who was creating a fiction of him or herself. I wanted to be the one who pointed out where they were wrong, when it meant something. I saw that I needed to be, quietly, right. Correct. I was stripped down once again, and I didn't like who I saw there. And I thanked the karate school, much later when I was able to think about the experience honestly, for showing me that. And that I needed to change, if I was going to grow up and be an adult. That sometimes, I needed to let the other person win, in tug of war.

CHAPTER 17

The Wrong Side of the Fork

I know we tried, but in the end we were just too polarized.

There was too much of ourselves in the way.

I remember, for example, one time when Steph and I were having dinner at a Thai restaurant near the rental house, and she caught me tracking the slim-hipped Thai waitress but misread what I was thinking. Sorta. I was quietly wondering if I would be willing to consider an extreme conclusion and admit I was gay if I was attracted to slim-hipped Thai chicks, because this girl was quite attractive, but she looked like a teenage boy, which is how my mind works sometimes. I figured I'd have to think about this one later.

But Steph was not upset, not in the way she could get when we first met. I'd never been with anyone with such a short fuse, when it came to jealousy.

We'd been neglected at our table for some time, and I looked over her shoulder in search of that waitress, then muttered something about "Halley's waitress," under my breath.

It took her less than a microsecond, but then Steph realized the joke—the waitress that returned every seventy-six years—and a mixed expression seized her face.

"Did . . . did you just make that up?" she asked, and I wasn't sure if she was impressed or annoyed, competitive.

I was caught short, halfway tempted to take credit, but instead I said, "No, no; it's a song title from an album I just bought," and her expression changed again, this time comforted, perhaps even relieved.

We started talking about something or other, and I quietly brought up that I'd like to, eventually, eat that #11 Shark Steak on the menu.

"You want to eat shark?" she asked.

"Yeah, I have this thing where I'd like to eat anything that might potentially eat me. Like worms, lions, hippos, crocodiles, Monte Cristo sandwiches. Establishing my position at the head of the food chain and the like," I said.

I continued: "Did you happen to read about that shark in Virginia last year, the one that spontaneously generated a fetus, with no males around, ever? It was in the top stories of the last year."

"Seriously?" she asked, looking up from her menu. "A shark just up and developed a virgin sort of birth?"

"Yeah," I said, "It's called 'parthenogenesis,' I think, but I've always liked 'spontaneous generation,' since I read the phrase when I was a teenager. It's how I tried to disavow my parents. I wanted to do a skin graft over my belly button. Anyway, apparently it happens a lot more often than previously thought, during periods when males and females aren't around each other and the conditions are correct, then—*BAM*—the womens knock theyselves up."

Steph listened to this, now fairly accustomed to my random impersonations after two years of being together. A year ago, she'd still have asked me why I needed to slip into my 1970s Philadelphia ghetto junkyard impersonations, Redd Foxx from *Sanford and Son*. Not so much anymore. Sometimes she asked me to "bust up her chiffarobe for a lemonade," if you know what I mean. But in public, she just listened and ignored it, because it was better that way, she'd decided.

Let Shecky be Shecky. But don't encourage him.

Anyway, the impersonations and jokes are for me, and for no one else, I told her.

"But I like making you laugh," I said. "I like pushing your limits of the acceptable. It's there that we'll really meet each other," I told her, like I knew what I meant.

"Hunh," she said. "You think they can draw that leap back to humans, and the 'virgin birth' of Jesus?"

"Nah," I said. "That would be far too . . . I dunno . . . easy. It would have to happen far too many times in humans to categorically discount the idea of divine fertilization."

"You think? I mean, couldn't it explain away the virgin birth thing? If it happened enough?" she asked.

"No, I'm not entirely convinced it could happen with humans. My favorite explanation of that whole mythos to date comes from that Guy Ritchie movie where they posit that it's far more likely that the myth of the virgin came from a typo in a translation rather than the sort of conditions in a Virginia aquarium. I think a lot of the world's mysteries can be solved by understanding the nature of typos. Like with the difference between 'whiskey' with an *e* and 'whisky' without. My guess is that the Scots probably couldn't afford the ink for the extra character."

No response from Steph. I took this as a challenge.

"As someone who works in publishing," I continued, "this makes much more sense to me than a spontaneous virgin birth in a female-only culture, even if it happened periodically in other species."

⌐⌐

We were both quiet for moment, and I was thinking a little more on the topic, sipping a crappy Sapporo beer.

"Anyhow, the real reason you know it didn't happen by 'divine insemination' is because Joseph didn't kill Mary. Stone her to death in an honor killing, back in those days."

I'm sure my reading of Talmudic law left much to be desired, but I was on a tear.

I noticed that this suggestion of misogyny and violence tweaked her, but I couldn't help it: I had to nudge at her. It was how we poked at one another, called it "love." Instead of sex.

"I mean, think about it. Do you think a man could live with a wife that would go, 'Oh, Joseph; do it like God did it that night. Not like that, Joseph! God didn't do it like that! He was *much* better at *that!*' and 'Ouch! Joseph! God *never* tried to do *that!*'"

Here Steph gave me a hard stare. I saw her upbringing fighting to surface and give me a stern, corrective, change-the-subject look, but there were no shock collars for me: I was smiling now and couldn't help myself. I was still too punk rock. Steph had very strict rules regarding what constituted "proper" dinner conversation, she once told me. This was a girl who said she was taught never to use the side of the fork, though I'd seen what she was capable of doing to my expensive pans and good dishes.

I could almost hear her thoughts running, *Don't encourage him. Don't encourage him. Don't encourage him. . . .*

⎯ ⎯

And then she couldn't help but smile, because I was trying so hard to make her laugh, though she hated how I was doing it because it conflicted directly with her programming of what was appropriate, and I was being terribly inappropriate, but I knew she found it funny. I was eroding her disciplines, and she hated me for it.

She'd come a long way from the humorless suffragette with the Georgia O'Keefe prints in her bedroom when we met just a year ago, now able to laugh at the things she once found sacrosanct.

So this encouraged me. I slipped back into my Shecky Greene.

"And then Joseph would be all like, 'That's IT! I've had it to here already! God did this, and God did that! One time God comes down and gives you a good schtupping, and I have to hear about it for the rest of my life? There are no worse things for a husband!!'"

Actually, that was delivered a bit more like Topol doing Tevye.

"'Well, Joseph,' says Mary, 'Truth be told, it wasn't just the one time.'" (I was doing Mary's voice here, too.)

Steph looked at me hard, her hands clenched on her silverware on either side of her dinner plate.

I took this as a cue to continue, and a punch line revealed itself to me.

"'What blasphemy is this? It wasn't just the one time?!'"

"So then Mary says, 'Well, the first time, He wanted to do something He saw in a porno once.'"

Steph threw her cutlery down noisily, loud enough to draw attention from fellow diners as I was choking on my own laughter, and she stood up, dumped her linen napkin, and made for the door. I was laughing too hard into my hand to watch her leave, but I flagged down the waitress, who looked at me with pity as I asked for the check and the dinner to be packaged in containers. I wasn't in the least bit embarrassed. This was not uncommon for us.

I found Steph a block down the street, leaning against my car, smoking a shaky cigarette.

Her mouth was pursed, frozen in a half smile before she let it go entirely and started laughing hysterically, which turned into a sob as she put her face in my shoulder.

I was with her at the laughing part, and I understood the sobbing.

"I don't know what I'm doing with you," she said into my shoulder.

"I was just trying to make you laugh," I said, which was partially true. The rest of the truth was, there was a joke in the air, and I locked onto it with my prey drive, the way a terrier would lock onto a squirrel and chase it into a tree. It's just what I did, and I couldn't control it.

Her cigarette was dangling from her fingers at my hip as she sobbed once again, and I was afraid she was going to burn the elbow of my leather coat.

I placed her in the car and handed her the food, and I drove us home. I decided to take a roundabout route for no reason other than to cool things off, and the next day I read in the paper that a teenager some two streets down from where we lived had been standing in the dark, firing a 9 mm pistol at passing cars, randomly and just for the sake of doing it. He'd put five rounds in five cars that police knew about until he had shattered the back window of a passing car and the driver had stopped, seen the kid running, figured out what was happening, and called the cops. They caught him inside, thirty minutes later, playing video games.

It was a street we might have taken, headed home from the restaurant that night, and I showed it to Steph, who didn't think as much of it as I did, realizing once again that as much as you can try, you just can't insure yourself against chance, and random lunacy.

"I can't protect you," I said. "I don't know if I can keep us safe."

"I'm not asking you to protect me," she said in return. "I can protect myself."

I had started to keep a catalogue of potential catastrophes that could harm us, up to date and constantly refreshed, in order that they might not be a surprise, thinking that if I could think of them first, they wouldn't happen. It's the surprise that gets you, after all.

I couldn't keep up with Steph and her potential for harm, not anymore.

CHAPTER 18

Showering Blows

At this time, my new job had given me much more liberty than what I was previously accustomed to, and I had far too much unregulated time, but I was also writing more and more, developing my unstructured project in a way that I hadn't expected, and my book was actually taking some sort of open-ended narrative track. I had been writing one-off short stories about growing up in Brownsville, and my family's history, but I began to see a through-line that would culminate in many of the choices my brother and I would make in our lives, and it began to feel important, like something real. So I continued writing and was excited, annoyed when real life interfered with my writing jags.

On the days I wasn't working for the now struggling "bilingual media company," I would wake up, send Steph on her way in the morning commute to her office, and then walk the mile down to the horrible bar in that terrible northern neighborhood and sit among the retired derelict drunks who'd been drinking since 6:00 a.m. That the bar opened this early, and daily, I was eternally grateful and disconcerted; it certainly knew its regulars. I had always found people who read in bars to be a bit pretentious, somehow, but to write a book in a bar—that was downright contentious, and I planned on doing just that, in longhand. Just to be able to say that I did. Dough would understand that.

At around noon, I would position myself at the end of the bar with a pint of something domestic and cheap, a glass of water, and my headphones, then begin scribbling stories into my small moleskin notebook, and write, write, write the day away. Some eight beers later, I'd realize I'd been gone all that time, and all the old duffers and laborers and nonurbanites would have swirled and commented and snickered at my hulking, leather-framed mass lost in my headphones and my notebook, but no one would mess with me, no one would challenge or accost me, as I was clearly, evidently, not one of them: I wasn't white, I wasn't broken down yet, I wasn't smoking low-shelf cigarettes, spending a controlled income on pull tabs, I wasn't . . . that stratum of America, in this crap neighborhood just thirty minutes north of Seattle but feeling like I was in deep redneck country.

So what was I?

I'm just visiting, I'd think to myself, as I closed my notebook, put away my pen, and shook out the cramp from my hand to pay my bill.

And the bill was always small. I could never believe it. Around a sawbuck.

I'd sit and sip thin beers for three or four hours while writing, and my bill would be about twelve bucks. God bless America. Or at least, these shitty redneck bars.

— ◆ —

The productivity and the creative hangover would usually leave me in a great mood, and I'd wander the evergreened, pine-needley, no-sidewalk-having neighborhood back to the grimy rental just in time to meet Steph, who was more often than not in an abysmal mood from her return commute. She was growing taciturn, resented that I no longer had to show up to an office, or present myself anywhere, really, and had two days a week free, plus weekends. I was good at what I did and could consolidate other people's forty-hour week into about ten good hours if I was left alone, and that's what I did, and that's what I felt was appropriate to what I was doing.

I wasn't about to apologize or negotiate my way out of it; if I was to remain labor, then my labor was to be dear. It was art, and they were lucky to have me.

In the meantime, I was writing this damned book.

— ◆ —

Steph fumed. Threw an odd assortment of outfits together and managed to get to work and be superior at what she did in her field, as she was incredibly intelligent, which is what drew me to her in the beginning. But my trouble with her was that I could never catch up to which of her insecurities was running the roost at the time. She was never with others who she was with me, and I had not the stamina to keep running after her and figuring out what she needed, which is another component of love I couldn't deliver for her. I just didn't know it at the time, and I'm not sure I had the energy. I was fat now. Maybe if we were both still twenty-five, but not at thirty-nine.

And so every time she returned home and found me beaming and tipsy and maybe cooking dinner or playing with the dog, or just going on and on about what I'd written that day, she would settle into a funk.

—◦—

One night, I wandered off from the local swill dump without my credit card, and I noticed it only after Steph and I had been in a particularly bitter argument.

The wine was in, I suppose, and I decided to make the drive back to the bar, which was less than a mile away and without stop signs, just the one turn.

"No!" Steph said. "You're drunk!"

"I am," I agreed, "but I have to get my card back. Otherwise that bartendress, Old Beryl, puts another 15 percent charge on it or something. Anyhow, I need it. For credit cardy stuff. Stand aside."

I blundered left right left right back to where my car was parked in the front yard—this was the custom in that neighborhood—and intended to coast the small distance to the bar, as it was just around the corner, and Steph came howling out of the house as I turned the engine over, and she jumped on the hood of my car, spread eagle on the windshield.

I yelled out my window, "Are you fucking serious?"

"I won't let you!"

"Seriously, get the fuck off my car. It's just down the street and I don't feel like walking."

She would not remove herself from my hood.

We were at an impasse.

"Fine. I'll walk," I said. I turned off the car and emerged from the driver's side, and when I put my keys back in my pocket, I found my missing credit card.

"That turned out all right," I said the next day, and Steph pointed out some deep bruises she had acquired from flinging herself onto the hood of my car, to keep me from killing children and dog walkers between the dilapidated house and the shabby bar, and I thought, *Well, shit, this isn't Texas.* I'd never thought of that before. You wouldn't have people walking in Texas, let alone walking their dogs. Anyway, in Texas, neighborhoods have sidewalks, and you're expected to have a few DUIs. It drives the economy. Mind the pun.

I didn't think I was drinking too much, or more than necessary. I thought, more than anything, that I drank like a British person. Or an Australian, when I'd really take it too far. Maybe I was just living in the wrong hemisphere.

Steph felt my drinking was entirely out of control.

I, well, didn't. I drank like labor. I drank like a working man, five days a week. Maybe six. Three of them acutely. I drank like a lord. I had every analogy available to put it into a context; she was the outlier.

She couldn't drink steadily; you put her in front of booze, and she drank it all, right at once. Then she had a seizure or a "life event" and wouldn't drink again for years.

"Who's the dangerous drunk, when you compare the two patterns?" I asked her.

⌒

So one morning, I was up pretty early, a bit sleep deprived—I'd been writing *a lot* lately—and Steph was in the shower, getting ready for her day at work. I knocked on the mildewed door to the bathroom with the mildewed shower stall and the undignified toilet where you had to pull up your knees to your chin to take a proper poo, and I said, "Hey, Steph! I got your coffee going, and I've walked Cleo," and I could hear her crying, in the shower.

"Steph, are you . . ." I asked through the door. I'm a bit lightheaded, sure, but I could swear I heard her crying.

"Darling, are you crying?"

The shower cut off with a squeak, and then a rumble. The listing vinyl platform we called a floor groaned as she stepped out and grabbed a thin, nasty towel off the floor, because the towel racks didn't hold into the linoleum, so we had the two swinging towel rack sides, but no bar joining them. Even the towels in that house were substandard, made of a tired, resistant fiber that moved the water around your body rather than soaked it up.

"Darling?"

And she opened the door, bright as a shiny day.

"I'm great!" she said. "I'm just fine! I don't know what you heard."

"Hunh," I said, "Because I could swear I heard you crying."

"No, no," she said. "Not at all."

"It's funny because I can still see tears on your face. But all right, well, I have your coffee going. I'm going back to the bar to finish writing this fantastic story about my grandmother and these ocelots—"

And I turned around here and she punched me, bare, sharp, white girl knuckly, right in the eyeball—*BAM!*

"You fucking bastard!" she yelled. "You goddamn lazy Mexican drunk motherfucker! You don't fuck me for weeks and all you do is drink and pretend to write and you're surprised that I'm *crying!*"

———

I took a step back as soon as I was hit.

She was standing there, so thin and wet and well, pale, with a towel wrapped around her torso, her eyes crazy and her shoulders bare and glistening with that toxic water from the mildewed shower, and she glowered at me with all the righteous indignation of a mother with a baby walker waiting in a crosswalk in Seattle.

My head was humming, and not from her blow.

It hadn't been much, but it had been received as terms.

We were done.

She had hit me, and my physiological response had been to hit right back, that very second.

But I hadn't.

I took that step back, made an instant assessment of the situation, and, while my eye was watering, I turned right around, grabbed my keys, and within a few hours was signing rental documents on an oversize studio on the same block I lived on when I met Steph, the only thought pumping through my head telling me to pick up where I left off, before I met her, try to pick up again where I was two years ago.

That was the end for me.

You don't hit people you love.

You do not hit people you love.

CHAPTER 19
Every Exit an Entrance, Someplace Else

About a month later, and against any sort of good judgment, we attempted an assuagement to the end of the relationship instead of a clean, cauterizing break. We were both sentimental like that and arrested in our adolescent dating phase.

The closest I can now explain it from the safety of this distance and this keyboard is that we both pitied one another as a bad fit for this world: What we saw and understood of the other made us sad for both the other person and ourselves, and if we could make it better for the other, well, it might be better for me, for us.

At least, that's what I thought: If she could make the adjustment and function, then so could I. I mean, Jesus—she was *way* more fucked up than I was, right? Sympathy and compassion are not love, though. There needs to be someone there, at the end of the compassion and sympathy, that you respect.

So I would help bring her to shore, help her feel better about our separation.

But Dear Lord: Get me hence, after.

—◆—

And so it started when I bought her that camping book, the one with the best hikes in Washington State, for dogs. And their owners, of course.

Her boss had kindly presented Steph with a book on her birthday some time before for the best alpine hikes in Washington, and that was a lovely gift, except that Steph took her dog, Cleo, with her everywhere, especially when she hiked, and dogs are not allowed in most state-sanctioned parks because of their "ecological footprint" on those heavily trodden and sterile experiences, where you meet one hundred other weekend hikers in their North Face polar fleece headed back down the same gravel path you've just trudged, smiling politely after going quiet when they notice you so their conversation doesn't intrude into your "wildlife experience."

It would generate a tremendous amount of anxiety between us that she'd bring the dog and then allow Cleo off-leash on these hikes, when we'd take them. Never mind the "ecological footprint" business, an off-leash dog creates a variety of potentially volatile situations with other humans and canines outside the designated off-leash parks. And I had a profound dislike for people who didn't take care of their dogs, or their children, in public.

＊＊

Which is why I bought Steph a book with the best dog-friendly hikes for her birthday, published by the "Mountaineers," who, as near as I could figure, were part of some shifty college of weekend/weekday warriors who kept their technology jobs in Seattle but *really* tested their polar fleece mettle on the fiercest hikes in the Cascades, on Saturdays. Maybe a slow Wednesday here and there. But definitely on those Saturdays: Saturdays are macho, for people who think in html and Java.

Steph accepted the gift in the manner it was presented, sort of a shot across the forgiveness bow, as we had broken up the month previous. It had been ugly, and it had affected our health, both mental and physical, and it hadn't settled well on me that we were separating like that, in that degree of ugliness after the level of affection shared between us. Back then, I wasn't smart enough to know that these dark feelings ebb just as quickly and as easily as the light ones, when they're not stoked.

So, the book, then.

＊＊

Steph found something in that book, out in the Cascades, outside an isolated town called Twisp, and asked if I'd be willing to come out with her and Cleo; it was late October, sure, but we could pack for the cold, right? Harvest moons and all that. There was enough polar fleece to spare.

What can it hurt? I thought. Play the good guy, have some fun carrying a backpack, take the dog out for a spin, stretch the legs on the dead relationship, and have some good old Lewis and Clark type of adventure, once again, because I'm nothing if not optimistic. It's why I'm here, isn't it? Why I moved west? Why we all, in fact, moved west? Trees and shit. Mountains and waterfalls and the like. With bears. Lots of fucking bears. Why the hell not?

This wouldn't be a rough, raw open trail place like Bacon Creek, which had grown tiresome and spent, and, if I'm perfectly honest, quite frightening, since it was an antediluvian hunting camp and felt a bit too "Live Free or Die," by either tobacco-spitting hunters or bears, after that last visit. This was a state park we had found, in that book, and it seemed a bit more guarded, kept up, a bit less . . . Donner Party, or Windigo.

We loaded up her Jeep with our preparations, our favorite pillows, and even visited a "foam store" in the U-District and bought a high-density foam that we cut to the shape of the back of the Jeep to make a safe, off-the-ground sleeping spot: Fancy!

This was actually my idea; I had a fear of apex predators, like grizzlies and yeti and hedge fund managers. I felt sleeping in the Jeep would keep us safe. If I had to sleep outside, my other plan was to sacrifice the dog first: If it was a bear, then break one of the dog's legs to buy us a couple of minutes; if it was a banker, sign her up for a predatory mortgage to cover our trail. That's what dogs are for. (Sorry, Cleo: You should have developed your neocortex and hired an accountant.)

It was late one Friday in a colder-than-usual and dwindling October afternoon when we headed north on I-5 for the North Cascades Highway and then exited eastward, rising ever steadily up, up, and up into these odd, insulated enclosures of towns and hamlets.

I was driving her Jeep this night, its headlights weak and more jaundiced than illuminating, and it was when I turned off I-5 on Highway 20 headed east, in Burlington—a proper train depot sort of town, on the Skagit River—that things began to descend into a clear Jungian exploration of self, for the both of us.

Even now, years later, I'm not entirely sure which one of us triggered this sequence of metaphor, this ascent into hyperreality—a declension of mysticism and trauma, lined with markers and signals and omen, from which neither of us would come out the same, or unbroken.

The mountains became a gateway, began our shared walkabout, as I drove that Jeep with both of us as willing participants, together. It was like we were both stuck and aggravated in our shared experience and wanted to kick the transformation into action: *Let's get a move on.*

Let's change the reality. Let's do what we both know we're capable of doing. Wine into blood, bread into body. Transfiguration.

Let's bring on the tragedy; I can take it if you can take it.

To understand this better, an appreciation of the geography is needed here.

The I-5 corridor runs nearly the entire length of Washington State into Canada, parallel to Puget Sound and the Pacific Ocean, nearly at sea level. When you turn right, or east, up around the northern bits, and drive for a few hours, you begin driving into the Cascade Mountain Range, and you start ascending into some deep, green, primordial country.

Bigfoot country. And remember, the Jeep had terribly ineffective headlights.

When I'd first moved to Seattle, my first experience with a karate school was under the tutelage of this older, spiritually minded mystic named Dennis, and he often said the reason he loved being in the Pacific Northwest was because the energy here was fresh from the polar ice caps—in the water, in the trees—and held a level of purity you couldn't find anywhere else. There was magic in the primitive evergreen nature here because it was brand new, unrecycled, untreated. All your wishes came true here, he said, so you had to be really careful about what you were really wishing for, because the place would give you what you wanted, whether you knew you wanted it or not.

And for Steph and me, it began right away.

We were just outside of Concrete, Washington, when we hit a traffic snarl on a two-lane highway. We crawled slowly for roughly fifteen or twenty minutes in the fading light before we came upon the source of the traffic irritation: a classic 1950s Chevy convertible in a head-on collision with a 1950s classic Chevy pickup truck.

Both vehicles were tremendously truncated at the fore, and both drivers stood by the side of the road speaking calmly to the state deputies, remarkably unharmed if a bit dazed and possibly discussing the cost of rehabilitation for either of the vehicles, with another seventeen-year-old deputy in a hazard vest trying his best to direct traffic around the accident.

Steph and I were silent, attempting to figure out what had just happened. The violence of the collision was clearly evident, but the odds of two classic, refurbished vehicles in that velocity of impact, on a two-lane state highway, with no casualties . . . it just wasn't making sense.

We moved on, went on our way, and the evening settled around us on this Friday night, and we eventually began singing along with my iPod, plugged into her dreadful radio that we could hardly hear because we had to keep the windows open for ventilation. It was an old, battle-worn Jeep, but Steph loved it, and at times so did I, when she would keep it clean and didn't have garbage spilling over in the front seat. Once, when I was driving, a water bottle rolled under the brake pedal, and as I was trying to negotiate a curve, the fucking brake wouldn't work and I had a moment of panic, until I understood what was happening and had to stomp on the brakes and crush the plastic bottle so I could make the turn. I was incensed at her, that her bad housekeeping would almost kill me.

But not this night. This night, we were getting along, talking loudly over the sound of the wind and feeling something very nearly comfortable, when out of nowhere I had to slam on the brakes again and bring the Jeep to something short of a complete stop and turn the wheel hard to the left.

Black car, halfway in and halfway out of the road, hazard lights blinking.

―◆―

It was still the two-lane highway, approaching some small mountain village with working-poor sort of single-family houses on either side of the road, where Highway 20 made a T intersection up ahead with a blinking stoplight, and there were these three kids, standing by the side of road, the fourth one down on his knees, cradling a black dog and crying.

I caught this in an instant, shaken. Shook.

Steph had all her limbs extended out, braced for impact as I wrestled the Jeep under control.

A Volkswagen Passat rested at an angle, and they all gazed up at us, snowboarding types, though it was early for snowboarding. We looked at them, and the one boy on the ground was holding the dog as the dog was convulsing, dying, in his arms, and this kid was visibly heartbroken, deeply affected, and crying, begging the dog's forgiveness, it seemed. It was a big dog, about sixty or seventy pounds, a Lab mix, with its tongue dangling out the side of its mouth, and there was blood. It would die in minutes. Nothing anyone could do.

The three kids stared at us, their faces silently asking if we knew what to do, helpless, and I slowly shook my head, saying, *Sorry, man; sorry. This one, you guys have to do alone.*

And Steph and I drove on, quiet now, with Cleo alert over the console between us, alert, aware, and sycophantic, trying to make peace from the hum of death in the air.

———

"That was horrible," I said as we were driving in the dark, about an hour later. Neither of us could get the image of the dying black Labrador out of our minds, out of our conversation.

The mood became morose in the Jeep, tinged with the mystic. It was a four-hour drive from Seattle to Twisp. Had I known, I don't think I would have agreed. Somehow, Seattle usually seems like it's two hours from everywhere else in Washington. Maybe I'm spoiled because I grew up with Texan distances.

Steph told me once again about the time Cleo was hit by a car, at the end of her leash, how they had turned one of those dark corners in the North Seattle neighborhoods she likes to walk with a sense of impunity. Once, she said, there was a couch on a street corner and she and Cleo stopped for a nap; that's how safe she felt out there, and I bit my tongue and kept quiet. But this night, she said, this night was a rainy wint'ry night, and Cleo had extended the full length of the extension leash and entered into the road and was clipped badly by a Buick.

"And I just flipped out," she said.

I knew Steph really well by this time, and Steph flipping out was not something pleasant. She could grow five times her size with histrionics.

Cleo's back leg was broken in a compound fracture, had been brought up into the back wheel well. She'd gone into shock and was looking at Steph like she was asking for permission to die.

Steph denied her that privilege and brought the dog back, she said, by bullying the poor Persian fellow who happened to be driving across their path that night and having him take them both to the emergency pet clinic on Aurora.

Steph can bully quite a bit out of most people is the lesson here.

They'd gone out on a date after, Steph said, but he didn't speak enough English to get along.

"Besides," she said, "from what I could make of it, he wanted a wife to stay at home and cook dinner for him and his mother."

"That's ... um," I tried to respond, "I don't think ... well, it's good that he took you to the vet clinic, I guess."

I was trying to imagine dating someone, even getting across the idea of a date, with someone who not only ran over your dog—hey, that's a rom-com waiting to happen—but also can't speak your language, when we rounded a wide, cliffside corner of a deep, dark mountain road with no lights whatsoever and turned directly into a four-vehicle traffic jam, about ten thousand feet into mountain air and an accident just waiting to happen, and I once again had to slam on the brakes and bring the Jeep to a measured halt.

Sonofabitch.

What *now?*

The darkness of the mountain night was ignited with the amber hue of hazard lights and brakes, and periodic, careening vehicles streaming past—at first slowing, then understanding the curiosity of spectacle, then deciding it wasn't their affair and moving on, headed off into the prolonged darkness down the mountain range, back onto their own business. But we—Steph and Cleo and me—we decided to make that little cluster of crazy ours, as I pulled over and set my own lights to signal "hazard."

"Are you sure you want to get into this?" I asked Steph.

We had driven around that long mountain curve and came up scared when we saw the cars, four of them: three lined against the shoulder and the fourth, the one causing trouble, tipped into the embankment, the front two wheels off into the ditch and the back two tires raised in the air. This was all happening in the blind corner of a curve, so that any cars coming fast around the corner had just a second to see the car and make an adjustment. It was going to be a fatality any second now, especially since it was on a cliffside.

This was nightmarish, especially for me.

And I recognized the Volkswagen Passat from earlier, parked alongside.

They'd apparently passed us, after Steph and I had stopped at a convenience store and let Cleo pee, and were now trying to make up for their vehicular dogslaughter, presumably.

—◆—

Steph was in the passenger seat and looked over at me, and I could see that she'd already come under her moral authority code: We do what's right. And right now, that meant we had to help. She didn't even have to say it; I saw it all in her face.

"We have to help this," she said.

I did the shortcut myself, and I knew I couldn't leave without doing what was needed. I don't feel that way anymore.

I said, "All right. Stay here for a moment. Keep her down." I meant the dog.

Steph's door was nearly flat against the mountainside, and Cleo was animated to annoyance with anxiety, so Steph grabbed her collar and pinned the dog down to keep her from leaping out of the Jeep and becoming another casualty that night.

I caught my breath, timed the cars whipping around the corner, and then left the Jeep.

It was dangerous, but not exactly "combat-dangerous." But almost. It was "danger-close" combat.

The car in trouble was a late-model Pontiac driven by a younger woman in Ugg boots, who may or may not have been inebriated, and who had lost control of the vehicle and miraculously survived a spin on the road but ended up teeter-tottering on the embankment, with another Mexican woman as a passenger.

Two of the boys from the Passat had the bright idea of hopping on the back of the car, pressing it down to get traction, while the driver was gunning it in reverse. It was a front-wheel-drive vehicle. Had their plan worked, the two boys would have been run over. The car was adjacent to the highway, and, after backing over the two hipsters, the car would have then been traversed into the highway, into oncoming traffic. Everything about this plan was a complete catastrophe about to happen.

— —

Somehow, I think because I was older than everyone else, I automatically slipped into sergeant major status and began barking orders as soon as I emerged from the Jeep. And cars continued whipping around that corner with no warning, the acoustics on that mountaintop that night giving no indication of the danger coming at us at seventy-five miles an hour.

They just appeared . . . and then they were gone—showing up with nothing nearing the indication that they'd even noticed the clusterfuck of cars on the blind side of that corner before they raced off into the dark of the night.

Even eighteen-wheeled rigs came out of nowhere: The Doppler effect was on their side, not ours. It was just a matter of time before someone was going to die.

"You two! Get the fuck off the back of that car!"

Voooooooooooooooofff!

"What?" they yelled back.

"Off the fucking car! Get this one out of the way; the Jeep has a tow hitch. Does anyone have a chain or towrope?"

"We . . . we have some hiking rope!" I heard someone else yell, from the other side of the Pontiac.

Inside the vehicle, the girl was still roaring her engine, and her front tires spun without purchase in the ditch, which was well lit with her headlights.

Then another trailer came around with a horrifying noise.

"*Goddammit!*" I yelled, because I was looking the other way. Even out here, you couldn't hear if someone was coming around that corner, and thus you had no chance to react.

"You!" I yelled to some bearded guy standing across the road with his hands in his pockets, trying to keep warm, and then I noticed he'd been talking to the kid who had been holding the dying dog.

"Get across the road and tell us when there's another car coming! You hear me?! Warn us when there's someone coming!" I pointed to a triangulated place where he'd be able to see down the road and still be able to yell at us, where he'd have a line of sight to an oncoming car. He nodded with exaggeration and gave me the thumbs-up signal. Fine.

I banged on the top of the car and told the girl to stop with the roaring and then directed the owner of the Hyundai that was parked between the Pontiac and the Jeep to get it out of the way; the Jeep had the hitch and the power to pull this car out of the ditch.

"Move it over to the side of the—"

"CAR!" the kid over on the side of the road yelled, and sure enough, *ZZOOOM!!*

This car seemed to slow down, and I saw brake lights over my shoulder, but I ignored them and focused on what was in front of me.

"Fuck," I said. "All right, get your—"

And here I was handed the hiking rope, which looked like threaded plastic, and the guy who owned it was now under the elevated back of the car—

"CAR!"

And there was nothing I could do but hope that—

ZZZOOOOM!

FUCK.

"Get out from under there!" I yelled at the kid, who was heroically looping the thin cord around a brake line. Jesus Christ.

"Come on, man, get out. This isn't going to work. Who owns the Passat?"

"Trevor," said the kid standing next to me. I can't even describe him now. I don't remember his face. Just his fear.

"Where's Trevor?"

"Trevor!" two of the kids began yelling.

Trevor was the kid who had hit the dog.

But never mind that now.

Trevor ran up, his hoodie still bloodied from the dog.

"In your trunk, under the cover, in the spare tire, you have a towrope. It's nylon and flat and rolled up with two hooks at either end. Find it and bring it here," I yelled.

Then I turned to the two kids standing next to me, who had been trying to pin the Pontiac to the ground.

"Don't let her out of the driver's seat. You two stay—"

"CAR!"

ZZZOOOOOOOMMM!

"Stay out of the road, and stay right here! I'm going to back the Jeep to this po—"

"I can't find it! There's nothing here!" from Trevor, at the Passat.

"Look in the side! In the side compartment!" I yelled back.

"OH, I found it!!" he yelled back.

"Then bring it here!" I think, *Jesus; that was lucky.*

"CAR!"

VARRROOOOMMMM!

Fuck.

I thrust myself into the driver's side of the Jeep and took a deep breath. It was suddenly quiet, in the Jeep.

Steph and I didn't look at each other.

"Are you all right?" she asked. She was still holding Cleo, who was trying her best to get out from under her grasp. There was just too much happening for her to be calm. She was shifting, struggling, but silent. A dog muted from electroshock therapy.

"I think I have this solved. I'm good. How are you? You're safe here, you know."

"There was a man who came by," she said.

I had turned on the Jeep and I was backing up carefully as she said this.

"What?"

"A man, with a beard, he came to see what was happening and stuck his head in your window, while you were back there."

"A man? With a beard? What . . . ? Were you . . . Did he . . ." I wasn't sure what she was saying. Was she threatened? I didn't see anyone stop or . . . wait—

"The old station wagon?" I thought I had seen an old station wagon slow down, the first car, earlier.

"Look, we stumbled into this, and I have to fix this. Nothing's going to happen to you; stay here," I said and extracted myself and leaned against the side of the Jeep all the way to the back, where it was now just a few feet from the Pontiac.

Trevor was standing there behind the Pontiac with the other two kids.

He handed me the nylon towrope with the hooks on either side as I disentangled the mess of the cord, from earlier.

"Get out from behind this car. Get to the other side of the road or across the ditch, now."

This is bad, I thought. A car or truck careening around that corner hitting the Pontiac would kill five people.

I looked at the guy across the road to measure his responses and he looked as if he saw nothing, which was a gamble. These kids were idiots. Affable, but idiots.

I took a deep breath and scrambled under the Pontiac and found a structural support, looped the nylon tow cable and squirmed back out, quick.

As I stood up, I saw Trevor, the only one left, standing there and waiting to help, awaiting my next bark.

I looked him square in the eye, and he looked at me, wanting to know what to do.

I said, "It wasn't your fault about the dog. He was loose, he had no collar. That happens, in the world. Dogs get killed by cars. It was good you stopped."

Maybe that was true about the collar. I don't remember seeing one. But it made Trevor move.

VARRRROOOOOMMMMMMM!!!! went another car behind us.

Catching my breath, I told the woman in the car that I was about to get in the Jeep and pull her out: She had to put her car in reverse and I would pull her out. We would travel a little way down the road so that she wasn't so close to the blind corner—*Do you understand what I'm saying here?*

She looked back at me, scared, but understanding.

All right, then.

In a second, I scrambled along the side of the Jeep and made it into the driver's side and buckled in.

I stepped on the brake and, for a moment, everyone behind me was illuminated: the foolish, out-of-season snowboarders, the guy who stopped by to help but couldn't do anything, and the two tipsy hot chicks in the Pontiac. I put the Jeep in drive and let the towrope engage, slowly, and the car began to shift, badly, on the embankment, and then *VAR-ROOMMM!!* another truck whipped by us when the goddamned Pontiac caught front-wheel purchase and they were on the road and began traveling with the Jeep. I dragged the car about thirty feet from the site of the accident, and I set the Jeep to park and I stepped out, undid the hitch, and Trevor was there, running up with his two pals who asked, "How did you know that the towrope was in Trevor's car?" and I said, "I have a Jetta at home; those Germans prepare for everything," and the girls were suddenly jumping up and clapping and I said, "Look, I don't know if you're drinking or what, but it's not my responsibility from here, so just . . . I don't know; it's your choice . . . from here," and I shook someone's hand who tried to pat me on the back and I left when *VAR-ROOOOOMM!!!* once again an SUV zoomed past and I just wanted to get the fuck out of there.

I stepped back into the cab of the Jeep and Steph released Cleo, who put her cold nose in my ear and began smelling all over me. I signaled and entered back onto the highway, and I was feeling like . . .*All right . . . I did something. I helped these helpless kids. Maybe they'll make an app to stop breast cancer or something,* and Steph said, "I was really scared by that man."

"Which man?" I asked, not tracking.

"The man with the beard, who stopped and put his head in your window, while you were gone."

"My window is up. My window has been up all this time."

"Still," she said. "He was there."

CHAPTER 20

What the Morning Brings

There was a sense of relief in the darkened cab of the Jeep, after we put some distance between it and the scene of the earlier accident, and I drove us farther into the mountains and into the primordial darkness. We were quiet for some time as we drove on, and the cars that were in front of us or behind us may or may not have been the other participants of that entanglement, may or may not have been the station wagon that had frightened Steph, and as the possibilities grew thinner, she became more open, and talkative, as eventually did I, until we were positively garrulous from nervous energy, and we recounted the experience of those ten dangerous minutes to one another from our different points of view until we agreed on a convergence of narrative, and were able to understand, individually and together, what the hell had just happened back there.

Eventually our ascending and winding path brought us to the strangest, most unsettling manufactured village in the mountain range, this incredible verdant and brightly lit town that felt half like a military base and half like a set from an apocalyptic film, after the town has been abandoned. It was the control area for a huge dam, right in the middle of nowhere, lit up like an airstrip, and I had just about hit my limit of things that were unnatural and abnormal for the evening. I was actually frightened at this point, because things had become foreign and nonsensical, a lot like what I imagine my being in Belgium would be like. Except with the precision of 1950s American engineering. Like Boeing, with waffles, and Jean-Claude Van Damme.

After the eventful four-hour drive that we'd had to this point, I was flooded with anxiety and at full emotional capacity with the sense of imminent . . . weirdness. Doom. Change. Religious iconography. I don't know what it was, but my Catholic sensibilities were just humming by this point, and if I was a smaller sort of mammal, I'd have bolted for the nearest burrow and hunkered down for a day. Maybe nibbled on a carrot, for comfort. As a thirty-nine-year-old human male in an urban environment, I would have normally replaced that burrow with a bar, but here I was, a Gulf Coast flatlander in a mountain land, a foreigner in a foreign land, and in a car with a woman who disapproved of my drinking, so that idea was out.

Three ominous car wrecks in two hours, and now this creepy isolated town lit up like a militarized installation, and if I had been thinking more clearly, I would have rented a hotel room, said good-bye to Steph, rented a car in the morning, and made it the hell back home.

But instead I had to pull over and have Steph drive the rest of the way, which was inexplicably just around a corner and then down a steep descent to the valley floor on the other side of the Cascade Mountains. Twisp, Washington: a land devoid of cell phone towers, but with more than a few illuminated crosses on surrounding hilltops. Oh, yeah.

We followed the instructions in the hiking book, which had now become an invaluable guide through the old, retired logging concern, and it directed us basically into people's farms and driveways, navigating around goats and annoyed cows, standing and chewing in the middle of unlit dirt roads in the deep darkness. These weren't mentioned in the guidebook, but we did the best we could in driving around them, and eventually found the trailhead we sought, designated by someone's hand-painted sign, then rolled up the Jeep to a stop, an elevated bivouac that would keep us from being cold, we thought, as we created a nest for the night in the back of the Jeep, for three. Or two and a half. Two legs good, four legs bad.

The Jeep, after two hours sitting in that mountain valley in darkest October, was like a refrigeration unit set to "Viking."

It was a miserable night, made more so by the mania of the dog, who was now smelling deer and bear all around her and demanded a pee every two hours.

The next morning could not arrive soon enough, and when it finally dawned, I was packed and loaded and ready to head on our further misadventure into the Cascade trail by 6:00 a.m., with only minimal kvetching and a good bit of huffing, and some puffing: I was the load-bearing wall on the hike, the pack animal, because, well, that's what we do, where I come from. Here was an expression of my Gramma's people: You need something carried? I can carry anything—bring it on.

So I had this fantastic rig complete with aluminum infrastructure and multiple holds, compartments, and lofts—all reinforced with zippers and sexiness—and I was John Marion Wayne, baby: Let's conquer this land, for Texas.

I looked like a tortoise, and I had about seventy pounds of extraneous gear on my back—multiple tins of soup, dry foods, dog food, ground coffee, a camping coffee-making kit, a BB gun with accessories, pots and pans, silverware, socks, extra clothes, the tent, sleeping bag, foam mats, full water bottles, paperbacks in case we became bored—it was like a ten-year-old had packed it, because that's kind of what I was: a kid living out what he thought was the fantasy of camping. I even had a utility belt, where I had a machete in a scabbard (in case of jungle vines, duh) and one of those retractable police truncheons—in case of bears: I wasn't going against a bear with just a machete.

And we might have even made it to the hidden lake and the raw, natural camping ground we were attempting to reach, if we hadn't taken a wrong turn within the first fifty feet of the trailhead.

That was my fault. I forget what confused me, but I led us east on a horse trail, when we should have just trudged up.

We basically walked five miles back the way we came, parallel to the dirt road we'd driven in on, and this is on me.

The dog became horribly annoying the entire trip, running forward and backward and clipping us at the knee every time, enough so that I finally lost my temper with her and directed a blow to her snout when she just about knocked me down at the halfway mark, and we both decided it was time for a coffee break, on a ridge overlooking a deep and staggeringly steep ravine, where Steph sat and undid her own pack, then helped me with mine, and we started a small fire and made that morning's coffee.

It was surprisingly beautiful, even though it was an absolute error, and she sat perched with her feet dangling over the ledge and asked me to take photos of her, using her phone camera, as it was useless for anything else since we were so far out of cellular reach.

She shifted dangerously close to the edge so that we could get her into the same frame as a stone waterfall that loomed directly behind her, if she positioned herself correctly.

It was an actual waterfall formation but in volcanic rock. It went up, into the mountainside, and it cascaded down—frozen in time, because it was rock—right into the ravine, and if you stood back, it looked just like a waterfall that had been transformed into stone, as if by the gorgon Medusa.

It was one of the most beautiful things I've ever seen, made me wonder at the never-ending capacity for metaphor in nature.

And Steph sat there, at its base, on that ridge, and asked me to take her photo, with a look of sadness sliding over her face that was now frozen like rock, as if she knew something that I didn't, or wasn't ready to admit yet, though in reality we were already engaged in it.

On that mountainside. With that dog.

CHAPTER 21

Neon Crosses

Steph drove the Jeep back to Seattle through the Cascades on our way home the next evening. Driving out of the valley into the mountain pass in the waning daylight felt like an entirely different experience, and though the vestiges of a tingle remained from the omens and danger we had seen and experienced on the camping trip, it was actually an enjoyable journey back through the mountain highways. We were even able to sing loudly over the rush of wind from the lowered windows, though never on key.

Well, my singing was never on key. Hers was always spot on.

Steph had a voice for radio, seductive, warm, sexy, and siren-like, and she could sing even better, when the mood overtook her. She had grown up singing in a singing family, like the Partridges, though not as ginger.

So when she sang, it was a wonderful sound, and she sang a lot on that ride back through the mountains.

And this is where it started, after our guard had lowered.

There came a chime emanating from her handbag, tucked away under camping gear in the backseat, and it was persistent, ringing often enough under the blow of the wind that I had to find it and come to terms with its insistence.

Sixteen messages, from her mother and brother.

I handed her the phone as she was driving and watched her face change as she listened to message after message: her mother crying, then her brother, telling her that her father was in the hospital, where the hell was she? Had she not received the messages? "Call us, as soon as you get this."

He'd been clearing wood on a piece of land he'd bought for Steph as a present, near a river, in case she wanted to come back home. It was an isolated parcel of land, quite woody and Henry David Thoreau: perfect for her.

He'd taken to spending his weekends clearing trees and shrubs— sometimes with friends, sometimes alone. This time, he'd been out with an old friend and they felled a large tree that had felled him, in return.

He was in ICU and severely hurt. Broken ribs, facial fractures. Uncertain of his survival.

Family had been at his bedside for the past two days, while we'd been out of reach, in that valley of the shadow of neon crucifixions.

She relayed the vital information to me as she heard it, rolled up her windows to get the full messages, and repeated back to me what she was being told in the voice mail.

My startle impulse locked in, and I could see hers forming in the hardening of her features. Finally, she flipped shut her phone and said, "I have to go. I have to be there. He might not make it."

There was a momentary pause for me, because I wasn't sure what role I played in her life any longer. But it was only a moment, and instead I said, "All right. What do you need from me?"

We were an hour still from Seattle, and closer to her place, which once was our place but was now just her place, so it was there that we headed.

———

I was beat, I remember. The hike from the day before had been a catastrophe, and we had humped a tremendous amount of gear for nearly eight miles on that trail that paralleled the road we had driven in, and we were effectively stuck in falling temperatures on a roadside that was not amenable to camping.

I finally acknowledged that I was not holding up my part of the covenant of discomfort for camping any longer and wanted a motel room, so I flagged a passing vehicle and was able to get us a ride back to the Jeep, effusively thanking the retired couple who obliged us and were entirely amused at our camping idiocy. ("When you get to the point where you whittle down your toothbrush to save weight and space, then you're ready to carry a pack out camping," the woman said to me. Steph and I had both brought our Sonicare toothbrushes.)

I'd rented us a musty, moldy, nasty redneck motel and snuck in the dog, and after midnight, when the adjacent bedsprings on either side of the paper-thin walls began squeaking their secrets in a building crescendo, Steph indicated she was interested in doing the same, and it just wasn't there for me, anymore. Normally, the very idea of a motel or hotel would get my crank going: I mean, there's no other reason for hotels, really. They're a structural, physical embodiment of sex. When I was younger, just entering a hotel room would turn me on at the suggestion of possibilities. But here, the chemistry had fizzled out between us, and I felt awful doing it, but I turned my back to her and pretended I was dead asleep, though I was wide awake and crawling with discomfort, itching at the idea of the mildewed sheets, bedbugs, and redneck lovemaking that had transpired in that room previously, lying there with someone for whom I'd lost all romantic affection.

When we reached her place, we did not unpack the Jeep, just rushed inside and began preparations for her departure across the country. While she showered I found her rolling suitcase and began the preparation for travel, thinking perhaps I should accompany her on the trip. It was late afternoon, around 4:00 p.m. when we made it back to Seattle, and she'd be flying into an airport a hundred miles from her hometown and then driving a rental in the middle of the night through some fairly dark and rural highways, and the one highway in particular where she had nearly died fifteen years ago, I knew.

Something in me couldn't allow her to do this on her own. When she emerged from the shower, I said I was going along; she shouldn't do this alone. I could do my job from any hotel room with an Internet connection; it didn't matter where. "So let's get you home."

Her features softened, and she looked me square in the eye, nodded her head.

"All right," she said. "I would like that."

By 5:00 the next morning, we were driving from a small airport to a medium-size city on the East Coast where her father had been hospitalized. It had been touch-and-go for the first eighteen hours, but he was a tough dude, had stabilized and seemed to be pulling through, the reports began to reflect as we flew over the flyover states.

She'd put both tickets on her card and I'd given her the daily cash limit on my withdrawals, which covered my ticket. We agreed that she'd cover the car rental and hotels while I'd pick up all the food costs because I didn't eat like her, peanut butter and Cheez-Its and a cup of coffee satisfying most nutritional requirements for days at a stretch, and this seemed fair to both of us, since it was her crisis, her family.

It was around 6:00 a.m. when we arrived at the hospital. She had paused for a moment in the car and allowed herself to break down, to shiver and shake and cry and steel herself for what was about to come, seeing her dad hurt, being thrust back into the miasma of family dynamics that had been painful enough for her to put ten states between them and her, and the corresponding micromemories.

The car had bucket seats, so it was difficult to hold her, but I did, awkwardly and painfully over the console, as she shivered through her process and then resolved herself to plant her feet and attend to what was asked of her.

It was still early enough in the morning that the hospital was quiet and there was little going on, so we were able to slip inside and find his room. Her dad was sleeping. Her mother and brother were curled up in back-pinching discomfort in the waiting room, and I recognized them right away, as I wandered out to find some coffee in order to give her a moment alone with her father. He was a good guy, and I was deeply saddened to see him like that.

I remained at a distance for the next few days, allowed the family to work through their internal dynamics and process the fear of the near fatality of someone so close to them. Families in that situation do not need interlopers or outsiders, however well-meaning they might be, and I knew I had no right or privilege to be included and conducted myself accordingly. I'd help when asked, might make an offer or suggestion of a lunch or coffee run, move a car that needed parking or couriering, but otherwise stepped back and behaved like a cat, absorbing everything and thinking nothing.

There was a weird, competitive quality in Steph's family that I hadn't seen before, anywhere, like there was a correlation between how much they were putting themselves out as a sacrifice to show how much affection they had for him. It was interesting, and I chalked it up to Lutheranism. Catholics endured suffering differently, I noticed. Catholics sprayed their anguish, shared it with anyone listening and in the room, handed it out, piece by piece like the Body of Christ so that the load could be shared with others, processed with a community who are there with you for that very reason.

Protestants, Lutherans especially, would rather have their tongues cut out than exhibit that level of pain and passion. Instead, they make casseroles.

I couldn't quite get the nuance, though. Maybe this was a different strain of love, in a manner that I've never seen before. Their sacrifice was forced upon you, and you would take it, by golly. Sort of like, "For all the times I couldn't say it, I will force my love upon you with jars of fish preserves." But the odd thing is, they did: They said it clearly in their dedication. They showed it, always. I was amazed. But still, I was more accustomed to cries of anguish, gunshots fired into the night, sometimes out of windows.

Over the course of the next few days, when it became clear that the sturdy old guy was going to pull through, the levels of anxiety shifted and redirected themselves to the more quotidian, and the seams of the family surfaced and the bickering and picking of nits that Stephanie had insisted characterized her relationship to her mother and brother began to emerge. Or rather, Stephanie insisted they'd appeared, but I was unconvinced, or, if they had, they'd slipped by me unnoticed or unknown.

"Do you see how she does that?" Steph would ask me, over a private lunch or dinner away from her family.

"What?" I'd ask, not tracking. I was usually distracted by some unfamiliar brand of soda or saltine, or other mundane product from that part of the country, which I'd only visited briefly, once before. I found everything interesting and new. Moxie soda, kids at convenience stores who couldn't see spending two dollars for aspirin, so they gave it to me for free, a woman standing at an intersection with the deepest, most tragic black eye I've ever seen on a living human holding a sign, "Battered Wife/ Homeless, Please Help." I gave her twenty dollars.

"The way she said that thing about how I have no friends!"

"She did? I didn't catch that," I'd say. Steph was in a state of constant vigilance for a double entendre or backhanded slights when she was around her mother, which must have been exhausting for both of them. And, truth be told, her mother *had* been correct: Steph really didn't have many friends.

"You mean you didn't hear her say it?"

"I, uhm, no. I mean, I just haven't heard what you've heard. I'm not sure she really means it like that, Steph."

"God, you're unbelievable," she said, disgusted.

"I just don't see what you're seeing; I don't think she's being malicious or undermining. I think you're actually *trying* to see an attack and so you create one where there isn't. I mean, your mother's a bit childlike sometimes, but I don't think she's actively trying to harm you, or diminish you. I think you're doing that yourself."

That was it: that last part, probably too much. If we had been trying to get back together, if there was the slimmest indication that it was a possibility, it died there. I'd sided with the "other" and was no longer reliable in validating her world view.

Something slammed shut between us when I wouldn't side with her against her biggest vulnerability, her biggest imagined enemy, in her mother. Both Steph and I had once bonded over the idea that we were that kid in the crowd who pointed to the Emperor in his New Clothes, pointed and shouted and stomped our feet and demanded that everyone else see what we saw, determined to call out the shenanigans where others failed to see them.

I think she wanted my validation then and I couldn't offer it, couldn't buy into her persecution complex, and that made her feel even more isolated, separated us further from the idea that we'd ever end up in a happily ever after where it was just us versus them, where "them" was everyone else.

I liked her family, quite a bit. I really liked Harold, and for a time there I think they really liked me. It was a real shame that Steph was batshit crazy and we were as incompatible as we were: I really wanted to be a part of her family, in spite of her. It might have even worked.

One of the last afternoons we spent in the hospital, her mother and I were in a waiting room and talking about her and Harold's time in England, back in the '60s, about Carnaby Street, and I was asking questions about the fashion and the music, and her mother was delighted to revisit the memories with someone who was genuinely interested when Steph, who was sitting nearby and pretend-reading a magazine, stood up, slapped it shut, and bolted through a set of swinging doors, bringing the moment to an abrupt halt. Of course, I made my excuses and followed her, both her mother and I puzzled about what had triggered such a response, and when I was finally able to make some sense from what Steph was telling me, I realized she felt we had been flirting.

Of all things.

"This is just craziness, Steph. Your information tray is jammed. You're just fucking *wrong*, man. This is out of control."

By this point, we'd been there for over a week, and I'd been sitting in a hotel working remotely to eastern Washington and executing my job as the designer for the bilingual periodical, which was floundering every week, the smell of print death more prevalent as the weeks passed, much more acute in ink than at the hospital, and everyone was itching to get back to their habits and routines, Harold and her mother especially. They wanted us gone, out of their hair, and Steph kept pushing our exit date back.

Also, I'd gone nearly two weeks now without a drink. It was the longest I'd been dry in years. And I thought, maybe, I was getting thirsty. I wasn't sure.

It had actually been quite easy to abstain. While we'd had a couple of spats or moments of discomfort—the biggest one when Cleo escaped captivity and wound up at a neighbor's house, and Steph asked me to take care of it, make a decision, and I was at a loss of management—that was the only moment when I very nearly went down to the hotel bar and loaded up.

But I hadn't, when I normally would have. I'm not sure why. Maybe it was because I wanted her family to like me still.

———

At any rate, when we finally caught a transcontinental 747 at JFK, we were stuck on the tarmac for three hours, and I could see her looking at me out of the corner of her eye, and I realized she was waiting for me to lose my cool and throw a hissy fit, which would then—if history served—make her lose her cool, but instead I shook my head and kept reading *The Book Thief*, which I was having trouble following, and we made it back across the country and spent the night at my apartment downtown, and during nearly two weeks of constant exposure to one another and sleeping next to one another in many beds across the country, we didn't have sex once, and we both knew that it was really over, if we hadn't acknowledged it before, back when the whole thing started with the car wreck and the dead dog and the descent into the mountains of madness.

We were done. We just needed to see what we had left.

———

We were back in Seattle for a week before it happened again.

Actually it was more like five days, reimmersed in our separate living patterns, which had me working from home for the illiterate newspaper for three days a week, then working on the unpublished book I'd been writing for too many years to count, on those days that I had nothing to do, and I was making a surprising amount of progress, in the abstract. And at local bars.

Still, I was happy; I mean, I wasn't proliferating, exactly, but for a graphic designer in Seattle in the post-Internet boom, I was doing all right. And I was looking forward to being single again, left to my own vices, and devices, as it were.

Steph and I had been gone for a good two weeks and I was missing my friends back in Seattle, particularly my friend Sarah, from the karate school, with whom I'd take those twice-weekly walks around Greenlake and talk like a new mother hen.

Sarah, at this time, was not doing well. She'd just been hit with a divorce from her husband of fifteen years, and she was no longer the enthusiastic, engaged conversationalist who would delight at topics that flirted with the inappropriate, suggesting some degree of misbehavior or misconduct, right along a deep and entertaining two-mile monologue on Mary Shelley, or the suffragette movement in America, or the continued misnomers of Greek culture, or an exchange of *mamaloshen*.

We walked around the lake a few days after I'd returned, and after about a mile I realized Sarah was not, in fact, engaged in the conversation.

"Are you all right?" I asked her. "You seem distracted."

"Oh," she said, after a bit, and we maneuvered around a group of pregnant women walking basset hounds.

"Yeah. My husband just asked for a divorce," she said.

There was a long, profound pause before I responded.

"You have a husband?" I asked.

It occurred to me that after a year of friendship, she'd never once mentioned she was married, and I'd never bothered to ask. I was surprised.

Anyhow, Sarah was in her own doldrums, and she was my friend, and I cared for her deeply.

So one afternoon, about a week after I'd been back, it was an unusually rainy day in Seattle, because it was *really* raining, like it *meant* it, which it doesn't do often here, contrary to the popular mythology. You know how Eskimos have like ten different phrases for snow? People in Seattle have three for rain: There's "Aw, crap; it's raining," and "*Fuck!* It's raining," and lastly, "*Shit!* It's *really fucking* raining!" These are usually the transplants, though; proper born-in-Seattle Seattleites wouldn't allow themselves the Anglo-Saxon.

This particular day, it was the last sort of weather: It was really fucking raining. I had just settled back into my own routines, living downtown in my apartment away from Steph and languishing in the idea of sidewalks, neighborhood pubs, and twenty-four-hour grocery stores, and I was feeling that I might, once again, be able to resuscitate the idea of the urban male single guy. Build up the wardrobe, get back to dating women who would be comfortable at a bistro, didn't wear flannel, and had a predilection for most things lit'ry. Just not Rebecca Brown.

But today, I decided I wanted to see Sarah, and as she had a schedule as irregular as mine, I called her around noon and asked, since it was raining, if I could just swing by for coffee and a catch-up.

She seemed happy to hear from me, delighted even, and said, "Please: Come on by and tell me about your adventures off with Steph and her family on the Right Coast."

"Sure thing," I said. "Be there in about half an hour."

———

I stopped at a liquor store en route to pick up some bourbon, something dark for the wint'ry afternoon and unusual for us, Sarah and me, since we were mostly exercise/walking friends. I saw that the prohibition on absinthe had been lifted (I'd been monitoring this, as I was fascinated with the idea of absinthe, since I had it at my friend Andy's house once and it had provided me with the most crystalline dreams I've ever experienced, and was never able to experience again), and as I was checking out with my flask of Kentucky something, I bought a couple small display absinthe promotions, thinking it would be a nice treat.

I had all the accoutrements at home—again, remember, I had that fascination earlier—and I went home and collected the absinthe glass, the spoon, and the raw natural sugar preferred, then drove to Sarah's house.

She was preparing dinner, for her and her child, and she had been working out in the basement before I arrived.

I sat down at her counter and then with a carnival, vaudeville clown–type flourish, I began to produce from every part of my huge leather coat ... a small bottle of absinthe ... then from this sleeve, an absinthe glass ... from this pocket, an absinthe spoon ... I'm totally Marcel Marceau here ... then from that pocket, another small bottle ... and from the other sleeve, another glass, and so on.

When I was done, Sarah had her hand on her hip and was looking at me with a combination of sympathy for my bad vaudeville and enjoyment at the idea I'd take such time to try to cheer her up.

After I set the ceremony together on her countertop, she continued with her baking and I suddenly realized she was wearing spandex, and a form-fitting aerobic top under one of those jogging Lycra jacket thingies.

I said, "Wow, Sarah; you're incredibly attractive." A naturally slender woman, six years of karate had not hurt her allure. (I've never been good at poker, obviously. I'm the guy who yells, "Whoohoo!" with a good hand, and says, "Aw, shit," when it's bad, before looking up and realizing what I've done.)

Sarah, in her kitchen, stopped for just a second and pursed a smile without looking at me, and I knew something had changed between us, as did she.

———

I poured the absinthe and some cold water over the sugar cubes and the spoons and explained to her the process of the drip, the slow mingling of the sugar and the opacity of the *louche*, the smell and taste of licorice. I loved the ceremonial aspect of it, I told her, like taking communion, or getting beheaded by a fellow dishonored Japanese man with a long sword, after you stab yourself in the liver: It's the ritual that's important.

I had most of my absinthe, but she did not like hers, and then my phone started wringing.

And I spelled that correctly.

It started worrying, and it was Steph calling, twice, three times.

I begged pardon and stood outside in the pissing rain, on the back porch of Sarah's house, and I answered the phone to have a hysterical Steph telling me I needed to come get her, that her mother had been in an accident now, and that she needed to get on a flight back home, again. Please.

Wait, what?

"She was in an accident," Steph said.

"That was your dad," I said. Maybe I was absinthed.

"No, my mother this time! She's in the hospital! She had an accident!"

⸻

"All right," I said. "I'll be there in twenty minutes at the front lobby, depending on traffic."

"Have to run," I said to Sarah.

"Oh, is everything all right?"

"I think . . . you know, I'm not sure. I'll tell you more when I know it."

I was pretty high and a bit tipsy from the absinthe as I drove downtown to Steph's work, and it made the traffic snarl that much more bearable, but I picked her up, and she was damp and soaked and my car was enveloped in cascading waves of some really ferocious rain when she slid in and slammed the door shut finally and managed to explain that her mother, who was doing the upkeep on the house while Harold was recovering, was moving some things around in his garden shed when she knocked something over and a heavy shovel fell off the wall and slammed her in her eye.

"She might lose the eye," Steph said. "I have to be there."

"Hold on a minute," I said. "You just got back from being gone for two weeks. This is crazy; what will you do with work? It's not life threatening."

"You don't know, all right? You don't know what this is like. Maybe in your family it's acceptable to not show up for an emergency, but it's not in mine."

This really hurt. She meant the incident with my younger brother in Austin, and how I had talked myself out of going there, overnight, and how awful I'd always felt about being 3,500 miles away, alone and isolated, when he was in a coma and my family was ripped to shreds.

"That's not fair, Stephanie."

"I'm sorry. I am. That just came out. But I have to go."

"Fine; I'll drive you home and then take you to the airport."

⸻

Five hours later, I returned to Sarah's house, and there was an impromptu party, mostly with people from the karate school. I could tell by the way she was moving that Sarah was a bit in her cups, and I had not yet had enough.

Brenda was there, among others, and it was not a party-party, just people gathered and drinking, and Sarah was feeling a bit brazen.

I walked in with more booze, and people were happy, and Sarah saw me from across the room and sauntered quite sexily over to me, pointed at me, and then pointed at the guest bedroom, and said, "Get in there."

"Oh, no," I said. *Aw, shit. I did this.*

"In there?" I asked, coyly, delayingly. My initial response was that if we had sex, that would end the friendship. It always did. And I really, really loved our friendship.

"Follow me," she said, and she walked in.

The party continued on behind us, but it was closing down, and I was trying to figure out how to get out of this in such a way that saved Sarah's blushings. I dearly, dearly liked her but wasn't sure I wanted to move into—

"*Holy shit,* Sarah!" I said as the door closed behind me and she peeled off her jeans, let them drop, and then took off her top and revealed the most perfect body I think I've ever seen in person.

"Jesus Christ, where did *that* come from?"

"Lay down," she commanded, pointing to the bed, and in a matter of seconds, our relationship went from the platonic to the sophist.

Part III

Looking Down

CHAPTER 22

Sarah's Place

Her house was built in the northern shadow of Queen Anne Hill, right into the angled slope just above a private Christian university and the intersection of two quiet, little-used urban streets that made an isosceles triangle. The house rested at the base, and a small, beaten-down lawn emerged valiantly in the limited sunlight, tucked neatly into the tip like the bow of a Euclidean ship, plowing through a frozen rock and asphalt sea.

It was a good house—the kind of clean, healthy house you'd find in one of the better John Irving books that played more of a central character than a location or vehicle of rehabilitation. It stood gray and tall and angular, had steep sides and unused balconies, and could make itself invisible if it wanted to, could hide from you behind its evergreens if you weren't looking for it. It shared the neighborhood easily, rubbed its boundaries comfortably with the block, except for the gay couple down the street with the pocket Chihuahua, two ridiculously large firefighting-type men with an unnatural fear of larger dogs, or the series of dogs that at one point or another lived at Sarah's house, which, for many years, was a living system of shelter and rescue for many upturned lives, both human and canine.

It was the sort of house with a screen door that was never locked and opened right into the kitchen, the hearth of the home, and invited you to sit down, make yourself comfortable—sit, sit, sit!—while someone cooked you something to eat. Sarah would, later, make me, as a lumbering dead person, something to eat, and often.

That was Sarah's house, back then, when I began visiting her, started making excuses to come by, excuses suggesting the innocuous and platonic and transparently friendly because, well, they were. Or we were, rather, every one of those things—platonic and friendly and transparent. So much so that the purpose of my first visit was to bring Brenda Brown some lesbian porn magazines I'd found under Steph's bed.

Brenda Brown, our karate instructor, lived in Sarah's basement and brought a real sense of color to the house, which would otherwise have passed for a stuffy, upper-middle-class house with doilies and a pervading smell of some grandmother's bad German candies. Instead, Sarah's house was lined with books, philosophy texts and women's literature, a triptych of iconic images of the nourishing cycle of femininity. There was power here, and I was drawn to it.

So when I found all the porno magazines, instead of being concerned or curious about Steph's choices in buying them, I thought I knew just the person who would like them, if Steph had indeed lost interest in their draw, as she was claiming. I'd been fascinated with them at first, from the position of a printer (saddle-stitched, gloss cover, 12 x 18 with a bleed and face trim, with a sixty-page newsprint black-and-white interior, printed in California—who was producing this? Was it self-sustaining? Certainly a niche audience. How were they keeping themselves afloat? Not by advertising, by the looks of it. Definitely not a Larry Flynt product, too homemade, too . . . unheteronormative. Much less gynecology in this magazine, for instance, and ironically. And these models—this is what Steph was into? Did I really look like a butch lesbian now? I mean, I know I gained some weight, but REALLY, I don't own anything flannel. . . .).

Steph had more than a year's subscription under her bed, and not a single penis to be found in all twelve or fourteen issues. Call me phallocentric, but I was much more intrigued by the cultural significance and production dilemma of a printed lesbian periodical than the idea of it being pornography. After all, I was most certainly not the target audience; it made sense that the eroticism was lost on me, and not because most of the models looked like a plurality of modern-day Venus de Willendorfs, in mullets.

Steph never felt compelled to explain why she had the collection, and I never pressed her for an answer. Interestingly, she often felt contentious about and diminished by the pornographic trails left on my web browser, and curiously, I thought she and I had been above such a discussion anyway—especially since she had had a much more, let's say, adventurous sex life than I would ever consider.

So when I came up with the idea to give the magazine collection to my new friend, Brenda, who I thought would appreciate it, Steph had agreed, and a bit too sheepishly and coy, I had felt at the time.

Brenda lived in the basement with her three dogs, in probably the only place in the city that living arrangement could have been possible. Sarah had her own dog, an aging and elegant English Lab named Genevieve who kept order as the alpha bitch. Brenda had a gorgeous pit bull puppy named Betty Brown that she had rescued from a future of being a bait dog, plucked right from the trunk of a drug dealer's car, and they were inseparable. And she had a lanky Irish wolfhound named Jack County, also a rescue, also relieved of ownership from a drug manufacturer, some guy with the last name of "County" who cooked meth in a trailer park and had left Jack chained to a tree with no care or water. Brenda saved the dog, brought him back from the brink of death to a life of health and sanitation, gave him the best years of his life. Jack County looked like the canine version of Tom Selleck and would follow me around, find me in the house when he heard my voice, then curl up at my feet or near me with a paw placed reassuringly on me to convince me to stay still and keep him company while he napped. He had this wonderfully demure manner of curling up his long tail and tucking it under his nether bits while he slept, which looked like a merkin. "Remember this is all gravy, Jack," Sarah would say when Jack would enter a room.

Finally, Brenda had Bill Brown, a dog that had moved far past his dog years and into archival history, had dementia and doggie Alzheimer's, would sometimes find himself trapped in a corner of the house and incapable of remembering that to get out of the corner, all he had to do was either turn to a side or back up. Instead, he'd stare at the corner and become confused, begin barking and growling until someone came by and pointed him in another direction. It would have been funny if it hadn't been so sad.

Brenda accepted the paper bag full of lesbian pornography in the manner intended: It was a fun gift—enjoy it. But the more I learned about Brenda, the more I realized that she didn't need pornography; Brenda was a magnetic draw of vitality. She didn't date other lesbians; she dated straight girls who suddenly realized how fantastic and sexy Brenda was. We called these women "brendasexuals," because after a brief fling, they'd eventually end up dating men again, and Brenda would be the only same-sex experience they likely would have in their lives. But that was Brenda: She was mesmerizing.

She was even more mesmerizing on the karate mat, so much so that I hadn't seen that Steph had developed her own fascination with Brenda, oddly enough. Which, at this point, just makes me sort of laugh, thinking back to when I tried to introduce them one afternoon at the karate school, and I said, "Oh, hold on just a second; I'll get Brenda and you can meet her," and when I turned around again, I saw Steph actually running out of the school. If this had been a cartoon, and sometimes later it felt like one, I would have turned around to a floating, spinning hat, suspended in midair with a word bubble that read "Whoosh!" floating beneath it.

Instead of feeling any sort of jealousy, from this distance, I think my only real envy is that I wished I could have met someone back then who would frighten me with similar feelings felt at that level. The only comparable intensity would eventually come with my feelings for Sarah, but that's not for a few chapters at least. Right now, we were still frightened of the torrid affair we'd had, and rather publicly, in front of most of the karate school people who had been at her house that night.

And as much as I really missed my friendship with Sarah as we adjusted to the new reality, I have to say that I really missed her house, really missed the sanctuary and safety of being in a clean, sunlit place full of dog energy and Brenda Brown in the basement, the house itself as a destination, a place to go and sit with coffee and talk about everything and nothing, feeling a sense of safety that you couldn't say anything wrong, and neither would she, because we were both very clever, and very raunchy in private, and then very polite in public, for the most part. I could get away with saying almost anything that popped into my mind, and Sarah would look at me like, "Did you just really say that?" and then giggle, and I'd respond the same, when she would lob a particularly astute or sordid bon mot, and we'd have a wonderful time because there was nothing in the balance, nothing either of us demanded of one another. We had nothing to lose in the exchange.

But that had shifted immediately the morning she woke up and I had disappeared, and she had to face her household alone, with a headache, and I had crawled back into my apartment on the other side of the hill, in the rental area, and sulked, and quietly waited for the rest of the storm to settle in for good.

CHAPTER 23

Buying Goblin Fruit

Morning arrived with something like an ice pick of awkwardness and fear of the consequences of what Sarah and I had both willingly allowed to combust between us the night before. In the months that followed, I tried to convince myself that I'd been a passive passenger in that evening's fevered affair, but this wasn't true. By this age, I'd come to accept that I would often give off an "I fancy you" vibe when all I really wanted to say was, "I want to know more about you."

With Sarah, it was much more the former rather than the latter, and she'd simply responded in kind.

That morning, I had managed to slip out when she was still asleep, and I drove back to my apartment thinking I'd allowed the friendship to ruin itself because friendships do not come back from fucking, I've learned. But this morning, I felt at once exhilarated and deeply ashamed, a cognitive dissonance, then finally conflicted because I felt almost as if I'd cheated on Stephanie, even though we weren't together. I couldn't imagine what Sarah was thinking.

Nevertheless, I walked around in a state of bewildered completion the weekend after Sarah and I had locked in spontaneous ignition. It was something like I had never before experienced in my life, and I was staggered at every level, wondering if it had meant and functioned and fulfilled her in the same way, but I had no vocabulary to ask her, and things had become stressed between us.

～～

Two days later, Steph returned from her second and most recent emergency trip to the East Coast looking worn down and spent. It had not developed into the mercy mission she had imagined. She had instead overstayed her welcome, and much of the old scar tissue in her relationships surfaced and needed a good scrubbing with a psychiatric loofah. When she disembarked from her plane, claimed her luggage, and then lodged herself in my passenger seat, once again safely in the fold of the cold, hanging Seattle rain, she began rattling off and apart on the details of the trip, why her relationship with her mother was once again in a standoff when it seemed to have swung around during the first trip, when everyone was helping her dad. Her mother, she said, seemed annoyed and weary of her presence, while Steph was only trying to get things done around the house as her mother adjusted to her newly developed monoculism.

I was nervous the whole time, my sense of guilt telegraphed on my features as I drove her home, calculating with a due sense of dread how I could disentangle myself from this situation before Steph found out I'd slept with someone else, though it was entirely within the bounds of acceptability. I simply couldn't withstand the impending sense of betrayal in which she'd view it. Steph's exhaustion was catching, and worse still, it seemed like she was convinced we had a fighting chance of reparations.

I was in a bit of a pickle, once again, because of my passivity and cowardice.

Back home now, Steph surprised me with an invitation to a beachside stay in Oregon for the long Thanksgiving weekend. I expressed my concern at her taking the time off, after missing three concurrent weeks of work during her busy time of year. "Not a problem," she said. "I'm catching up. We should take Cleo and drive your car down to Oregon. It'll be fun."

Meanwhile, my interactions with Sarah had become awkward and cold, distant, as I had dreaded. We had been building what was, for me, a deep and sincere lifetime friendship that I feared lost now because of that epic, drunken fumbling in her guest bedroom, wrestling like naked teenagers, fueled by pent-up sexual sublimation and vodka. Sarah, in the wake of her divorce, had realized she had subdued her sexual identity for many years as she played the good mother and wife, and had found in me a willing, if entirely confused, partner to apply a defibrillator on her libido. And I had, with Stephanie, questioned whether being miserable and sexless in a relationship might be more important than fanning the spark of human combustion between two people who deeply, passionately wanted to fuck one another's hearts out, as I had now realized I wanted with Sarah.

And yet, still, I drove on that trip with Stephanie, to Haystack Rock, thinking that I would use this time to tell her that I was gone for good.

On the final day, when we stopped at a Mexican restaurant near Mount Rainier, matters finally came to a head. Steph and I had, in keeping with character, kept from being intimate during the trip because I had been afraid to remove my shirt in front of her, uncertain of what she might see that I could not, from any angle in a mirrored bathroom. An imagined tapestry of evidence on the palimpsest of my back would have indicated that I had been participating in something other than sexlessness, and I was cowering from the confrontation, any confrontation. How I would normally break off a relationship in my youth was, I'd put on a drunk, stick on a cheap hat, and then trusted it to luck, like I did with everything else.

But at this age, and with Steph, I was extremely worried. I would have normally been uncomfortable addressing the issue directly with someone who could, on a good day, have been described as level-headed and reasonable, but Steph would never have been accused of that, not even on her best day, so I was summoning the courage to have "that talk" and kept finding myself lacking. I was once drawn to the "Sinead O'Connor and Wolverine" fantasy combination of epic femininity, but I had seen what a genuine, self-assured, and self-actualized adult woman was really like, and I had grown tired of explosive confrontation disguised as passion and caring.

But the situation pressed itself finally, after three days of tension and awkwardly parried invitations from her to lock into sex again, hide in the penumbra of something that was clearly long dead, and I had to ultimately say what I was avoiding.

She was sulking in the front seat while Cleo was shedding in the back.

I was driving my car through the rain and the traffic of Portland and had been muttering and cursing under my breath at the inconsideration of other drivers, particularly this one individual speeding in a late-model pickup while pulling a Bayliner, and she was becoming more agitated by the grumble. They weren't well versed, I kept pointing out to Steph, in driving "Texas Friendly."

"What's 'Texas Friendly' driving?" she asked, taking the bait.

"Common fucking awareness," I responded, and it annoyed her, so she stayed quiet and wrapped herself in her own arms, locked down tight and staring out the window for the last two hours as I drove us into the chalky parking lot of a roadside restaurant with bad, idyllic paintings of a Southwestern theme, saguaro cactus next to abstractions of donkeys and female forms making an ideal tortilla. Desert socialism, permutations of Diego Rivera.

<hr/>

We were alone in the restaurant, which was between shifts, and the waitstaff seemed mid-siesta while Steph sat in her red vinyl booth and stared moodily out the window on the grayness of south Washington. I took the moment.

"You've been pissed at me since Portland," I said.

She didn't respond to this.

"We agitate the shit out of each other," I said, thinking that her icy silence and defensive body language were in their own way a manner of encouragement.

"My normal, regular states of being upset you. And I have to say, most of the time, yours frustrate me. We're not good together anymore, Steph," I said. "Why do you want to salvage this relationship?"

She went quiet, her stare stricken, as if I'd spoken something verboten.

"We must not look at goblin men," she finally said in a whisper, and surprised me. "We must not buy their fruits." She was quoting from a Victorian poem that had been written into the dialogue of a *Doctor Who* episode, an episode that had been particularly frightening and I had asked her to watch with me and hold my hand while doing so because I'd actually been that frightened, quite some time before. She had obviously paid it much attention.

"I'm not a goblin," I said, weakly. "Or maybe I am. But I'm certainly no longer selling my fruits. I want to try to remain on good terms, but this is obviously done, don't you agree? We don't get along anymore, we don't have sex, and . . ." I stopped short of bringing up my feelings for Sarah.

"I don't know what to do," she said, verging on tears. Her pride couldn't take that I was the one giving her the go-bye. We'd always talked about it being her that would be doing the leaving.

"Neither do I," I replied. "It's like one of us has to die in order to get out of this."

"Don't do me any favors," she said, and then stepped outside for a smoke, while I ordered a pint of Dos Equis and something vaguely resembling Mexican food, then sat and watched her through the window as she stared off at the big, brooding snow-covered volcano to our east.

—◦—

The week after that miserable Thanksgiving was the first expanse of days when we tried separating, and I think I fared worse than she did. Steph had a good poker face when it came to hiding her hurt, until she didn't. I wore mine on my sleeve, and it had grown difficult for me to accept that I was putting down yet another relationship at this age, had to realize that as much as I wanted it, I couldn't move past a certain level of intimacy with another human being, and the fear of this being the truth nearly propelled me back into Steph's orbit for yet another chance.

Instead, I threw myself back into therapy with renewed vigor and talked for unending hours with my therapist about trust and sex, why it had felt so open and monumental when Sarah and I had finally shifted our relationship into intimacy.

But I did call Steph once a day at least, I think for the reassurance that she was still there, somehow. I knew at some level that I should cauterize that particular compulsion and felt like what I was doing—the slow, agonizing separation—was the wrong way to go about it. Somehow. Or so I convinced myself.

Meanwhile, my relationship with Sarah mollified into a weird stagnation until we both decided what to do with each other. This had been incredibly painful and frightening, as I thought I was losing that friendship now, as well, and I could hardly bring myself to leave my apartment. My compass readings were all wrong.

Since I was working from home, producing that wretched bilingual publication from my laptop at my desk, I could go for unending days without leaving my apartment, let my mental and physical health draw down to dangerous levels before I would come back swinging and struggling and gasping for air, and then I would repeat that same cycle.

I had always been able to come back from this pattern, but as I grew older, it was becoming more difficult to break the surface, and I felt I was losing this particular fight now, felt that the draw of the hole was growing more powerful, and the darkness inside was getting blacker, thicker, like a sludge of obsidian.

———

One morning in early December, I'd been harassed by an illiterate teenage web designer working on a website for one of my freelance clients, an incredibly seedy hot yoga studio owned by a secular Pakistani businessman, introduced to me by our shared printer, Nasir, whom he knew from their mosque. I woke up to a flurry of impassioned, unpunctuated five- or six-word e-mails from this vulgarity of a child running some sham business creating uninspired websites for other, dreadful small businesses, and who had previously offered to sell me a suite of pirated software for $200. Irritated beyond measure at the illiteracy and the fact that he had mistaken me for another Latin-named designer, I let the little fucker have it and was feeling pretty good about myself after he responded with a red-faced, but still illiterate, apology.

I called Steph around 11:00 a.m. and told her about it.

She sounded sad, deflated. I didn't have to ask why, and I instantly regretted having made that call.

She told me instead how she'd had a similar experience, but in less "dude" terms, with a Japanese exchange student who Steph felt was attempting to undermine her position by questioning a few of Steph's concrete assertions.

She told me her own story in flat, unemotional terms, but I could sense that she was roiling with anger: Nothing bothered her more at work than when her word wasn't taken as gospel, but she'd never mention it to anyone other than me. She'd instead smother it down and let it fester into rage and anxiety or ulcers, perhaps bake a number of complicated dishes simultaneously to channel her anger.

It felt out of place to talk about such personal things now; the distance between us was really showing itself, and I felt that it was a good start, amplifying the individuation finally.

I hung up feeling optimistic.

That was the last time I ever spoke to her.

CHAPTER 24

The Hurricane

Steph's father phoned me at 2:30 that next morning. She had driven her Jeep over the side of an overpass at 11:30 that night. By the time I spoke to Harold, Steph had been unconscious for three hours, hypothermic and crushed.

I was dressed and down to my car in the garage in less than ten minutes, driving through the dark, empty streets of Seattle toward Harborview Hospital at top speed with the radio off, feeling an innate, profound sense of things changing in that densely packed silence as I drove to a part of the city that I had had very little reason to visit previously. After I made it through the receiving station on the ground floor, I was directed to the ninth floor, which would be my new "third place" for the next year, though I had no way of knowing that at this time.

It was past 3:00 a.m., and people were stretched out in the waiting room like refugees, covered in matching hospital blankets. They were sleeping on expanded couches and sitting up in chairs, the family of trauma patients awaiting news or miracles. An older black man was sitting up awake, wrapped in a similar blanket, and he watched me as soon as I exited the elevator and looked around in bewilderment at the hospital floor. I paced the length of the hallway twice then decided I needed to sit down; my knees were feeling a bit liquefied, so I found a chair sitting opposite the grizzled older black man, who had not stopped looking at me. An arcade of grief blanketed that waiting room.

I waited roughly ten minutes, rocking in my chair. *What if Steph's dead? What if she doesn't survive this? What just happened here? I just spoke to her around noon and she said she was working. She was headed home, she said, soon. How could this have happened?*

A nurse walked through the doors and I immediately stood up and began asking questions, and she first tried to calm me. I asked her to stop calming me and start talking about Steph. She said the injuries were survivable. Steph had lost control of her car and went down an embankment, the nurse said, but she would be able to survive this. I started to calm down, but I still felt terrified. I was scared, like nothing ever before in my life.

"You need to breathe," she said to me. "You need to calm down. We're stabilizing her, and you can come see her in a minute."

I was nearing a panic attack but tried to remain calm because I knew I was the only channel that Steph's parents had for communicating with the trauma unit, so I asked the nurse to speak directly with Steph's father and explain to him what she'd just said to me. The place positively hummed with the psychic energy of trauma. Or maybe that was just me.

I lingered nearby and overheard him as they spoke. He sounded relieved. She handed the phone back to me and smiled. Ten minutes later he called back and told me he'd just received a call from a neurosurgeon who said that Steph was in a coma, and that the prognosis was grim, and the neurosurgeon recommended that her family get out to Seattle to make decisions about her care.

This did not jibe with what the nurse had just said. Right about here, the world went white with light. I felt the blood in the back of my head grow colder and colder, and I thought this was what the start of a stroke must feel like.

I grabbed my coat and charged through the doors that read "Authorized Personnel Only" and I found that same nurse who'd just spoken to Harold and reassured both of us, and I asked her what the fuck was going on; how could her father get that call?

She informed me that the diagnosis he had just received was over two hours old: "She's being stabilized; she's here, now, in the ICU. You can come see her," she said and walked me to the room. She parted a curtain and pointed me to a bundle on the bed.

Steph lay on the bed. Except it wasn't Steph. It was her head, but her head was twisted, the top part of it broken and to the side. There were tubes in her nose and mouth, and both her eyes were protruding so far out, her eyelids didn't close. One eye was swollen purple, but you could still see it emerging. This was from the swelling of her brain and the cracks in her cranium. It was the most painful, most horrible thing I had ever seen in my life, and she was right there, with people walking around her like they saw this sort of thing every day. There was no light in her eye. She looked like a fish kept on ice for some days. She looked dead, her arms and legs in awkward angles. A doctor on his own errand pushed his way past me and to Steph's side and began a procedure, put a stint into her aorta, which quickly became bloody. Steph began to squirm and fight, her pain response still as vivid as anything, though her body looked like this.

The nurse could see how it was affecting me. She started to pull me out. I couldn't speak; I had no more words at that point, just fear.

"She'll survive this," the nurse said to me. I noticed that she had a name tag. Her name was Juliet. That was the first fact that made it through, something I could hang onto for a moment, could trust, if it wasn't, on its own, a laminated lie. There was always that possibility. But it was something.

<hr />

Next thing I knew I was in the waiting room sitting next to the older black man, who introduced himself as Sidney. When he spoke, he sounded like a jazz musician out of central casting. "You look like you need to sit down, man," he said, which confused me because I was already sitting.

"You doing all right, man?" asked Sidney.

I managed to nod, weakly. "Yeah, I'm just . . . I don't know what I'm doing here. I don't know how this works."

Sidney nodded sagely. "You'll figure it out eventually. We all had to. Is that your girlfriend you've been talking about?"

I nodded again, said, "Yeah, my . . . uhm . . . ex-fiancée."

Sidney raised his eyebrows. "Ohh, sorry to hear it. About her, I mean." After a moment of quiet, Sidney said, "You know, you should talk to her, when you're by her bedside. That's what they tell me to do. Just keep talking to her, telling her how things are at home, like she's not in this place. Tell her how her plants are, and that she's safe, that you're not screwing around while she's in here. Women like to be reassured."

It was a bit awkward for a moment, but then I remembered my manners. "Who are you here for?" I asked.

"For my son," he said. "Was in an accident, motorcycle. Broke his neck. Been in a coma for a month now."

I made a pained face. *A month?* "I'm really sorry to hear that," I managed.

"Yeah, it's been bad. The way he had been carrying on for a few years now with the drugs, I'm surprised he lasted this long. Something was gonna get him. Anyhow, I've been staying here, waiting for my ex-wife, who's coming from N'arleans to see if we're going to take him off life support. Cheaper than a motel and more interesting than the Discovery Channel, watching people come and go." He pointed his chin at the clusters of sleeping families. "Hear all kinds of stories here."

Around 4:30 that morning, Sidney finally nodded off and I walked downstairs, wrapped myself up deeper in my coat, and stood in the ambulance parking lot and made a number of calls. I called Steph's only friend that I knew of, Lisa, and left a tearful message, which felt incredibly weird, and I checked in with Steph's parents to see how they were getting along, see what time their plane landed.

Then I began calling my own people, on automatic pilot. I called Amy, my best friend from my time at *Seattle Weekly*, first. Left a message. Called Sarah, left a message there, too. Called Brenda and a couple other friends from the karate school. After some minutes of thinking about it and realizing my list of support candidates had grown far too short, I called home, to Houston. Called my sister, Marge. Called my mother and left her a weepy message, asking her if she would consider coming up for a while. I had no idea what I was doing; I was calling people and leaving nonsensical high-alert messages on their voice mail, standing outside in a wet parking lot on the deepest, darkest night in my memories of this town.

De profundis.

Though there were far many more sub-basements of profundity already in the mail.

I even called Dan, but didn't bother calling Derek.

It was of course Amy who showed up first, around 5:45 a.m. I had a moment of mild surprise when I saw her walk in from the elevators, catching myself briefly wondering, *What are you doing here, Amy?* when I realized I'd left her that message, and she was first to understand, like Amy does. She brought a bag with her: magazines, water, snacks, anything she had handy that could be of comfort to me in the waiting room. And her knitting: Amy had started knitting a year or two before.

She hugged and held me and was then quiet, before asking questions.

I answered as best I could, but then after a while just shook my head helplessly, admitting I knew nothing else, could speculate on nothing at all. Instead, I walked her through the doors and took her to Steph's bedside.

They had her in an upright position by this time. She was in a harness of a sort, her arms extended forward like she was imitating Frankenstein, or Stephen King. A metal spike protruded from her forehead to indicate cranial pressure. Tubes and sensors emanated from her like vines. Amy didn't wince; I watched her out of the corner of my eye to see if I could adjust my startle mode to what Amy was seeing, but I couldn't get a bead on her. If Amy was as frightened as I had been, she was keeping it to herself. Instead, she put her hand warmly on Steph's shoulder and began speaking to her, reassuringly.

"Hey, Steph," she said, barely above a whisper. Amy is shy, keeps her voice down usually. "You're safe now. You had a car accident, honey. But you're at the hospital now, you're in ICU. No one else was hurt. You're doing fine, and the doctors are optimistic. We're here for you. Your parents are on their way, and we'll take care of Cleo. You have nothing to worry about except getting better, Steph."

I hadn't done any of that. At that moment, I simultaneously felt an immense amount of love for Amy and like I was the worst person in the world for not thinking of that previously, reaching out and reassuring Steph.

My friendship with Amy went back years and years, and she was the target of terrible jealousy on Steph's part. There was no reassuring Steph that Amy and I had never been romantic: We'd simply bonded over Nick Cave and the Bad Seeds while working at *Seattle Weekly*, then found we had an identical wit and penchant for being crafty, and we disliked all the same people. What better way to establish a lifelong friendship?

But Steph was never having it, and I gave up trying to convince her otherwise. So be it.

Amy had never been bothered by it, more amused than anything, and watching her be so kind and tender to Steph like this wrenched my heart open, made me feel another level of affection for my dear friend, who was here at the hospital first, before 6:00 a.m., before she had to be at work.

She took me back out to the waiting room and we sat in silence for a good long while, saying very little. There were no platitudes, no words capable of reaching across this worry, and Amy's presence, her sitting there with her knitting, was enough witness to Steph's pain, my grief, and without even speaking about it, we both innately understood it.

Finally, I had to tell her that my mind was exploding with guilt.

"Did she do this because we split up? Did she find out about Sarah somehow? Maybe someone from the karate school somehow told her. What the hell was she doing at 11:30 last night? Was she at work all that time?" She was driving back from Aurora, the bad part of town she felt she could travel with impunity, against all my warnings. Steph would always conduct her life like she was inoculated from harm, the sort of entitlement white people and children on playgrounds have in their sense of justice. What the hell was she doing out there at that time of night? Maybe she was buying silverware. I had taken back all my silverware when I had moved out. Maybe that's what she was doing when she drove off the overpass.

"This is my fault, Amy."

"Stop it. You did not give her epilepsy."

"Well, no, but . . ." I said, weakly.

"Stop thinking like that. Did you call her boss?" Amy asked.

"I left a message for her two workmates," I said. I figured they'd be able to deliver the news to the right people. This had been the second tragedy to hit that department, I was thinking that morning. A few months before, one of their department heads had suffered a stroke in the bath and had remained undiscovered for a few days. Her husband had been out of town, and she had died alone in their bathroom. It had been left to Steph to cycle through her voice mail to separate any work calls from personal ones, and her husband had kept calling and calling, leaving increasingly hysterical messages as the weekend progressed and he had not reached his wife. It had been torturous to go through them and had left Stephanie a tearful, weeping bundle of nerves, and I'd held her and talked her down for hours when she came home sobbing that afternoon.

Around 7:00 a.m., Steph's boss showed up and sat with us, after she visited Steph's bedside for a while, stroked her hair, and talked to the doctors. She was an MD, now doing research, and an incredibly reassuring and strong presence. I remember feeling my whole body relaxing for the first time since 2:30 that morning when she entered the room and began asking the right questions from the doctors, began using her resources to help manage this new tragedy.

I was like a terrier introduced into a family with no strong alpha, thinking that it was up to me to take that role, nervously yapping and nipping at the other omegas. (I had been watching a lot of Cesar Millan's *Dog Whisperer*, at this point.) I gratefully relinquished the position to Steph's boss and encouraged her to be the lead advocate, until Steph's parents arrived.

Within a half hour, Steph's work people had made preparations for her family to stay nearby, arranged for rides from the airport, were bringing food in shifts, creating a network where for the last six hours it had just been me, then Amy and me.

I was finally feeling something along the frequency of support and order when Amy and I returned from the cafeteria and I saw Sarah, standing there looking absolutely attractive and concerned, walking toward me with a face full of worry.

I thought, *Oh, fuck*. The two split halves of my simultaneous worlds I was desperate to keep apart had become one, and that stroke that started some six hours ago felt like it was ramping into high gear. Sarah had herself shifted into caretaking mode and was incredibly helpful and kind, made herself useful and supportive. The fear and worry that I carried alone that morning had shifted partially, and I was breathing a bit easier, and yet it felt like this ordeal was really just beginning.

Amy had to report to work, but not before she insisted I speak to my mother and family, and when I finally had my mother on the phone, I broke down and cried like I'd been needing to since 2:30 a.m., or since I was twelve years old.

Mom heard the anxiety and grief in my voice and asked, "Do you need me to be there?" and I had to admit that I wanted my mother with me, for the first time in my life since I had forcefully broken my emotional tethering to them when I felt they could no longer be trusted, as a kid.

I said, "Yes, I think so. I need you, Mom. I can't do this alone," and over the course of a few hours, she was on her way from Houston, arriving that next afternoon.

When we had a moment alone, Sarah asked if there was anything she could do, and I gave her my key, asked her to please go to my apartment and remove all beer cans or bottles so that my mother didn't see how far down I'd fallen in my depression.

I was barely holding on, as it was, both Sarah and Amy could see, and I needed all the help I could get if I was going to make it through this and be of any use to Steph and her family, which I clearly felt honor-bound to do.

By the time Steph's parents arrived, I had done as much as I could to prepare them for the advocacy of and participation in Steph's care. I had doctors and nurses designated as primary contacts, had given as much pertinent information as possible to her care providers about Steph and her medications and previous medical histories, what I knew about her, sort of laid the foundation for her parents' arrival with the help of Steph's work friends. And still, I felt like I was guarding an element of Steph that her family didn't know, this life she had built out here, the way she had reinvented herself, the secrets that she had shared only with me, and I couldn't disengage, not like this. It just didn't feel right.

When they finally made it to the hospital, I was down at the lobby to meet them, and Harold hugged me close, but there was little to say.

Instead I simply took them up the elevators to the ninth floor, pointing out landmarks so that they would be able to navigate their way through the labyrinth of this old hospital on their own later.

With her parents there, I felt I could now step back a little, take up my position as . . . whatever role it was that I was playing in her life. I was entirely uncertain as to whether I was the grieving ex-fiancée or the deeply concerned friend, and I wasn't sure how much Steph had told her family about our situation.

If they were shocked, neither parent gave it up when they saw their daughter in such a state. I was unsure whether I deeply admired this quality or wanted them to show their grief in a bit more Catholic manner, maybe render a bit of cloth or put a knife through one of their burning hearts, a la Jesus. Maybe cover a mirror or two.

They were stoics, and by this time, both quite well-versed in speaking to doctors and navigating a hospital ward. And while I'm sure they were entirely grateful for the help, I could also sense that Steph's mother was quite practiced at receiving the attention that was waiting for them that afternoon.

It was still too painful for me to spend much time by her bedside, but I would try. Steph's only friend, Lisa, came to visit sometime that afternoon and walked around with a dazed sort of half-moon smile, and I studied her for some time before I realized she was out of her mind on antidepressants, and that if she understood why she was in the hospital for her close friend, it was only partially leaking through to her ability to appreciate it. She was able to sit by Steph's bedside and stroke her hand, speak in soft platitudes about the tulips that were going to bloom that week and that Cleo had been walked that morning, what they had seen in the neighborhood.

Now, *this?* This befuddled me entirely. I was incapable of talking small on most days, but with this much agony in the room, it was impossible. I mean, I understood what they were doing by talking to Steph about the small stuff: I was just unable to bring my anxieties down to that hemisphere, and I began to notice sideways glances and indications of disapproval from others.

Even the waiting room camaraderie began to show symptoms of fatigue.

CHAPTER 25

The Third Place

There was no comfort coming from anywhere, those first few days. I thought when her parents and friends arrived, I'd be able to find somewhere to catch my breath, square my heart and thoughts, and be able to take the next steps. That place never showed itself—every minute just shifted into the next torturous minute, awaiting the results of the next CAT scan to reveal the amount of neurological damage, MRIs to diagnose the extent of her body's injuries. There was no place in my mind to run to, no safe place to hide from worried thoughts. There was nothing that didn't put me right back here, right back at this bedside with this broken ex-girlfriend who looked like she had no chance of recovering.

Worse yet was that I felt she would have wanted me in the position of being her guard dog, being the person who stood watch and kept others from seeing her like this. She had said so, quite clearly, some months earlier when we were talking about her prior accident. She'd been in the hospital unconscious and recovering, and she'd been visited by people she'd known and had hardly cared for, but they'd come by to pay their respects and when she'd woken up, she had been horrified that she'd been visited by people she knew only through work.

This also befuddled me entirely—why not accept all the goodwill offered?—but she was a strange one, that Steph. So I tried to monitor who would see her this time, though it made me feel entirely like an asshole, and I stopped doing it after the first day. It just felt wrong.

When her family arrived, they took over the decision making and advocacy, and I was able to take care of myself a bit more. I called my therapist. I called my friend in Los Angeles, Philippe, who was wonderful and comforting, and Mrs. Philippe was kind and reassuring from the background. And in the middle of all this, Dan called me, after nearly three years of mutual distancing.

We lapsed right into talking as if no time had passed, his voice somber and reassuring, and neither of us mentioned the silence. I took his call from the large, yellow hall with a floor-to-ceiling window looking southeast, onto Mount Rainier, and I remember the mountain blazing red with sunset that afternoon while talking to Dan for the first time in the longest estrangement we'd ever had, and how I cried when I heard his voice, how much I wanted to tell him the whole story, from the beginning about meeting Steph through all the bad issues we had, to the breakup and Sarah, and now this, and how I just couldn't leave now. I gave him the short version, as much as I could, and it felt like confession, felt like I was granted a form of absolution in that talk, prepared me for meeting my mother, when I picked her up at the airport a few short hours later.

Before we hung up, there was a moment of quiet, right before he encouraged me and reminded me of who I was, what we'd been through already, and that I could get through this, which choked me up. Then he said, "junebug versus hurricane," almost in a whisper, which is a line from one of our favorite Lucinda Williams songs, and that was enough.

Junebug vs. hurricane.

For my mother, I drove to the airport myself and waited for her at baggage claim. I think I was suffering from some sort of contextual or proportional distortion, because she looked much smaller than I remembered her, even though I'd just seen her a year ago, when she'd visited for the green belt test. I had an impulse to put her in my pocket and keep her there, until this madness was over.

Instead, I hugged her and wept, couldn't really tell her everything at once, and then she grew in size as I buried my head in her shoulder and she became my mother again, made me stand up to full size and face what was awaiting us at the hospital.

━━━

I drove us back, took my mother straight to the ninth floor and led her to the ICU. In the waiting room, I introduced my mother to Steph's parents, and Steph's mother was as ingratiating as ever, spoke to my mother in loud, clear, emphasized language with large sweeping hand motions, as if Mom didn't understand English. My mother smiled and looked at me in bewilderment, like "Is she all right? Why is she talking like this?"

"I'm just so impressed you had so many children!" she said to Mom, and my jaw hit the floor. Steph had warned me previously that her mother was capable of saying idiotic things, since she only had the one eye, and back then I was able to overlook or shrug off her insipid attempts at what, at this point, I think she didn't understand could be insulting forms of backhanded compliments. But this was my mother, and my fight drive was triggered, especially in these circumstances.

Mom, however, was more amused than insulted. "Hunh," she said. "Well, thank you. They were tough at first, but they're really great kids." And I took her by the elbow without making eye contact, which would have been difficult even under better circumstances, since she only had the one eye, and led her away.

I think what bothered Steph's mother so much was that theirs was an American family in decline, burning out and dwindling in resources and ambition. They'd seen their heyday and prominence, and she was now standing in front of the next wave of American evolution: My mother, in her own choices with my dad, had given birth to the next generation of American progress, in my sisters and even us, the decrepit boys, and we were pushing forward, and my sisters were nothing if not incredible indications of prosperity, when Steph's own family was in obvious decline. This was a meeting of two maternal wavelengths, one in the ascension, the other in the declension and with nothing else except an attempt at being petty, even if she didn't mean it, or more to the point, couldn't understand it.

I forget how long I'd been at the hospital at this point, but it was late, and we'd each put in our share of vigilance by Steph's side, and it was time to call it. I'd been there a day and a half and was depleted, needed to get my mother home after her flight across the country.

I took her to dinner and she allowed me to tell her the story of the last few months, the absolute truth about my relationship with Stephanie, even about Sarah and my profound confliction, and Mom listened to me as an adult child and son, and this, too, felt like confession, like a relief, like absolution for being human.

Sarah had indeed removed all my empties from my apartment. And she had done my dishes and prepared my place for my mother's arrival. I felt a bit exposed, weirded out by this. I summoned the courage to call her and ask her to back away, expecting—I don't know what. But I didn't have the bandwidth or emotional capital to take on our relationship along with everything else, and for a moment I was expecting an emotional blowback like I would normally receive from Steph, but instead Sarah was understanding and apologetic, said she understood entirely and that I should instead focus on supporting the family and my mother; we would sort ourselves out later.

I was suspicious: No one I knew was that rational. *What gives?*

But, no: Sarah was simply that levelheaded and rational, even in the midst of something like this. It baffled me, as I was accustomed to emotional knife fights and fisticuffs in order to get anything done, so this was unusual for me. This is how trust begins.

That night, my mother slept on my couch, which is huge and oversized, dwarfing her further and reinforcing the perceptual distortion I kept experiencing with her. I left the French doors leading to my sleeping nook open so I could see that she was there, because I was afraid to be alone. When I closed my eyes, seriously nodding off from exhaustion, I could hear Stephanie yelling for me, "*JUNE!*" when I would briefly lose consciousness, right before the hypnic jerk, like it was a frequency open for panic, and she was trapped in her own nightmare, and I was the person she was calling for help, from under the wreckage of the Jeep.

The next morning, we were back on the ninth floor before 8:00 a.m., and Steph's parents were already there. They were sitting quite a distance from Sidney, my friend from the first night. I went right over to him and introduced my mother, and pointed out Steph's parents, who managed a small, pursed smile and slight hand wave. They were unaccustomed to black people, I knew, from Steph's stories. Once, Steph liked to recall, when she took her mother to a larger urban center outside of their idyllic New England town, Steph and her mom had passed a group of three black teenagers, and when they were just out of earshot, her mother had asked, "Are those *REAL* rappers??"

But Sidney hadn't noticed, or made any indication he felt slighted. I brought him a cup of coffee in my rounds and then went in to see Steph, who looked the same, if a bit more bruised. There was more diagnosis, more discussion with doctors and immediate care nurses, and nothing was guaranteed or assured, and we counted the amount of broken bones and were told what to expect, what was coming next. "Pneumonia," the attractive younger internist had said. "It's a process of the body, with so many broken ribs. It's guaranteed."

About the only thing they could guarantee, it seemed, was the bad news.

Steph's head remained distended, her eyes protruding and needing to be covered in an unguent to retain their moisture. An orthopedist to help set her crushed foot. An optometrist to work on her eyes. A neurologist to review yet another series of scans.

And it went on like that: We normalized to the everyday trauma, learned once again how to listen to the doctors and interpret their dithering hodgepodge of Greek and Latin terminology, nod our heads like we understood, and tried to draw something optimistic from their desiccated sense of duty, their fatigued ability to offer hope to the families of the broken.

Next door, a revolving cast of extras moved through the trauma unit. A gang member who'd been shot and refused to stay longer than it took the doctors to stitch up his torso. A stroke victim who moved in and out the same afternoon. His wife and daughter moving from the terror of initiation to the trauma unit, to the good news that he'd be released and sent home tomorrow, and the look in that woman's eyes when she looked at me and nearly apologized for the good news, and I shook my head at her, and her nodding back at me, an entire conversation exquisitely delivered in seconds, wordlessly. Another car accident survivor from eastern Washington whose family had no place to stay, could hardly speak English, so it became my role to help them like Sidney had helped me, that first night. It was what you did.

———

A routine eventually develops, even under circumstances like this, because routines give humans a semblance of control and normality, and for that first week my mother was there, we all worked together to make sense of the symbols and signals we received from Steph's bedside and each of the machines and reports, learned the personalities and habits of the nurses and a language from the sounds and alarms of the ICU station, exchanged information and kept watch as much as we could. I was still trying to be the good guy, and I think my mother was proud of me for that period. I spoke to my family daily, even called my father and grandmother in Brownsville, Texas, and sent Gramma fifty dollars to make a petition at her creepy, Aztec Catholic church service and walk on her knees until they were bloodied so that Steph would recover. I'm actually making that part up: I think she just gave her church thirty dollars and kept twenty for herself. This was, after all, my Gramma.

I tried to sit shiva, next to Stephanie, in that chair, but I couldn't do it for very long some days. It was tragic to me, somehow, more than to the others. I'm still not certain why. Her chemicaled friend, Lisa, could come in there with that distance, looking like Luna Lovegood, and talk to Steph about a project she was working on at school or update her on how the dog was doing, who was now staying in that huge pack at Sarah's house and learning dog manners, which was something Cleo was clearly unaccustomed to. She had no dog sense, would get corrected often by the other dogs who did not like the new addition to the pack. It was like junior high, for teen girls, except with more shedding, and better teeth.

Still, Cleo was safe there, even if she'd been nipped at more than a few times for being undogworldly.

What I would do, some afternoons, was sit next to Steph and play some of that Harry Potter audio book, while I rested my head on the side of the frame. When we had lived together and had trouble sleeping, I would play it for us on the long nights we'd lie awake in her bedroom and stare off through the windows at the night sky. Steph would also place her broken-down clock radio directly under her pillow some deep mornings and listen to a small community college radio station that had very little range, and she'd dial in and fall asleep listening to some really obscure radio programs through the PRI network, some Canadian programs that we'd grown to love.

So I figured out how to dial those in through my iPhone, and I would sit there with her and play that until the internal cranial pressure monitor would start beeping, as if the radio was increasing her blood pressure or anxiety, and I'd turn it off. Then the monitor would resume something nearing her regular status, and I'd play the programs again, to the same spiking effects.

During this whole time, this was the only communication I ever had from her; the only way I knew she was still cognitively "in there" was her responding to Harry Potter and her Canadian public radio, like I'd heard her yelling in my sleep.

When my mother left, everything changed again.

We stopped by the hospital so she could say good-bye to Steph and her parents, and it was touching to see how much affection my mother had developed for this woman, and in a way, the life I'd tried to build here away from home. Mom genuinely cared for her, in spite of the fact that she knew I was trying to get out of this relationship when the accident happened. So when she was saying her good-byes to Steph's mother, who thanked her for coming and spending a week helping, my mother said, "Well, Steph is family to me," and I saw Steph's mother wince at this, and my fight response was once again triggered and I blushed with anger.

That was difficult to forgive.

Mom had changed my entire opinion and estimation of her during this past week, and I had found a new love and respect for her. It had started, interestingly enough, on a walk with Sarah, back at the very beginning. I had been telling Sarah stories about growing up on the Texas border, still uncertain as to whether I wanted to share my writing with her, and I began telling her about my mother, how distant she had seemed when I was a kid.

"Your mother was constantly up to her elbows in diapers," Sarah said, point-blank. "You're lucky she didn't drown you like Andrea Yates." This made me rethink everything. "Hunh," I think I said. From that moment on, I looked at my mother very differently, and it was during this crisis, when I needed her most, when I saw that Mom really had listened to my grief, knew that I was really breaking apart and heard me call out for help, and she had shown up for it. It changed everything. I had so much respect for her then.

In fact, one moment stands out among many, and it happened in the waiting room. It was a Sunday, and Sundays become entirely too crowded in ICU waiting rooms. Sidney's ex-wife had finally made it up from Louisiana, and about three generations of Sidney's family had traveled with her to help with the hastening of their son's life.

Our little crowd had been in the corner of the room that afternoon as we were leaving, and as we were packing up, my mother turned to Sidney's ex, who was a black woman in her late fifties, with cropped hair dyed hot pink, and Mom was taking the time to show her how to work the tricky pull-out couches when the woman turned on my mom, who was much smaller than her, and let out a string of vitriol, doing that finger-wagging, neck-shifting "attitude" display people do when they have little agency for anything else.

I heard this happening and I was immediately on high alert, thinking the situation needed neutralizing, and Steph's parents both darted out of the room like shots had been fired. Sidney reared up and attempted to pull his ex-wife away and she was of course arguing, and my immediate strategy, as a West Coast liberal, was to begin apologizing—"Obviously this was our fault, so sorry; please, we were only trying to"—and my mother stood there, absolutely defiant and cold, staring hard into this woman's face with terrific dignity.

I should mention, if I haven't, that my stepdad is an African American from the East Texas/Louisiana bayou border country, and my mother is absolutely adored by her in-laws. Mom works for the City of Houston and manages a huge crew of people—builders and carpenters and engineers—and she does not take shit from anyone. I was astonished at this person in front of me, who did not back away from the confrontation.

"If you had let me finish," she said to the woman, who was still huff-ing and puffing, "I was showing you how you and your family could be more comfortable tonight." I led her away, and I caught Sidney's eye, who gave me a "women always be crazy" shrug of his shoulders.

The next morning, when we arrived with coffee to resume our vigil, Steph's parents were not in the waiting area, and as soon as the woman in the pink hair saw my mother, she ran up, earnest and smiling, acting in an uncomfortable infantile sort of shame dance, looking down, and said, "I just wanted to say I was sorry for yesterday," and of course, my response was to say, "Oh, no, no, no; don't think anything of it," but I looked instead at my mother and her face was once again hard, unyielding, and she said, "You know better than that. You know how to behave yourself better when someone is trying to help you," and it was just stunning, in that room for that second, and my mother grew ten feet tall in my estimation.

So it was with a tremendous amount of fear and regret that I was let-ting her go that morning, on her flight back to Houston. I was going to be on my own now, with Steph's family, in all this craziness.

I wanted to go home with her.

"You can't," she said to me. "You know you have to stay here."

"I know," I said.

"They need you to help," she said.

"I know," I agreed.

"You're my son," she said. "You can do this."

I put my head into her shoulder, a full head shorter than I was, and I cried and hugged her before she left.

Sarah had given us a lift to the airport that morning and watched all this from the driver's seat. She watched my hulking, 220-pound form break down into a boy needing his mother, and she mentions it to me still, says I can revert to that more quickly than anyone she's ever seen.

—◦—

The next morning, there was a definite sea change in the routine, palpable from the minute I entered alone for the first time, carrying just three cups of coffee. This was the long haul, and it was just Steph's parents and me now. It wasn't anything immediate or overt, but I could tell there was something going on. Very likely, it originated from a symptom of stress they were experiencing between themselves—they were, after all, nearly in month two of hospital stays, since they started with Harold's hospitalization, then Steph's mother's, and now Steph—and though I was trying to be as helpful as possible, there are just some things you can't handle from a waiting room. In fact, my friend Andrew built up a small laptop and lent it to Harold so he could continue handling his e-mail and business from the waiting room, and as helpful as that was, I'm sure Harold was stressed from feeling unproductive.

Personally, I was thanking God that I had the job I did, and I was able to do most of my management and planning and design from the waiting room, using the hospital's Wi-Fi. The first production cycle after Steph's accident, something like three days after, I was absolutely incapable of concentrating on my layout and design, would work for blocks of ten or eight minutes, then lie down next to my desk for five while my mother watched helplessly from the couch and encouraged me to get up, get back to it. I just couldn't. My mind was coming apart with anxiety and fatigue, but I also knew that I couldn't take the time off because if I did, if someone else saw all the scripts and shortcuts I had made for my production role, I'd lose my job. As a graphic designer, keeping your solutions opaque is a part of your worth; when upper management sees how "easy" it is to do your job, they undervalue it and try to replace you. It was a lesson I'd learned twice before.

So it was with a great sense of self-preservation that I would climb back into my chair and treat jpegs with my Photoshop scripts, lay in type and apply styles, cut and paste something from a previous issue, do everything I could until I was able to meet my deadline and head back to the waiting room, to wait.

CHAPTER 26

Now the Wolf

When it was just us three, Steph's mother made it a point that first morning to sit me down and give me a speech about how close their family was, and some other important errata that was completely lost on me because I kept focusing more on her contextual meanings and her overly saccharine delivery, rather than her message, and when she finished, I didn't understand why I was feeling like I'd just been attacked, but I knew that I had. Though I wasn't sure why.

I said something like, "You have the most sweetened way of saying the most god-awful things," and both of her parents stood up and walked away, and for a moment I thought Harold was going to hit me, and I thought, *Yup, this is how it should end; I get hit by him, too*, but I wasn't, and after a while things cooled down, and we each sat at opposite sides of the room.

While I was in the ICU with Steph that afternoon, she received a visitor from work, and for a moment I was confused as to who this person was, when I finally remembered Steph's last phone call about the Japanese PhD candidate, and suddenly here she was with a handmade card that had been written with exquisite care, a small orchid, cookies, and a Hello Kitty doll. I'd been sitting by Steph's side, studying her head and fractures a bit more and noticing that her head was indeed growing back into a regular shape, when I noticed the Japanese woman looking a bit lost, at the same time Steph's mother did, and instead of running interference—if Steph had wanted *anyone* bounced from ICU, it would have been her last enemy—I decided to see how her mother would handle it, from a sense of devilish enjoyment, from being, as my dad would call me, *cabrón*.

The Japanese woman's English was slow, halting, and apologetic, and Steph's mother decided right then she knew how to navigate this one. She started speaking to the PhD student like she was a kindergartener in her class back in Yankeeland.

"I have VISITED your country ONCE!" she said with a big smile, while pointing out the window, I think toward the east. "Thank YOU for the GIFTS!" Here she held each one up for inspection. "These COOKIES look DELICIOUS!" Here she rubbed her stomach in circles. "Are you FRIENDS with Stephanie?" She pointed with exaggeration at Stephanie, still in a coma. "She is still VERY SICK," she said, and made the "sleeping" hand signal with a pouty face. "I will tell her," she said, using her hand like a puppet mouthing words, "that her JAPANESE friend was here! Thank you!" By this point, the woman was in tears, though I don't think it was from the moving acceptance speech, but much more from the agony she had witnessed in the coma chair, suffered by the person she'd argued with about protocol two weeks before. She had obviously been feeling guilty about it. So much so that she bought a coveted Hello Kitty doll from Japan; those aren't cheap.

Back in the waiting room, Steph's mother looked over the booty and decided she didn't want the doll and handed it to me, said I should take it. She did that, often; people would come in with food or gifts or flowers, and she'd thank them gratefully like fallen Southern gentry, and after they'd gone, she'd regift them to others or to me, and I was developing quite a pile of food at home that I'd never eat, lots of plastic Tupperware containers growing in my sink.

With my mother gone and everyone else seeing to their own responsibilities, I was left alone in dealing with her parents, and I was doing what I could to keep it together, but I was still suffering from some severe anxiety and guilt. I had seen a doctor while my mother was there and she had been astonished at my blood pressure at the intake. It was something like 190/110, and I hadn't been taking anything or wasn't even hungover. That was normal for me, during this time: That was my level of stress. With my mother in the room, I explained to the doctor that I was going through an incredibly stressful event and that I had people counting on me, and that I was also an alcoholic who binge drank in periods of stress. When I admitted to being an alcoholic, I caught my mother's eyes, and she looked at me with a combination of sadness and mild disapproval, almost like she was saying, "You're not supposed to talk about that," or maybe even, "How did you end up so weak, like your father?" But mostly, it was sadness, I think. I hope.

The doctor listened to me, nodded, and then handed me a prescription for Xanax.

Great, I thought; I'd heard of these.

Although Dan and I had been talking again, I didn't think of calling him and asking him about the Xanax, or how it could react with alcohol. Dan would always give me the real skinny on this sort of thing, but for some reason, I just didn't think this one through, so I was taking the Xanax as prescribed, and then not.

—◦—

Back at the hospital, Steph's parents had developed a habit of moving from living situation to living situation in places across the city that were not amenable to easy public access to Harborview Hospital. I couldn't understand their choices after I'd had Andrew's wife, who developed websites for a travel agency, find them a number of low-cost options that were on bus lines or a ten-dollar cab fare away. I offered my own apartment. I pointed out the best and safest neighborhoods. I explained and pointed using maps. Harold loved maps. For reasons known only to them, they ended up in West Seattle, or Northgate, and a huge part of my responsibility became chauffeuring them from the hospital to home, usually at rush hour.

My routine basically settled into getting to the hospital around 8:00 a.m. bearing coffees, sitting with Steph's mother and listening to the latest test results or procedures, seeing if I could do anything else, visiting with Steph for a while and telling her, jokingly, that I was going to force her to deal with my parents on her own when she woke up, then seeing if there were any developments otherwise, finding lunch, and sitting around discussing things in vaguely optimistic terms. Then around 3:00 or so, her parents would begin closing down for the day, and I'd drive them to whatever part of town they were staying in, then I'd drive by a liquor store and buy a quart of gin and go to my empty apartment and slowly come apart, watching something on Netflix. Shows on Netflix became my only constants, my television friends who were the furthest thing from the ICU at Harborview.

I'd come wide awake around 6:00 a.m., after sleeping about four hours, take a hot shower, and then do it again.

This is how I was keeping it together, and it wasn't working.

One afternoon, I saw a tall, elegant priest making his way through the waiting room into the ICU and decided to ambush him on his way back. I stood in front of him and engaged him in conversation long enough that he had to sit down and talk to me, and out of the corner of my eye, I watched as both of Steph's parent were stricken with a shocked look of disquiet ("How *CATHOLIC!*") as I sat down to explain to the kneeler that I had long lost any sense of comfort from the church, that I didn't agree with the institution and its practices for human management with reproductive issues and its subjugation of women, certainly had issues with its unwillingness to punish pederastic priests and its behavior through World War II, but *right now, right here, this right here is where you are supposed to provide a place for me, as a Catholic, lapsed or not. Isn't that what you Jesuits say? "Give us the boy until he's eight, and I'll show you the man?" Well, here's the man, Padre. Show me what I paid for, show me what my parents bought for all those Sundays.*

"And it's not because I believe in it," I said to him, "but because I want something to believe in. There should be a safe place, shouldn't there?"

He agreed, began unpacking the Hail Mary for me like it was the Talmud, told me how it was a story about two women, one of them shunned for her choices to be an unmarried mother, the other not understanding she's been the vehicle for the largest social change in human history. He told me about their spiritual choices, broke the stanzas into smaller metaphysical meditations like something from John Donne while I told him that this was what I missed, this was what I needed: I needed somewhere to go, somewhere safe, and I didn't have anyplace like that, not any longer. There were no safe places, and could could could the Church give me that, now?

He said, "Listen, I'm right over here, at St. James Cathedral. Here's my card. When you're having these crises, come to the chapel and I'll talk to you; we can discuss this renewed desire you have to return to Mother Church."

"Great," I said, "thank you," and for the first time in a long while I felt like maybe I had someplace to go, someplace to feel safe and protected from the anxiety, the craziness, the pain and agony swirling in hurricane formation around me, settling on me like a season.

Junebug vs. hurricane.

I e-mailed the priest three times and never received a response. I visited the cathedral, and each time I went, it was locked, and I was left outside in the rain to look onto the baroque and Gothic spires, the worn faces of saints in the nooks overlooking the doors, and I had to keep my pain and anguish to myself, carry it back to my car because I couldn't leave it at their door as had been our deal, and I took another Xanax and went home to find a moment of quiet in a bottle of Bombay Sapphire gin and another Netflix series.

Many days ended with something like, "Oh, no! The doctors have overlooked something and it looks like she'll never speak again," so I'd go home that night and try to incorporate that new idea into my tapestry of fears. Or they would say, "We just had these new results! She's developed a new hypothalamus and she'll be ready to go home in a week!" and I'd drive home that night higher than happiness, listening to Burt Bacharach and yelling out the window with joy: "It's over, it's over, and she's going to be all right!"

At this point, Steph had been removed from the harness and she was lying in her bed, braces and medieval medical devices forcing her limbs and feet to heal back into their proper shape after being crushed.

Much earlier, it had been revealed that she had very little of her anti-seizure medication in her bloodwork, and everyone had been puzzled and cautious about saying anything that might have led to some sense of responsibility or litigation, I could tell, but I was able to say it quite clearly: Steph had stopped taking her full script because she felt the Lamictal made her thinking fuzzy, and she was more than three weeks behind on her work, so she was working long, late days and playing a dangerous game of chance, which she wound up losing that night.

A photo of the wreck appeared in the local news blogs, and it was deeply painful to see, astonishing as to how she had survived such a catastrophic impact. Her Jeep had plummeted nearly twenty feet, onto its rooftop. Our camping equipment littered I-5, as flares lit up the site and cars drove cautiously around our detritus, my favorite pillow, out on the icy interstate. It was horrible to imagine, horrible to think what she'd endured that night, under there, awaiting rescue.

Meanwhile, both her parents were still going through their own medical procedures, recovering from their accidents, in which they'd each lost an eye. Steph's mother needed some preparation for her ocular cavity before she flew back east to see her optometrist, who was supplying her with a false eye, and in the meantime she still walked around like Yoko Ono, wearing sunglasses indoors. Her dad still had his own physical therapy to cope with his healing ribs, and some other procedures to do with the eye in which he lost vision. So it was a family in a number of stressful situations, and they weren't easy to navigate, and still, I didn't understand my role, why I remained by her side, an intruder into their family's pain.

As the days wore on and our better natures began to crumble under the stress, I came to feel like a reprobate, or a scoundrel, around them, not a scoundrel like Rhett Butler or Han Solo, but more like Peter Lorre in *Casablanca*. And after spending all that time with them, I realized that this had been a part of Steph's plan all along: I represented further discomfort for her parents, making them squirm at the Mexican, whom they now had to depend upon. She'd put them through the lesbian relationships, now it was time for the nonwhites, and Catholics, male though they might be, subverting a deep prejudice with a lighter one.

<hr />

It took about a month but I finally had to call Sarah once more, one afternoon, when I could no longer endure their bickering, exclusion, and target for attack, and feeling like I still had to be "the good guy." I dialed Sarah around 2:00 p.m., as I knew her to be the only person with a schedule as open as mine was usually, and said, "Can I please just come over and climb into your bed to sleep? I can't go home and be alone anymore. I need Jack County. I need to be around dogs and listen to people," and she said, "Absolutely. Come right over."

She didn't have to say a word when I arrived, just led me up to her bedroom and pulled the shades, and I stripped to my underclothes and climbed into bed. Then some moments later she climbed in as well and we made love in the most manic, silent way possible in that afternoon daylight. When it was over, she slipped away and locked the door after the dog came in and lay down next to me, curled up like a croissant at my legs, and slept with his large head on my knees and his big bear paw on my hip, reassuring both of us that the other was there. I finally slept, slept like a pack member—and the wolf, for the first time in weeks, was left outside the door.

That was what it took for me to realize that Sarah was not someone to defend against, that there was safety in our pack of two. Sarah's own situation had been in fast dissolution after her husband had asked her for a divorce, and in my condition and general state, there was really no way a woman of Sarah's estimation would ever look my way as a potential mate, unless she wanted a tawdry affair to get her girlfriends talking or rouse her ex-husband's ire, which was what I was accustomed to. But in her own current typhoon of her life's deconstruction and how I was walking the earth now, looking haunted and broken, it triggered something in her, and we were actually a viable commodity, began seeing each other almost every day after this. I would come over after my shift at the hospital and bring wine, and she'd make dinner and feed us these wonderful home-cooked meals, while I sat at the counter in that kitchen and recounted the day's events, explained how matters were now dire, or were now looking up, and she'd tell me what she could about her divorce, and how it was profoundly affecting her life, her kid, her family.

I'd slump on a stool at her counter and try to reconnect to humanity.

I'd bring a bottle or two and she'd make pork chops or salmon or something nourishing, and we'd talk and eat, listen to music, and take care of one another as best we could.

Sometimes, when she cooked, it was something as simple as toast, twelve-grain bread from the Essential Bakery with a slab of butter. I couldn't remember toast being so goddamned delicious and fulfilling. It made me stop one afternoon, as I sat there and marveled at the simple transformation.

"Sarah," I asked her as she was getting out our favorite goblets for the ten-dollar bottle of red grocery store wine.

"Yeah?" she responded.

"Darling, don't make fun of me for asking this, but what's the difference between bread and toast? I mean, it's just heat, right?"

She thought about this for a moment, understood what I was really asking.

"It's the caramelization of sugars," she said, and we were both quiet for a moment, taken by the kitchen metaphor. "It's like the William James philosophy of the 'once born' and the 'twice born.'"

It also reminded me of the myth of Martin Luther, when he visited Rome and was astonished at the corruption, the wholesale consumption of indulgences. When he took too long doing his transfiguration ceremony, some cynical, veteran Roman priest whispered in his ear, "Bread thou art, bread thou shalt remain." Hence the splintering.

Somehow, it all fell into place for me, that simplicity.

What it takes to transform a person into actualization.

Those recondite nights are my only fond memories of this time, how we'd stretch out on her bed, in the dark, after making love, and she'd nod off right away, from the exhaustion of the sex, the life we were living, and the red wine, perhaps, and I'd stay awake, sitting up in her bed, watching movies on her laptop and taking Benadryl after Benadryl so that I could sleep, but they would never work, not even with the red wine.

She'd come awake sometimes, rest her hand on my back.

"Have you slept?" she'd ask.

"I can't," I'd say.

"Why don't you take a shower?" she'd suggest, and at first I'd disagree, demure and pass, but then eventually I would nod my head and follow through, stand under the burning water, my hand resting against the black-and-white tile in her shower, and just allow the water to change the feeling of my skin.

I'd come back to bed and she'd be awake, yawning.

"I feel better," I'd report, and she would say, "I wonder if any other animal has learned to stand under water for reassurance," as she yawned and fell back asleep, leaving me there to wonder at that thought, and at her, and I would maybe then be able to sleep.

⌐ ⌐

We were like two POWs, holding one another up during a death march, knowing we were smack-dab in the middle of the march and uncertain as to exactly how long it was going to be or whether it was ever going to end, but at the very least, in the immediate future, we had to hold each other up: That was the first principle. And the sex began to reflect that: We'd close down for the night and lock ourselves up in her guest bedroom with very little light coming through the shutters on the closet door, and we would go at each other like karate students, in the dark, these shapeless shadows, legs and arms and borderless lands, perspiration and fingers and hair, with all the ferocity of fear and animal mind. That was the only place throughout all this insanity, in that dark bedroom and in the velocity of our lovemaking, where we would entirely lose sight of one another and leave our bodies to become these patterns of sensations and images of sensuality and exertion bordering on physical threat, would lose each other and ourselves in something so primitive and, really, the only resource left to us, which was this trigger of desperation and passion, could finally lose identity and all that marked us, all that defined us in that obscurity, and the wolf would finally know that there was one boundary it couldn't breach, would have to instead cross its paws and sleep that moment while Sarah and I blended into one another with physicality, until we each woke up the next morning and dressed and returned to our duties in keeping the wolf sated, keeping our lives from really breaking apart. I would put my other mask back on and drive downtown to see what Steph's parents needed that next day, then pull out my last emotional equities so that I could get it for them.

⌐ ⌐

The days I couldn't see Sarah, I'd go home and drink alone. More naughty water. Spending time in isolation wasn't good for me, but I didn't know how to ask anyone for help, felt that I needed the alone time, which was idiotic. I called my family, spoke to my mother and sisters and sometimes Dan, but their concern could reach only so far.

213

I decided I needed to see a psychiatrist and get on some sort of anti-depressant or mood stabilizer, and Sarah recommended someone who did God's work, since I was losing my health insurance, which I'd had through Steph. I met with the guy one afternoon and recounted the recent traumatic events, said I was in near constant hysteria and I wasn't sure how I could endure it much longer. Not a problem, he said, and he prescribed Wellbutrin, one of the many scripts Steph's friend, Lisa, was on. *Fantastic,* I thought.

It was about here that I started going crazy.

The Wellbutrin combined with the Xanax and the gin kept me awake for days on end.

I could get it together to drive to the hospital every morning by 8:00 a.m., listen to Steph's mother and father discuss any updates, sit with Steph for a while and stroke her hand, let her know I was there, then talk with her parents in order to figure out what the next steps were and where she was headed. I would pick up any visiting friends or relatives from the airport and bring them to the hospital, and then at about 3:00 p.m., I'd see if anyone needed any rides anywhere, needed anything further, and then I'd head home, with a stop by the liquor store en route.

I had managed to move Cleo from Sarah's house to the home of a friend who ran the karate school and was a veterinarian, along with her husband, and had a pack of three rescue dogs where Cleo would feel right at home. Couldn't have been more perfect for her.

This was a great solution, since the only time I was left alone with her, while I was house-sitting at Andrew's for Christmas, a few weeks after Steph's accident, I managed to lose her. Fucking dog took off through the side door and it was twenty degrees outside, and I'd been drunk for two days and had forgotten that Andy didn't have the end of his yard secured. The dog took off and started running around a busy street, and I lost my shit and chased after her in the dark and cold, ran around the neighborhood for an hour before I gave up, thinking, *Fuck, now I've done it, now I've lost the fucking dog,* when she showed up at the door with a stupid smile, asking to be let back in. I was so upset with her, I put one of Andrew's daughter's fake mustaches on the dog and took humiliating photos of her and put them on Facebook, as retribution. See if she does THAT again.

Later on, when things started getting really serious for my mental health, I was much more destructive, much more in need of professional health care, much more dangerous.

I'd gone for more than four days without sleep. I just couldn't fall off, couldn't stay down. When I'd lie down to sleep, lie on my side and curl up with a pillow, I'd get these violent hypnic jerks, the long muscle twitches, short muscle spasms. Nothing would help. I'd chug a bottle of wine and take ten Benadryl. I'd drink most of a bottle of NyQuil. I'd drink a six-pack and gin, then take sleeping pills. I'd be groggy, chemical sludge in my veins, but dead awake. I'd watch horror movies on Netflix, or rom-coms, or a full series, but nothing stopped my brain from exploding like fireworks. I was finally going completely crazy, and when I realized how far down my mental health was, it was almost reassuring: At least I knew what to call it. Like when an exorcist gets the demon's name.

One day, Sarah came by to tell me that I needed an intervention. It was 10:00 a.m. and she'd made her way through my building, had knocked on my door, and I was sitting talking to her while my body was blooming in sweat. I had a towel and I'd wipe down my head and back—I'd removed my shirt to show her what I was going through—and I sat there, opposite her, while my body blossomed from the top of my head to my knees in a sweat flower, in eight-minute cycles, and she was at once repulsed and fascinated, and asked how long that had been happening.

"Three days," I said. "I can't sleep."

She helped me make a number of emergency appointments and even drove me to an emergency room to have my blood pressure checked. It was through the roof: 210/160. I saw the nurse actually blanch when she took it again, to make sure she had it right the first time, and I thought, *Fuck, I'm going to have that stroke after all,* and I waited for them to give me something to get it down, but instead they just had me sit and talk with Sarah for a half hour, and sonofabitch if it didn't decrease considerably, just with us talking quietly.

When she left, I took a long shower and tried to get it together so I could visit Steph once again.

At this point Steph had been moved to a long-term care place, a nursing home in West Seattle, and they were not managing her very well. There had been no "magic moment" where her eyes fluttered open and she regained consciousness. She had simply started moving around more, and it looked as if she was trying to focus her attention on you, and then something else would catch her eye, and she'd spend all her time looking at that. It was unnerving, watching her focus like that. She never stopped squirming. They had her in an ordinary bed, and she shifted and moved and squirmed so much that she was in constant danger of falling off the side. Also, she never slept. Neither of us was sleeping; we had that in common.

These types of facilities, nursing homes, were very common to me because of Dan's career. I knew how they operated, and I knew the characters and nurses and people to talk to there, how to navigate them. I actually felt a bit safer in this environment than I had at the ICU, and I was both encouraged that she'd been released there and also frightened: I had this image of Steph recovering only so far as the sad, shattered patients I'd seen who lived in nursing homes the remainder of their lives, medicated and broken, the light in their eyes a soft glimmer of the person they once were, smoking in the restricted areas and wearing pajamas, their hands clutching a newspaper or dog-eared paperback, looking at you sadly as you left from your visit, remembering who you were together, and it just tore my heart apart, imagining that this could possibly be in her future.

She'd begun therapy there, was developing enough cognitive ability that the therapists had started her on small rehabilitative programs. She still hadn't slept, that I remember, never stopped looking and shifting and writhing in her bed, not so far. This was now late January, early February, and I'd missed my fortieth birthday, like in *The Great Gatsby*. It was also my writing deadline: I had made it a point to decide whether I was going to continue writing, keeping alive my secret wish to publish as an author, or give it up entirely and start really sharpening my skills as a designer and learning web design in earnest—basically, the "I give up my dreams" point. I still took my notebooks with me everywhere I went at this time, would cite notes and make little observations and comments while I sat in waiting rooms, sat at hospital bedsides, bars near my home.

But that day just slipped past, like every other.

Instead of any celebration, I went home and lay in bed, about my sixth night without sleep, and I lay there thinking about Steph and feeling horrible and guilty, decided that I would frame photos of her and bring them to the home and place them all around to warm up the place. Her mother had made all these posters and lurid banners, used Tibetan prayer flags as decorations, and created these placards with an entirely fictionalized depiction of Steph as a human being and had posted them all around the bedside. Steph would have been insane with anger at the sight of them, at their failure to describe who she really was, and I was equally upset with the inaccuracy of the description, for some reason. I'm not sure why.

Her mother listed a number of authors as "Steph's Favorites," which Steph had at one point or another made clear she despised. Her mother recorded a number of "favorite movies" that Steph had never seen, music, painters, and so on. It was awful, and a reproduction of the daughter her mother wanted, not the daughter she had.

All this was creating an atmosphere of tension and growing menace.

I drove to the nursing home around 2:30 that morning with my stack of framed photos and saw that her room was lit up and a number of people were already there. "Oh," I said, "Nice to see everyone here."

They looked happy to see me and welcomed me in, not telling me anything at all, and I came in with the photos and placed them all about. I didn't think anything about the fact that Steph was on the floor on a series of mats, because that made much more sense to me, given that she had been shifting and moving and in constant danger of falling off the bed since she had arrived. Around 3:30 a.m., they turned off the lights and I lay there next to her, with her not sleeping or making any sort of acknowledgement that she saw me even when she looked right at me. I kept whispering to her, "Sleep, Stephanie; go to sleep, sweetheart; stop moving, please. Come on, you can sleep, just close your eyes, just close your eyes and sleep," but she wouldn't; she'd just keep staring at me and through me, and I couldn't sleep either, because my body was doing the same thing, shifting and twitching and moving, and I couldn't stop, not for longer than three seconds or so because of the Xanax, as I lay there on the mat next to her in my karate jumper, trying to keep warm and keep her safe. We spent the night lying next to one another like that, until about 7:00 a.m., when breakfast time came, and I had to go home because I had to work that day.

CHAPTER 27

People Ain't No Good

I could hear it in his voice that morning, when I first spoke to him. Alfred was the publisher of the bilingual "newspaper" I was producing and the owner of the Hispanic media company out of eastern Washington and was my boss, and he was never any good at diplomacy. I heard the switch in his voice when we were talking about that issue's content, and I knew my number was up. He didn't have the business sophistication to disguise or massage the message that he'd made the choice to let me go, as a contract employee, and in order to delay the news I changed the subject and said that I had to take another call.

But I knew it was in the mail. I just knew it. Unbelievable, that he'd do this to me, after his whole, "As Hispanics, we're all a big family and should look out for one another" speech, that while Steph was in a fucking coma, he'd let my contract end and refused to renew it for the next year. I was making decent money for a print designer, but obviously, the Republican side of Alfred's "Mexican Businessman" thing saw this as too large an expense, and I knew I was out. Also, I had no benefits to speak of, since I was on contract.

I couldn't fucking believe it. Another bottom falling out from under.

Alfred and his wife were second-generation Mexican Americans living here in Washington State, the children of fruit pickers and farm laborers, and they reminded me entirely of the people I knew back home. That's why it had all worked so well, when we'd started. But this—he knew what I was going through, he knew about Steph—for him to cut me out like this at this time, my head was just exploding.

Un-fucking-believable.

Everyone fucks you. Here's the trick: When it comes right down to it, when you're down, *everyone* fucks you. It's better if you just accept it.

It's entirely biological: When your luck turns bad, the herd wants you out, subconsciously.

I didn't give Alfred the opportunity to introduce the topic of my penury that morning so I was able to ingest it myself, first. I didn't want to attack him and needed a chance to center myself. I knew his speech would be pathetic and bilingual and Christianly and Republican—he was like Reagan, in the '80s, who conspicuously gave veterans awards for service, then cut VA benefits left and right.

And I wasn't sure I couldn't keep from yelling and cursing him, though I had started cursing him, deeply and profoundly, in my heart, cursing his kids and his wife and his family, hoping the most horrible fucking things would befall him, that he'd know what I'd been living, would eventually face what I was facing, but I knew that I had to keep this quiet.

So I made an excuse and cut off the call, and he sounded relieved that he hadn't had to have that conversation with me just yet.

When I spoke to Steph's mom next, asking about what was going on at the nursing home, I immediately heard an earful of shit.

"What the fuck were you doing here last night at 3:30 a.m.?" she yelled at me.

"I, uh, was dropping off . . . the . . . um . . . what?"

"Did you know she fell off her bed? Why were you here at that time? Who called you?"

"No one called me; I just . . . I know how these places work; I was feeling lonely and sad for Steph, so I brought her those framed photos. What's going on?"

"You were lonely and sad," she repeated back to me in tones meant to humiliate.

"Yeah, I was sad and I brought over those photos. Why are you yelling at me?"

"She fell off the bed last night and hit her head! They were going to send her to the hospital for X-rays, but you showed up and said not to!"

"That's not at all what happened! When I arrived there, there were people in her room! No one asked me anything!"

"Just stay out of it, Domingo! You don't have the authority to determine her care, you hear me?"

"Whoa, whoa! Hold on! I never made any such fucking call! Who said that?"

"The nurses here! They said 'Mr. Handsome' showed up with pictures and you told them not to send her out!"

"Not at all true! Nothing in the way of true. Nobody calls me that. Holy shit, that's just wrong."

And then she hung up on me.

———

So I began drinking at 9:00 that morning. Refuge, in a box of wine.

I'd been watching all these series on Netflix to avoid thinking about what I was living, but strangely, in every instance, no matter what the subject matter, every fucking show somehow turned around and had a story arc about a brain injury.

No shit. I just couldn't get away from it.

———

And I had started really breaking down, making some horrible decisions and hurting every relationship I had in my life. I had a growing sense that I might really go mad if I recognized what was happening around me, if I turned too sharply to the left or right and caught it full in my scope.

That Christmas before, when I had lost the damned dog, Brenda Brown had come to find me while I stayed at Andrew's house, and we'd stayed down in Andrew's "man basement" because he had a drop-down cinema and projection booth. I had invited Brenda over to watch a series of war movies, and she'd shown up with "three bitches and a bag of blow," after she brought over her drug dealer, dog, and girlfriend, and it had been a fantastic night of revelry, and then isolation when they left me alone. She had left me her necklace, this long chain fitted with trinkets and baubles that meant something to her, and she pulled it off her and put it around my neck, for strength, in an incredibly sweet gesture. Before she'd shown up, it had been the most miserable and isolated Christmas holiday

I'd ever experienced—it was just another ordinary day at the ninth floor waiting room. Then I had driven home, picked up Chinese food with all the Jewish families, and settled in to watch the loudest, most gory movies I could think of, on Andrew's projection system. That somehow made sense to me then. Dan tried to reach me, as did Mom and my sisters, but I couldn't talk to anyone at this point. Didn't have it in me anymore. I was feeling mean, bitter. Even had turned on my closest friend, like a family pet turned vicious on a leash.

I'd harmed Dougherty after he expressed his concern and grief, and I used him as a scapegoat for my anguish when I zeroed him in my crazy target, said something to the effect of, "*YOU! You never thought we were good together and you hated that she was here for me! You hated that she took me away from you!*" Just all this nutso illogical crazy spasm directed at Dougherty, none of which I really believed, but the drugs and the alcoholism were making it easy to spin out these fabrications of fiction and go off the rails.

I did that about three times, damaged about four other deep friendships as I spun entirely out of control and headed toward what I thought was my new gravity, in craziness.

I wanted to get arrested, or committed, in some way, I thought. I'd lost everything—relationships, work, life—and I needed something else to ground me. Maybe institutionalization was the answer.

CHAPTER 28

Stalling

I woke up one morning with this line written in my notebook:

There comes a time when every damaged little boy has to dance in both directions.

I've looked for it in the books I was reading, searched for it online, the films and shows I was watching that night, and asked other people if they recognize it, but no one knows it. It sort of sounds like me, but I'm not entirely sure.

———

In the early days of flight, there was this man named Lincoln Beachey.

Lincoln Beachey solved the issue of the tailspin.

Beachey was a barnstormer and a pioneer aviator when avionics were a brand-new science, and the mortality rate for aviators was in the 90th percentile. In particular, they grappled with the issue of mid-flight stall, and the going logic at the time, based entirely on intuition, was to turn your propeller away from the plummet and try to restart the engine with friction.

This eventually happened to Beachey, and defying his own intuition and popular logic, he instead turned his plane *into* the dive, *into* the plummet, increasing his downward plunge and decreasing his response time to seconds. But it worked: The dive decreased the kinetic friction against the propeller to restart his engine, and suddenly, the stall was no longer an issue for flyers. Lincoln Beachey solved it by defying his impulses of self-preservation and diving headlong into what was a risk.

I had the same idea, in my mental health, I told myself. It hurt to fight it, so I was just going to let it take me on its path. Maybe I could get my propeller started again as I plummeted.

Sometime after Steph's mother yelled at me for interfering, I ended up in a tavern about two blocks from my apartment, drinking alone and sulking in a corner at the bar. I couldn't believe things had become this bad. And when I thought they'd been bad enough, they became worse, just kept falling out from under me.

There was no one there this night, except two other guys by the pool table and the hard-bitten Vietnam veteran bartender who hated his customers. It was one of the last remaining taverns in the neighborhood, and the clientele had definitely taken a turn for both the urban hipster and the unwashed equally, the unapologetically vulgar, as was evidenced this night, even with the limited patrons.

Somehow, it had suddenly neared closing time, and I decided that I needed to listen to Mexican music. They had one of those new electronic jukeboxes with the infinite library, right out of a Borges short story, so I knew it wouldn't be a problem to find Vicente Fernandez in the middle of Uptown, Seattle, and sure enough, there he was.

I played the saddest song in the world, "La Misma," which is sung from the point of view of a brokenhearted man sitting in a Mexican tavern, begging the mariachis to play him that same old song that reaches down into his soul, and he's so goddamned sad, even the waiters are crying. It's a great fucking song, and I wanted to hear it, so I played it.

It was three lines in when I heard the two guys playing pool snickering, and as I marched over intent on starting some shit, I realized I was wearing possibly the worst, least combat-operative shoes this night, square-toed and fancy, but fuck it: I wanted to get into a fight.

I had a suitably deranged look about me as I marched right up to both these kids and said, "You have a fucking problem with my song choices?"

The kids, who were drinking their pints and holding pool cues, were startled, suddenly wide-eyed.

"Ah, um, no, man; no!" one of them stammered. "I was just telling my friend here how much of a surprise it is to hear this music here; I'm from South Texas, and I've never heard anyone play this in Seattle."

I remained in fighting mode, but I was trying to figure out what I had just heard.

Did he just say he was from South Texas?

"Did you just say you're from South Texas?"

"Yeah, man. I'm from Brownsville. Do you know it?"

———

By the time the vet kicked us out about an hour later, we were arm over arm singing a playlist of Vicente Fernandez. I'd bought us all a couple pitchers of beer, and the only way the bartender could get us to shut up and leave was to sell me a "to-go" six-pack of Pabst Blue Ribbon because it was nearly 2:30 a.m. and he wanted us out. We exchanged numbers at the door, and my two new friends went one way and I went the other, went home and tried to kill myself, as I had been planning.

I stumbled into my apartment, disrobed and ran a hot bath, I remember.

I left a voice memo on my iPhone, saying I was sorry but I had finally broken.

Junebug vs. hurricane.

———

I might have called Sarah. Or maybe that was later. I found an old, double-sided razor and sank into the hot water, drinking from the six-pack of Pabst, and I put my wrist under the tap and started digging with the edge of the razor, and with each cut, I dug harder and faster so that I wouldn't lose my courage. I kept going and going while the water ran over it and the blood began gushing and right at the point where I nicked at the vein I was aiming for, something primal snapped in my mind once again and I realized what I was doing, and that there was no coming back from here, and I panicked, panicked, dropped the blade and pressed my thumb into the cut, now an inch or two long and welling uncontrollably with blood.

I managed to slosh my way out of the tub and call 911 with my pinky, then sit in the hallway and wait in my robe for the cops, who called an ambulance and carted me away to an emergency room downtown. I hardly remember any of this, and I don't know how it was that my neighbors never knew, but it's a testament to the tacit isolation and privacy agreement that Seattle neighbors have with one another that we'd never involve ourselves in one another's business, which, in times like this, is a godsend because you're able to suffer your indignations privately, but it can also harm you entirely, when you're begging for help and don't know how to ask for it.

———

At the hospital, I wasn't a model patient, and I had two overweight security guards standing by me when the surgeon came in and numbed my arm, wrist to shoulder, in order to stitch up my wound. I'm not sure why I was still mouthy and shitty, but when the social worker came in and asked me her standard "suicide attempt" questions, I looked at her like, "How dare you think you can assess me with your mindless optimism, Night School? Do you know what I've been through? Do you know what broke me down so bad that I've ended up here?" I just wasn't having it. I needed help, and I wasn't going to find it in the Swedish ER.

I was still a bit out of my mind when I demanded my phone, felt entirely lost without it, somehow, since no one knew where I was, and I was finally able to convince the desk nurse that I'd calm and quiet down if they allowed me my phone, so I could leave someone a message, and they agreed.

Of course, I called Sarah. Then I called and left a sobbing, apologetic message to my mother and sister Marge, and gave them Sarah's number. I don't remember calling Dan, or Philippe.

A few minutes later, the one nurse I'd listen to stepped in my room with a tray of food and told me to eat, sit quietly, or else they'd have to send me to a psych ward, and she could tell I was just being difficult. "You don't have to make this worse than it is," she said. "Just eat and get some sleep." It was typical hospital cafeteria food, with a little milk carton, and I didn't remember the last time I'd eaten, so the food felt innocent and like manna. For a moment, before I nodded off, I realized fully what I had done and I was deeply ashamed.

———

Some three hours later, Sarah appeared.

She had told the ER nurse she was my mother, which was a stretch, but it worked. She would have had to have had me at age thirteen, and I don't think they allow that, even in Idaho. I was sitting up and feeling miserable, memories of everything I'd done and said the night previous flooding my conscience, and I tried to remember who I'd called, who would be worried, who knew I'd broken down this far.

Sarah stood there and looked at me with pity and anger.

I couldn't look her in the eye. Instead, I asked her, "Are you wearing a bra?"

She looked stunned at first, then grinned mischievously, but still seemed aggravated.

I smiled and thought, *Maybe I'm not in so much trouble after all.*

She drove me to her house an hour or so later, dressed in my bathrobe and pajamas, looking like either a hobo or a postsuicidal Arthur Dent. I'd always imagined I'd be better dressed for my suicide, but I didn't have much choice at that time in the morning. I was hurting, and not only from a multiple-day binge. Still, I attempted a patrician bearing as I walked past all the real hobos waiting outside the ER. My psyche hurt, my soul felt damaged, imperiled, and I don't buy into the whole "suicide sends you to hell" argument from the church.

I'd read often about suicides, had a real sadness for people who went through with it, felt a twisted sort of bond with them because it was a shadow that had followed me throughout my adulthood. I felt a kindred spirit with people who suffered with that sort of depression, wrestled with that decision as an actual possibility.

That I had swung so far into nearly doing it scared the hell out of me. Certainly it was a cry for help, from that bathroom, doing my imitation of Dorothy Parker, but the intent was there, and it frightened me.

Most survivors of suicide attempts will tell you that the minute they jump from building or bridge, the minute they've committed to the gravity, there's the moment of regret, and it goes deep.

I knew exactly what that feeling was now, that deep-blue tethering to the world and life and your people when you think, *Oh, shit; what did I just do? How am I going to fix it?* And I had the chance to fix it.

Many people don't get that chance.

I rested in Sarah's house for a day or two, as I recovered. I was finally able to sleep, and I curled up with Jack County, who found me asleep on Sarah's bed and put his paw on my hand and kept me company as I lay there weeping, feeling awful, feeling like I had soiled twenty years of independence, my reinvention of self, of work, and feeling like this event had indeed killed both Steph and me, and I didn't have enough emotional capital to pull out of this stall.

I was able to reassure my family that it was a one-time thing, that I had just lost control and was, more than anything, really, asking for help, but couldn't do it somehow. Marge asked if she could fly out to sit with me and I said, "No; no, please; I'm all right. Will be all right. Please don't worry: I really learned my lesson here," and then I did as best as I could to keep this secret from Steph's parents, keep my weakness hidden from my compatriotic enemies.

Sarah, from her point of view, felt the same, watched me with clinical fascination as I finally slept with the dog's paw in my hand.

CHAPTER 29

Easy Money

There was no time to recover.

My boss finally mustered the courage in the days following to let me know he couldn't budget my salary in the coming year after the company went public and the new investors were unconvinced they needed someone who rated at my pay grade doing my job; they could hire a recent college graduate with minimal literacy.

"This wasn't a performance-based decision," he kept repeating, while I had images of his family curling up in a house fire.

Everyone fucks you when you're down.

I managed to get to the nursing home wearing a long-sleeved sweater, checked in, and tried to talk about the other night, but when I brought it up, Steph's mother pretended it had never happened and changed the subject, walked out of the room. Avoidance behavior; how Lutheran. Not even the chance for discussion. I suppose that's too Catholic.

They had taken to singing to Steph during the afternoon, after Harold had found Steph's acoustic guitar at her house and decided it would help pass the time. They'd leap up and sing like the former flower children they were, making me incredibly uncomfortable, especially when they'd launch into Bob Dylan's "Don't Think Twice, It's All Right," which was a knife in my heart, and I would wonder if they were that short on songs they knew or if they were simply that insensitive.

One day, Harold asked me to help him move into the rental property Steph was still paying for because her landlord was a massive prick, he had insisted they continue paying rent or he'd move her stuff out, so

I drove him out there. It was about a two-hour bus ride to the nursing home, but Harold was determined to move in there, he said, so I said, "Fine; I can help," still wearing my long-sleeved sweatshirts and hoodies.

We moved Steph's bed up from the basement room she preferred into the top part of the rental, which she usually reserved for fly-by-night Craigslist roommates, who were always awful or meth addicts, and we secured the lower portion of the house. I went through, looking to preserve some of Steph's dignity by collecting her journals and "secret stashes," and found that the rats we had been warring against had moved in during all this time of nonoccupancy and had taken to eating her more intimate toys and oils, and I quietly gathered up all these items and threw them out, so her parents didn't have to face their daughter's personal humanity.

When we were finished moving the bed and some of the other furniture and then winterizing the bottom half of the house, Harold asked to speak to me. Steph's mother immediately ran out of the room.

"Sure thing," I said. He told me he'd been going through Steph's credit card statements, especially the trip we had taken east when Harold had been in the hospital, and both he and her mother felt that I owed Steph $750 for the trip.

It's how men deal with crisis, I've come to find out, doing things pecuniary and vehicular. They'll review bills, get things in order, and park your car, maybe wash it. Anything to avoid feelings, or talking about feelings.

"What?" I said, uncertain I'd heard correctly.

"She paid for all the hotels and flights and rental cars," he said. "It's right here," and he produced the statement.

"I gave her cash. I paid for my ticket and all meals—that was our agreement, Harold. This is just . . . wow; look, if you need money, I can see what I can manage, but I just lost my job, and now you're asking for this? This is unbelievable. I don't owe her any money."

"Then why did she pay for the tickets?"

"I gave her the cash for my plane ticket," I said. "In fact, while you were laid up in the hospital, I saw Steph give most of that money to your wife because she didn't know how to use the ATM. Believe me, something like that stays with you. This is just fucked up, Harold," I said, as I produced my checkbook, mostly to see how far he'd go before he'd stop me, and then wrote him a check for the money, and sonofabitch if he didn't just reach over and take it, with no shred of embarrassment or dignity.

I'd been "jacked," like "real rappers."

———

I had a couple thousand saved up, minus the money that Steph's parents had just stolen from me, but I knew I had to find work, and soon. I had one final pay cycle coming from my former job, and Alfred had asked me to return all the company equipment—the laptop, the archives, the external drive, that sort of stuff—so I thought driving the four hours to eastern Washington was in order, though I knew I had to get back and get busy, posthaste.

I was forty years old and in a young person's industry that was becoming less and less "specialized," and I was competing against recent college grads who had none of my background or competency, but who would take a position at "labor surplus" salaries. And I hadn't taken my opportunity to shift my skill set like I had been planning because of all the calamity of the last five months.

It was the darkest, worst period of my life: unemployed, no health insurance, nearing indigence, recently hospitalized, in near isolation and walking around in a haunted, spiritually desiccated husk. I thought maybe my great West Coast experiment was over and I'd have to move back to Texas, and the idea frightened me more than being homeless here, in Seattle.

There was this artist some years back, whose memory haunted me for reasons that are difficult to explain. He'd been a member of an arts collective here in Seattle, and he was a bright, smart guy, and one day on some nationally recognized holiday for labor unions, he and some others had arranged to attach a huge cardboard ball and chain to the Hammering Man, the big silhouette on the Seattle waterfront. It was brilliant, very clever. The following year, he'd driven an old pickup truck to the city retail center and parked it, flattened the tires, then walked away.

The whole city shut down that afternoon, thinking it was a bomb threat.

He owned up to it, said it was a part of their art piece, but the courts weren't lenient and jailed him for a few months. He was too smart, too soft a guy to endure that, and when he came out, his nerves were shot, his spirit broken, and he could no longer support himself, went home to Michigan.

Inside a year, he stepped in front of a freight train, though his parents cling to the idea it was an accident.

I knew better, and I knew that's where I would be headed if I had to move back home. That's what frightened me the most. *L'appel du vide.*

One early evening at Sarah's house, I was recounting my fears while she listened and told me hers.

It was dark out, and she decided to take the dog horde down to the park for their evening pee: Betty Brown, Jack County, Genevieve, and I think I had Cleo for the weekend. The dogs were delighted to be out, and we walked down the street that ran parallel to Sarah's house, the leg of the triangle that pointed directly to the Christian college campus at the vertex. Dogs trotted and sniffed all around us, and then in front of Jonathan Raban's house, her neighbor a couple doors to her north, and after a bit of quiet, apropos of nothing, Sarah said, "You know what's going to get you out of this, don't you?"

If she had a magic bullet, I was ready for it, because I certainly had no idea what was going to bring up the sunrise on this longest night of my life.

"Nope," I said, as I *tch-tch*ed for Jack County, who was wandering behind us now, lifting his long, silky Tom Selleck–looking leg on a shrub. A modest dog, he'd then tuck his tail to hide his pongy bits.

"If you have any ideas, now's the time," I said.

"You're going to have to write your way out of this," she said, in that distancing, clinical way she has, and then wandered off with the dogs to allow me to think this one through.

My immediate response was, "Pfft. Do you KNOW how difficult it is to get ANY sort of attention in publishing on the West Coast? In Seattle, of all places? And then make enough to live off of?" Seattle, I figured out a bit too late, was not an easy place to launch a literary career. It's where you settle after you've proven yourself in real cities, like Los Angeles or New York or Chicago.

Before all this happened, I would often strut around like a rooster in her kitchen, saying how I wouldn't waste my time with regional workshops and writers' groups or attempt to make a presence known or felt with the local alternative presses and the subsidized "writer's support network" and that sort of shit—*NO!* I told her, "*Fuck that amateur shit!* I'm going big first. I'm going to fail UP, not DOWN! Or wait . . . is it the other way around?"

And Sarah would look at me like, "Oh, honey, you're so interesting to watch in the safety of your unpublished bravado."

If Sarah felt that this was my only lifeline out of this miasma, then I was in trouble, because I knew the odds against and the impossibility of publishing.

My heart, already sunk, disappeared altogether, hearing this.

"I want you," she said, continuing her hip-swaying saunter down the dark street, "to go home, clean up your five or six best chapters that illustrate your material, your themes, your writing style, and your wit, and print them out for me."

"All right," I responded. "I'll have them, tickety-boo." I couldn't argue. I didn't have enough energy to pose an argument.

"When you do," she said, "give me five copies and I will send your samples in an interoffice memo to Mary Karr, buy a bottle of something dark and red for Jonathan Raban here, and send another copy to the chair of the English department at Seattle U." Mary Karr was in the Jesuit system, Sarah said to me, and would receive her mail. (This actually wasn't correct, we found out later. She's at Syracuse, which is not even Catholic. Sarah blames her mistake on red wine and Buspar.)

As a fellow Texan, and memoirist, I had a deep fondness for Mary Karr. But it was the night that I lay in Sarah's bed, deep one early morning, suffering from a particularly bad spell of anxiety, when Sarah woke up, reached over, and turned on a lamp and then began reading to me from *The Liar's Club*, as I lay on my side and shivered, and she read for hours while Mary Karr and her own family pulled me out of my stall, just for a second, and I was, will be, forever grateful for that moment. So when Sarah said she could get my stuff in front of her, I was hopeful: Mary would understand.

"Hunh," I said. "You have a deal."

———❦———

In the meantime, though, I had a plan to find work.

I couldn't, at all, find the fight in me to compete for a job in my market as a graphic designer. So I resorted to something an old friend once told me, about a secret means to make a stable income that wasn't too competitive: the boutique pizza delivery network.

My old friend, John, who had been my manager at Pagliacci Pizza here in Seattle back when I was nineteen, had since stayed with the company but had become a satellite delivery station manager, then realized he could make much more just delivering the pizza, instead of being a wage earner.

"I made nearly $50,000 last year," he had said to me, some years back.

Aha, I thought. *I know the pizza circuit; I'll keep that particular bit of knowledge in my back pocket if ever I need it, methinks.*

Well, this was it, I decided. That's what I'd do to make it through until my mind righted itself and I could figure out my next move.

———❦———

For now, though, I had to drive out east and deliver the company laptop and peripherals, make a trip of it.

Steph was still in the nursing home, and it had taken a lot for me to see her parents again after feeling robbed like that, but after a few days, I stiffened my lip and returned to our rhythms, though I didn't feel quite as generous as before. Steph's mother had talked the nursing home manager into springing for an enclosed bed to keep Steph from falling again, and when I saw her after, she was now trying to speak, was now speaking in "word salad," where she'd string a lot of nonsense words together, but with real intention behind them. It had been a surge forward in her recovery.

What word she did say, and clearly, was "Daddy!" whenever she saw her father, or me. It was both entirely warming and creepy. One afternoon, after her mother had to fly back east to be fitted for her new prosthetic, Harold and I were alone in the nursing home with Steph, trying to feed her lunch. She had an uncanny resemblance to an itchy toddler in church, speaking in that husky, whispered word salad and refusing to eat. Harold handed her a chocolate-flavored Ensure with a straw, and she had a look flash across her face, decided to blow through the straw instead of sucking, and the Ensure blew up like a liquid hand grenade for the elderly. We were all covered in chocolate, the lunch ruined, and for a moment, Steph looked at the mess she had made and started smiling big. I thought, *Yup; she's still there.*

Prior to the check fiasco, I had noticed that she'd been trying to focus on people in the room and had this really unsettling habit of closing one eye to get anything into focus, and then I remembered how bad her vision was before the accident, so one day I drove out to her house up north and found her spare glasses.

I brought them in that afternoon, thinking they were going to make all the difference in the world with her recovery (you tell yourself things like this, that there are these "miracle moments"), but they only made us wonder, "What happened to her contacts?"

We asked around and there were no records anywhere of her contacts being removed, so they called an optometrist who gave her an exam, and the hospital finally realized that her contacts had rolled onto the back of her eyeballs and had been festering there for the last three months. They were removed before they could cause any serious damage, but we were all horrified and unsettled at how things that go overlooked can suddenly come around and bite you in the ass, like, say, not asking for a receipt when you pay someone cash for a plane ticket to fly across the country and help her family.

CHAPTER 30

Queen of the Savages

There was a pall in the air during those final months of agonal respiration for Kinesis, the karate school, as we had known it, oddly paralleling my situation with Stephanie in the ICU. Or perhaps that's my solipsism once again, my memory restructuring the external world to fit my internal model, as memoir tends to do. But there was no denying that the glow and charm that I had found when I returned to the karate school of old was in some sort of danger of blighting itself out, and that corresponded entirely with Brenda's participation as the lead black belt, which had become conflicted and erratic, due to personal issues with some of the senior students and the owner of the business, the head of the school, who was now in San Francisco, attempting to penetrate the market there with a new chapter of the school.

At times it was more of a pong than a pall, but it was something that was circulating fast, like a bacterial infection, and building momentum as every elemental personality that consolidated the dynamic core of the school went through some independent personal drama that forced him or her further and further from the fission that kept all of us in love and sweating and participating with the program. And that's what makes a karate school, I've realized: the people participating. It's the personal expression, the unfolding of your real self in a safe re-creation of crisis, exposing your vulnerability and weakness, then feeling a sense of power as you fight your way through it, sometimes with fists and kicks, sometimes with defeat and tears, but you get through it, get off the mat, and shake the gloved hand of the person who just put you there, and you thank them, earnestly, even the stupid fuckers you don't like.

Personally, I couldn't get it together to exercise because I hated going into my head, and exercising, even in a group environment, would put me deep into brain territory. It felt like a maggoty cabbage in there, something lugged about in Patricia Highsmith's legendary handbag. And it's bitter irony that exercise is sometimes the only thing that can help your mental health, but when you're in the grips of something deep and dark, exercise is the last thing you want to do.

The karate school had long been losing its magnetism, even before Steph's accident. Divisions and loyalties were splintering the school and tearing it at its threadbare seams, a karate suit that had already seen more than a few years' blushing long before I returned. Things came to an outright collision when Brenda Brown, as head black belt, rumbled a potential child predator at the school.

He was a new member, some slender slip of a fellow from northern Texas named Dylan who was attending a *shi-shi* arts college nearby.

He was pretty and twinkish, had studied or practiced extreme yoga or some such, pansexual, and didn't mind flirting with both men and women; he was one of these people who slipped, unduly exhibitionist, through their lives banking on their looks and winning, mostly because of the idiots who fall for their cheap coin. Personally, I'm immune to their bewitchery because nothing turns my stomach more than wholesale, indiscriminate flirting as a means of navigating the world. Also, I didn't overlap with this guy so much because he started at the school after I'd been processing out, losing my interest.

He'd been immediately taken in by one of the older students who followed him around like a lovesick orphan, fell immediately and comprehensively under Dylan's spell, and Dylan started showing a bit too much interest in one of the younger students from the kids' classes. It seemed innocent enough at a cursory glance, but Brenda had noticed something, had a tingle of intuition that something wasn't on the level, maybe heard someone say something who hadn't quite put it together.

Brenda approached the kid's mother, who immediately confiscated the kid's cell phone, then managed to get the full history of erased text messages, which clearly crossed the lines of acceptability and law. Dylan had been grooming this kid, who had grown up in the karate program and had Brenda as a friend, right in her school. It was like the moron had a death wish.

It was an issue, and it really chafed Brenda's sense of right and wrong, and her idea of the safety of this school. There was enough to charge Dylan through the Seattle Police Department, but the kid's mother decided she didn't want to put the child through it. Brenda came up with another solution.

A few days later, on sparring Saturday, Dylan found himself, as a yellow belt, on Brenda's mat.

It was a full class, and a lot of frightened neophytes were present when Brenda bowed opposite Dylan, who couldn't possibly understand what he was in for.

I think I've mentioned before the level of ring generalship that Brenda had when she sparred someone; she was able to control your posture and position on the mat by moving herself, aiming herself at you. I'd never met anyone so willing to drop her guard and leave her head unprotected in order to draw you in, get you close so she could hit you. She was fearless this way. And she never looked at you in the eye, or in the face, just at a point directly above your sternum where she could watch all movement, intended or otherwise, emanating from that one spot on your body. You became a pattern of targets and mass to her, watching and waiting for your body to reassemble itself at a point she would be targeting, and before you knew it she would be there. It was magical to watch her, even better to match sparring wits with her.

But Dylan would never reach such a degree where he would be able to appreciate the elegance of the assassin bowing him in that Saturday.

She started slow, warming him up and circling him as a soft target, but then she started slapping him, hard, then harder still, across the face, across the head in three-shot combinations that ended each time with Brenda pulping the meat in his thighs with her big toe. She wore these battered, malleable Jeet Kune Do gloves that kept her fingers separated, allowed her to grab or grapple with an open hand, then close her fist for a solid punch, and she kept Dylan confused, battered with each hit going through his guard. She kept the abuse within the corresponding rules of high-belt/low-belt engagement, but she was hurting him, and making him hurt.

Each time she'd give him a slap, she'd talk to him, whisper in his ear: "Do you feel outmatched?"

Then she'd slap him with cupped hands over the ears before he could answer, until he finally whimpered, and loudly, "*Yes!*"

She would also give him the opportunity to stop, bow out, but the concussion and impact of her hits had him flustered, muddled, confused, and perhaps even his sublimated gender politics kept him from bowing out, from stopping. He had the power to back out; all he had to do was agree, but he didn't, and she kept hitting him, harder every time.

He was in tears, at the end, after she'd dug the ball of her foot into his liver and kidneys through his slender little ribs repeatedly and mercilessly, and she called the round, then stepped up to him and said, "That's how children feel when adults prey on them. These kids here are as dear to me as my own children. You're done here. You're never to come back here, and if you contact that kid again, I will hunt you down. Now grab your shit and go."

He didn't even bother changing, just ran out of the front doors barefoot and down the steps into the cold Seattle night, leaving the whole room thunderstruck, except for Brenda and the kid's mother, who looked at Brenda and nodded, satisfied that this had been justice.

The other students, already squeamish and frightened of the sparring classes, looked at each other in terror, wondering if they would have to go through the same thing, rattled and addled at what they'd just seen, sensing also that something important had just happened.

It had: They had witnessed the first convulsions of the dying magic in the karate school, the first bits of light leaving the school with Brenda making the choice to spank that guy, on her mat, on the safe place where he was grooming one of the favorite child students, and it launched a lot of dithering discussion, exposed ugliness and partisan politics, brought out longstanding divisions and dramas that had, up until that point, lacked the necessary oxygen for conflagration, a fire that would take Brenda's beloved haven away from her, send her spiraling into a world that would consume the best parts of her for years to come.

De profundis.

CHAPTER 31

Northern Exposure

I thought the drive east would do me good.

In Texas, getting on the road and putting some miles under you is as therapeutic as life gets some days, makes you feel like you've done something right, can be regarded as self-care.

I set out that morning across the Cascade Mountains pass, into the eastern part of the state, and told Steph's parents I'd be gone for a day or two.

I asked Sarah to meet me in Roslyn, Washington, on my way back, for an overnight stay, and she had agreed.

The iPod was loaded with Texas outlaw traveling music, and I stretched the legs on my little Jetta as fast as they could go as I drove across the mountains and into the desert landscape of Washington State, past the vineyards of Yakima and the military installation that separates east from west, in this state. But instead of the music, I listened instead to podcasts and informational programs; I couldn't listen to music, somehow.

The only song I could listen to at the time was called "What Were the Chances?" and it's the most gentle, heartbreaking little song about abandonment, alcoholism, and affairs. Both Sarah and I would listen to the lines and think of one another, and we'd just bawl, for one another, for ourselves, for what was happening in both our lives, clutch one another like rosaries.

When I arrived at the media offices unexpectedly, I handed the equipment to the kid who had replaced me and with minimal fuss left inside of five minutes, deciding it was better to just slip out and not interact with anyone I knew. I climbed back in my car and headed out once more, after refueling.

I traveled back west to Roslyn, where I would meet Sarah in a few hours, as we had agreed, and I drove at top speed, feeling like I was doing better for the first time in a long, long spell, like there might be some hope at the end of this, just because I was driving.

During the last few weeks, I'd had another line from a song locked in my head and it had been driving me crazy. It was a line from a David Bowie song, and it repeated itself in my head at hyperspeed, at normal speed, and then super slowly, all at the same time, and it was tearing my mind apart from within, like a chant or a mantra: *"Ashes to ashes, funk to funky. We know Major Tom's a junkie . . ."* and I was simply incapable of turning it off.

The drive seemed to help, had been meditative and healthy, and now I was turning off the highway and into the little former logging town that had served as the backdrop for some of *Northern Exposure*'s exterior filming.

It was also the only trip Dan and I had ever taken when he lived here, and so I thought maybe there was something there, something yet to discover to help get me through this darkest period. I was in a spiritual search for something, and I needed some time alone with Sarah.

We made plans to meet at the Brick Tavern, also a *Northern Exposure* icon.

I asked her to pretend we didn't know each other and I'd pretend to pick her up, and she laughed, said, "Fine; you're feeling frisky, but sure, we can do that."

I waited for her and then became nervous, so I stepped outside to see if she was coming and suddenly, down the street, there she was, sauntering in a big-hipped swinging sort of way with a look of devilishness on her face as she walked by me and stepped into the Brick.

I blushed and giggled and followed her in.

All eyes were on her as she sat at the bar, a single, incredibly attractive woman sitting alone in a desolate mountain town. Yeah, it was going to draw attention.

I gave it a second and then sat next to her, and while she tried to keep in character, I could not and broke and started to talk to her like we normally did, when this tiny little Mexican *charro* with a huge belt buckle walked up to us, ignored me, introduced himself to Sarah, and asked for her telephone number.

I burst out laughing, which was probably not the best response, and explained that the lady was with me. I bought him a beer, and, a bit wounded, he took it and wandered off as Sarah and I went back to the place I'd rented, which had originally been the town brothel.

Perfect, I thought, *considering what we're about to do.*

CHAPTER 32

Roslyn

Some hours later, we woke up, cold and thin.
Or I did. I woke her up.
Nudged her to a place, and she came awake again.
"I have to tell you this," I said.
"What?" she asked.
"It's different, between us, the hurt, the damage," I said.
"I know you have yours, and I have mine," she said.
"Yeah," I said. "But mine, I mean . . . I don't know what I want to say."

She was lying there, just extraordinarily beautiful, in the dark. . . .
She was naked, with these lines back and forth, a geometry of beauty.
She was angry at me.
We fucked again, hostile, like fists swinging wide,
and it was almost morning,
we just did that.
"I fucking love you," I told her.
"Shut the fuck up," she said. "I know you think you do."
"But I do," I insisted. "I think you're the love of my life."
I can't explain it, otherwise.
She said, "I can't be with you. We can't be together."
I said, "We can make it if we don't look down."
Just don't look down.
She turned over and cried.

CHAPTER 33

Good-bye, Jack County

We spent the next day playing like off-season tourists, driving a mountain road and visiting spots she knew from skiing. The day was brilliant blue, the sky a magnificent Pantone 292, and logging trucks were churning past on their usual workday and it felt the lightest, brightest sort of way that I had not experienced in an incredibly long time. Sarah was driving, and I was entertaining her, and I had a moment of realization that this was the complete opposite of what I felt back when I was with Stephanie and she was driving these same mountain roads.

Sarah stopped by a large working ranch, pulled over to the side of the road, and walked over to a wire fence when a mangy, old, broken-down horse came over to see if she would feed it. I experienced a moment of anxiety—everything, at this point, gave me anxiety, even broken-down horses—and I yelled to her to come back, get inside the car.

"There's a bear hole!" I yelled and pointed, and she looked back at me in befuddlement.

"Right there, next to you! A bear hole!" and she saw I was pointing at a culvert, under the roadway. I didn't know what it was, but it could have been a bear hole, and that's sort of how my mind worked at the time. I saw bear holes.

—————

We made it back to the brothel/hotel, and after dinner, we settled in for the evening and I drank a couple of Bombay Sapphire airplane bottles while I sat her down and played a song for her, hoping she would get it.

"It's about where I'm from," I said to her, as she leaned back in the bed, and I explained, line by line, how this song was awakening something in me.

It was a song about cowboys and border bandits. I explained, "See, he's at his end, when the song opens, and he's having a moment of existential crisis, as much as a borderland bank robber can have, and he tries prayer when he's backed into a corner with just four bullets left."

"Uh hunh," said Sarah, looking at me like she wasn't sure whether to giggle or encourage me.

"No, seriously," I continued, "and he suddenly realizes the absurdity in hoping that things will change for him from an external source, and he instead decides to count on his own moxie. It's Texas, baby; no one's going to do it for you, you have to do it yourself, no matter how the odds are stacked against you. It's my people, from the border. This is who I am," I said to her, weakly, mostly because I was trying to convince myself, too.

"Come back to bed and keep me warm," she said, and I did.

She didn't try to tell me that every culture everywhere has a mythology of resilience, or that Texas in particular glamorized that "outlaw country" image with Willie Nelson and his contemporaries as an entirely commercial fabrication to sell country records in the '70s. She knew I needed to cling to something right now, besides her, so she let me cling to this, this idea of "my people," from the border, being survivors, because I needed to survive this.

There was no other choice.

—◆—

Later that night, I received a call from Steph's mother, asking if I'd be back in town later the next day to take Steph to an appointment she had at a specialist. "Oh, she's had a remarkable couple of days," she told me. "She's talking and making sense now; it's amazing. She's even getting around on a walker."

This was surprising; when I left, she had still been in that covered bed and appeared to be cognizant, but you could never be certain.

I had allowed the call to go to voice mail while I steeled myself to speak to Steph's mother, and I excused myself from Sarah so I could have some privacy, but she overheard everything. She heard the switch in my voice, baleful and subservient.

When I walked back into the bedroom, Sarah was shaking, putting her clothes back on.

"What's wrong?" I asked.

"I feel dirty," she said. "I feel like we're having an affair."

"No, it's not . . . I'm not . . . I'm sorry; I don't know what I'm doing. But I can't just leave her like that. They've been shitty and mean to me, but I can't just leave her," I said.

We crawled back into bed, but the chemistry died out for that night, and we just talked in low voices until the morning.

———

The next morning, I was feeling like things might be changing when my car gave out on the way into Seattle. Just like that, my temperature gauge started spiking, and my car began smoking and spewing shit out from under the hood.

One more level descended.

De profundis.

I had just made it over the pass and was entering some unknown town on the outskirts of Seattle when the car gave up on me. Steph's mother was expecting me in an hour, and I summoned all the resolve I had and phoned her, and when I said my car had broken down on the highway—this little Jetta that had been very, very good to them for the last five months—she let loose a string of vitriol and anger directed at me and my car and then hung up, for emphasis.

I sat there, in my car, and shook, until I realized I was outside some roadside mechanic and managed to get the guy to look at my car and give me a quote on the thermostat, which was a month's rent. I called Sarah, who came and picked me up an hour later. I was quiet and spent as she took me back to her house and I sat on her couch with Jack County, who put his head on my lap as I cried into a glass of something very red, almost laughing as I saw a tear roll down my cheek and into the goblet of wine, thinking, *I bet the French have done this,* and I felt entirely defeated, and I tried tried tried to give up. Let go.

Her phone calls started that day, I remember.

It was like getting phone calls from the dead.

My iPhone lit up with Steph's ringtone, and I was taken aback at first, confused. Then I answered it and heard something that sounded like Steph's voice, except in a forced whisper; remember, her larynx had been crushed. But there was something else I couldn't immediately place.

"Hello, June, I love you. How are you?"

What?

"Hello, June, I love you, it's Steph. I'm back. I love you. Thank you for taking care of me and my parents."

I thought, *Oh, dear fucking God, no; not this.*

"Steph? Is this you?"

"Hi, June, I love you. Yes, it's me. You were supposed to take me to the specialist but it's been rescheduled for tomorrow. Can you come and see me?"

"I . . . I'm sorry, I can't," I said. Then it hit me, what I was hearing: She was speaking with a British accent.

"Why not? I love you," she said. "Please come. I love you."

I had to think about it, but I finally said, "Because if I'm in the same room as your mother, I'm liable to take out her other eye," probably because I was a bit drunk, but also because it was funny. The thing is, you probably shouldn't joke with someone freshly out of a coma.

"Oh, all right," she said, then followed it with, "I love you. Come see me tomorrow," and she hung up.

I was knocked on my heels, couldn't even explain this to anyone as I tried to take in what had just happened. About an hour later, my phone rang again and it was a number I didn't recognize, so I let it go to voice mail.

When I played the message, it was the Seattle Police Department, some desk sergeant asking for me, wondering about some threats I may have made to an ex-girlfriend and her family, and I started laughing and crying and I swear my face was exactly that sad Pagliacci clown, as I sat in

Sarah's bedroom and giggled and cried and giggled some more as Sarah came in and thought I'd really lost it this time.

———〜—

A few days later, I picked up my car and managed to get hired on by a small boutique pizza restaurant near my neighborhood as a delivery guy. No shit. I sublimated every feeling of indignation and shame and decided that this was the low, tough gear that I'd inherited from my Gramma, that this was what I needed to do in order to rebuild and recover, in the absence of health care and mental health professionals. I would have to work a shit job to process through my anguish and recovery. It somehow made sense to me.

Besides, finding addresses, folding boxes, and mopping was about all my mental bandwidth was capable of enduring, so I worked with three or four kids in their early twenties and I became the far-out old man who was fresh out of work, doing what he had to do, talking to these college kids younger than my little brother like I was Dennis Hopper, saying, "Yeah, man; I remember seeing Nirvana at the Vogue before they broke big."

I'd encountered people like this before, in my own travels and odd jobs, older guys who took on these shit low-wage jobs while they were waiting for things to turn around. There was a dignity to it, I felt, and now it was my turn.

So I did it. I wore their T-shirts. I took my marching orders from kids younger than Derek, and I was kind and quiet and did everything I could to keep my dignity intact.

But, oh, dear God, did I hate it. Actually, that's not true. As a pizza delivery guy, you sort of slip by and through and no one really pays much mind to you once they diagnose you as "pizza delivery guy." It's not like New York, where there's been a rash of break-ins and assaults, all done by opportunistic pizza guys. I can't answer to that. Here, in Seattle, these kids were just stoned all the time and somehow still managed to deliver their pizza products, usually intact.

My manager was a kind woman, and I managed to make friends with the kids and didn't come off as too weird, though I did find it quite difficult to talk small and keep conversations from getting heavy. I just don't own that particular grace.

For instance, when one of the younger drivers said she was taking a design course and was complaining about having to learn typography, I said, "Oh, you couldn't be further from the truth. Typography is fascinating, the semiotics and signifiers, down to the relationships between the characters—it's incredible. Do you know the history of the ampersand? It was actually supposed to be the twenty-seventh letter, though it's the French or Latin word *et*, if you look at it. And the name: It's a corruption of the phrase, 'And, per se, and.' Get it? 'Ampersand?' It's really quite smart," and when I was done talking, I noticed everyone in the room was looking at me strangely, probably because they were stoned, so I stopped.

Stuff like that.

And it really wasn't so bad for the first month, because all I did was listen to audio books and drive around feeling pathetic, delivering pizza besotted with tears and feeling like the act of working was in itself, working, or rehabilitative. I was starting again, and so I didn't put pressure on it. I just did it. There wasn't anything else to do, so I just did as I was told.

At night, I'd go over to Sarah's when I could.

Eventually, I did as she had previously asked and polished up six of my best chapters, wrote a short introductory letter, and presented her with the printed versions she had requested.

After I gave her what she'd asked for, I sat around thinking, *Well, maybe I should send out some of my own, since it is, after all, a numbers game, when you don't know what you're doing,* and in my bookshelf, I found my old directory of literary journals that I had used when I first started sending things out for potential publishing and had little understanding of the codes or language used. I'd basically been sending my stuff to everyone listed, whether they published nonfiction, science fiction, or poetry, and hadn't realized my error until I was well into the E section.

So I began to refine my attempts, especially since postage was now quite dear.

Every pay period I'd put aside twenty dollars or so for postage stamps, and I'd make a studied list of potential journals and began sending chapters out that way. I had divorced myself from any hope of publishing at this point and was doing this mostly out of an autonomic impulse. I just kept putting things in the mail and not thinking about them. Trudge, trudge, feet on the road, et cetera.

Meanwhile, I reported for duty as a driver, as needed, at my little pizza place, and I watched the kids mingle and diagnosed them from my perch, at forty years old. ("Oh, honey; he doesn't know he's gay yet. Wow, that chick has issues. Jesus, that guy has some serious anger problems, from his mommy. Watch how he drinks.") It was interesting to see all this from the clinical distance that comes with age and experience, and I wondered if when I was that age, my own pathologies and anxieties had been so clearly visible and surfaced when I worked in a similar situation, and why the fuck didn't anyone tell me? Like I was about to do, with these kids.

Kidding.

No, actually, besides the driving and weeping bit, because I spent so much time alone in a car, I actually didn't mind the pizza stuff so much, until one Sunday afternoon I received an order to deliver a pizza to an address that I knew very well. Ten years ago, they had been my archenemies. Back when I lived with someone else, these were our next-door neighbors.

I had been living with someone in a house that shared a driveway, an easement. Being Seattle, this meant that neither household used it. You used it to unload your groceries or lawn-care products, but as soon as you were done, you backed out of it and cleared the way. You certainly didn't park there or use it for anything else.

When that original family moved, the house was purchased by a younger couple from Oklahoma who had purloined their senile grandmother's retirement money—ostensibly, to be used for a retirement home—and used it to buy property in Seattle. They'd turn the garage into a mother-in-law apartment and she would live there until she died, they thought. Happy, happy. But building mother-in-law units in the city was illegal, and the garage was on the property line. They were ingratiating and loud, and had a young kid named Sam, and they took over the easement and the mornings with noise, which was an issue since both my girlfriend and I worked nights.

It became horrible, angry, and uncomfortable. We eventually moved, and then split up, but of course the memories remained.

And now I was delivering a pizza to that address.

And I knew that they still lived there because that kid, Sam, as it turned out, had been my boss, at the pizza place, all along.

And I had to deliver a pizza there.

De profundis.

———

I stood in the parking lot that Sunday morning just flooded with rage, cortisol, and anxiety.

I know you're there, God, and you're doing this to me.

I'm doing what I fucking can, God, and you keep piling this SHIT onto me, you motherfucker.

If you were here, God, I would kick you in the dick, you fucking bastard.

———

I stood there and fumed, then packed up the pizzas in my car and made the delivery. This was my job right now. I would do it.

It turned out that I was off by a number and was instead delivering a pizza to the house I had lived in before, and a man with one arm answered the door, and he didn't know why I was sweating the way that I was. I thanked him for the four-dollar tip and nearly had my own arm removed by his huge German shepherd, but I was grateful, then sat in my car and apologized to God, said maybe, *I hope you can understand.*

We pals again, God?

No?

Well, fuck you, then, God.

———

I couldn't even explain that one to Sarah. It just went too deep, too far back, and I continued with what I was doing until I was going to do something else. I found out that my old friend, John, may have been embellishing his earnings back when I spoke to him about pizza delivery being something unexpectedly lucrative, and I was now burning through my savings rather quickly, as I perspired through that summer in a kitchen, prepping salads and folding boxes and talking to children about their pot use and making very little money in return.

Throughout this, Sarah's own situation was deteriorating, as her school had been downsized and she was teaching only part-time now, her divorce dragging on and taking a huge emotional toll. She had taken to watching every penny that she had, knew there were some real adjustments to her lifestyle headed her way, and was preparing as much as she could for the blow. She had even started going to the food bank, twice a week, to save on groceries. She did this without fuss, without talking about it, feeling that the hundred dollars she would save on groceries could go to Genevieve's bills at the veterinarian. Vivie was getting older, needed lots of care, and it was expensive. When she told me this, admitted to it like it was something shameful, I was in awe of her resolve, her ability to suffer in silence, and wished, wished that I had even a shred of it; it made me love her even more.

That's about as much as I'm comfortable saying, as I want to shield her privacy, but she was enduring some hard moments, tough times, as she watched everything she had built dry up and flake away in sections, and we had only one another to cling to at this point, in the evenings. Then we'd wake up in the morning and face our deteriorations again, daily.

And Brenda Brown had also started falling victim to her own personal demons and had quit the karate school in a miasma of drama after the incident with Dylan, forcing the students to choose between studying with her or staying with the school, and since karate is very much a vehicle of personal charisma, lots of people left when Brenda did, for their own reasons, and the sparkle seemed to go out of both the school and Brenda.

Her health began deteriorating, and she became erratic, weird, and potentially harmful to herself and others.

It didn't help that Bill Brown had to be put down, and she hadn't been prepared for that, would never have been prepared to let go of her own dogs, but it had been painful to watch this poor dog fall apart from age like he did, and so our friend from the school, the veterinarian who was taking care of Cleo, too, was able to put Bill down, and Brenda fell apart further.

Then Jack County was diagnosed with leukemia, and this just sent Brenda into a freefall, and it was then decided she had to move back home to Indiana.

This destroyed me, too, as Jack County was my favorite dog at this time, as bonded as we were, and both Sarah and I held each other and cried the day he had to be put down.

We had taken him out for a walk the day before, and he limped and moved gingerly because his hips and joints were killing him, and we walked him for a bit in the most scenic part of Queen Anne, my neighborhood, this lovely saunter at the very top of the hill that's a part of historical Seattle called "the Crown Walk," which I'd never realized was there, after all this time. I admitted to her just how frightened I really was, how terrifying these last months since I lost my job had been as we walked Jack County, and Sarah said, "Does it mean anything to you that what you're experiencing is a part of a historical moment?" I think she meant the financial crisis from a few years back, and I thought of it as we walked with a lumbering Jack, and thought, *Not at all*. I couldn't see past my personal penumbra.

At the end of the walk, we watched Jack County come alive for the last time as he flirted with a female labradoodle, and you could, for a moment, see the spark come back in his eye and the spring come back in his step. We laughed at Old Jack County, but then when the girl dog left, his spark vanished and was gone, and Jack was no more, ever again.

Sarah's house was empty, and only the two of us remained some nights, clutching one another and trying to stay above water.

CHAPTER 34

The Low Gear

Nasir found me at the pizza place when he needed someone to help with his new enterprise. It had to be some sort of tax shelter, but the way he pitched it to me was that he and a friend from his mosque were opening a new print shop in a town north of Seattle, and he needed me to run it, as a manager.

Nasir had been my printer when I was a freelancer, and I'd never have met him if I hadn't moved to that shit part of town with Steph. He certainly stuck out, in post-9/11 America and Seattle, because you didn't see many people in town who proudly dressed in traditional halal Islamic garb, wore the beard and the beanie cap. He was my age, spoke unaccented English, and seemed earnest in his proposal, saying I could do with something back in my regular vocation.

"What are you doing here?" he asked me one afternoon at the pizza place, made it sound like it was a spiritual question.

I was reminded of a movie I'd seen some years previous, some remake of a Victorian novel called *The Four Feathers*, and I remembered a particular scene where the hero is bereft, left out to die, and a wandering warrior finds him, confers with his conscience, then decides to save our hero.

Asked later why he'd reached this choice, the warrior responds, "God put you in my way."

I studied Nasir and wondered, briefly, if God had put him in my way, or me in his, but either way, I took his offer.

Besides everything else, I had grown weary of searching for house numbers while delivering pizzas in the impenetrable Seattle night. Bastards don't make any sense.

So I accepted.

The drive north and south every day to and from Snohomish took me right by Steph's accident site, and every time I drove past it, my stomach would knot and I'd get a real sense of sadness and gloom, and I'd try to keep from looking at the bent, unrepaired railing where the Jeep went over, but I had to, every single time, and then one day it suddenly occurred to me to wonder, *What if I had been with her? What if I'd been in her passenger seat? Would I have had time to stop the Jeep from going over?* I shivered at the possibility that I could have been there to stop the wreck.

The print shop was more of a failed sitcom than a business, as it turned out that Nasir and his business partner, Zahid, had taken on what they were told was a "turnkey" print shop in Snohomish, Washington, which, if you look at a map—and I had to—is about two hours north of Seattle in a forested, economically depressed stretch of mountain towns that now specialize mostly in antiquing.

There was no reason for the community to need a print shop there.

Even worse, the shop came with a pair of married, retired printers who, in their spare time, ran a magazine for hot-rod enthusiasts, actually watched NASCAR like it meant something, and asked me if I had "caught the races" by way of small talk. They had sold their lifelong business—whose technology, I should add, ended roughly, and badly, around 1980. They simply stopped keeping up with the technology and printing software back then and cruised their way into the millennium, not caring or understanding that while they charged hundreds of dollars for a set of business cards, other print shops were doing them for under twenty bucks.

And they'd sold their shop to a pair of Muslim businessmen, one of whom dressed like Osama bin Laden.

I couldn't pitch this story to CBS, because they'd tell me it was too outlandish.

Moreover, as their "manager," I was put in the position of having to diplomatically handle this xenophobic couple with these Arab businessmen, who, it turned out, were entirely Machiavellian, if you don't mind the cultural contradictions. Nasir and Zahid had told the old guy, a crusty, mean little man named Phil, that he'd have a place in the new business, and then they asked me to take as much knowledge from the old man as possible and push him and his wife out. There was little enough to take, since all the technology and equipment were outdated, and the place was wired badly because Phil had done most of it himself, and absolutely no business ever walked in that door.

Graphic designers are not printers, and there's really no personal takeaway from learning the obsolete trade anymore. Still, I taught myself how to network that shitty place, I taught myself the old-world printing, and I taught myself how to buy and quote *paper*, for fuck's sake, and I was asked always to do more, and then more than that, and then never a word of appreciation. I didn't understand this. I'd never had bosses like this.

After a while, I realized that they'd never acknowledge or credit me for the work I'd been doing because it would mean, at some point, they'd have to reward it in a wage, and no matter how much I gave or tried, or went above my earnings, it would all go unanswered, and they'd only ask for more. Conversely, if I said I didn't know something, they were not disappointed.

It was the first time in my life that I thought I would never understand another culture. When you're a kid, when you're younger, your window of acceptance and appreciation is laid wide open, and you crave to absorb all sorts of things, listen to all sorts of music—both country and western—and you want to know more about things that you're unfamiliar with: You want to try different foods, watch foreign movies, appreciate different things. I'm sure there's a biological imperative for it. But as you grow older, that window gradually begins to narrow, until you're a crusty older person set in your ways, like Phil.

Twenty years ago, I would have entirely "grokked" Nasir and Zahid, would have forgiven their disregard, their bad management, the low wage. At forty, I was looking at them and thinking, *We really have no way of understanding each other. Our aims are entirely different.* My upbringing on the Texas-Mexico border was primarily honor based, and honor represented itself primarily in my work, in being the fastest, the smartest, and the most creative, which corresponded perfectly with publishing: If you weren't the most effective and efficient, ten more people were willing to take your place. Nasir and Zahid's sense of accomplishment came from getting more for less, and coming out on top in any negotiation.

There was no way I could last in this relationship.

I listened to their verbal exchanges in Urdu with interest and curiosity; they'd infuse the term *inshallah*, or "if God wills it," after anything that they hoped would happen. My father and grandmother uttered similar incantations, only in Spanish: *si Diosito quiere*, or "if Jesus wants it." (Actually, it literally translates to "if Little God wants it," but let's stick with "Jesus.")

Anyway, after a while, I decided I'd just start enjoying the spectacle when an errant local logging redneck would wander in and ask to fax something to his probation officer or make copies. Then I'd watch as he'd stammer and sweat when he saw Nasir in his traditional dress, who then spoke to him in good, unaccented English, and they'd both look at me like it was my job to advocate, but I wouldn't. I'd just smile at both of them like, "Go on; let's bridge this divide," and the redneck would sputter about having forgotten something in his truck, and then you'd see his truck spill out of the gravel parking lot, and I'd look at Nasir, who'd then pretend it hadn't happened. Like a Lutheran.

Once, Nasir surprised me by coming in the back way when I was busy setting up an e-mail account on one production machine, with my back turned to him, and he yelled, "Hey!"

And I shot right up in my chair and yelled, "Jesus fucking Christ!"

Then I turned and looked at him, and we were both caught in the moment of cross-cultural blasphemy, and then again, we both pretended it hadn't happened. Like Lutherans.

—◦—

The commute north was devastating, the low wage and disregard for my worth was humiliating, and I was beginning to rethink my commitment to this job daily. Since my previous job was executed from my apartment, my wardrobe was entirely lacking, and what clothes I did have were terribly old. I would come back exhausted every day and complain to Sarah, who had grown weary of my weariness.

I tried to convey to her how deeply interesting and horrific this scenario was—"I mean, one of the presses that Phil still uses was in an episode of *Deadwood*!" I would tell her, to illustrate how byzantine the place was—and about trying to talk to these people, I said, "I have more in common with Nasir and asking about his mother's hajj than I do with the rednecks asking me about carburetors!" This wasn't supposed to happen, I kept saying.

"Fuck me, I'm done. I think I'm headed back to Texas."

Then one day, as I was asking Phil and his huge-breasted wife, Dee, to please remove yet another piece of machinery or carburetor parts from the front office, I watched my Gmail account light up as I received word from *Epiphany*, a literary journal out of New York, that they'd received my manuscript, picked it out of their slush pile, and they wanted to publish three of the chapters from my book, and I thought, *Hunh. Maybe there is an end to this absurdity and personal inferno.*

CHAPTER 35

Dining with Cannibals

I found it far easier to break up with Steph's family than I ever had with Steph, and after her mother hung up on me, I took to seeing Steph in the evenings, after they'd gone home, so now Steph could have double the care and advocacy. I hadn't really planned it that way, but it turned out better for everyone, and I never spoke to them again.

After that incident with my car breaking down, I let them navigate the city on their own and never looked back. They had worn me through, finally. But I still felt Steph was far from ready to be on her own, so I would stop by and sit with her for a couple hours fairly often after work. At first, her cognitive abilities fluctuated, and some days she'd be as quiet as she was in the first stages of the coma, but then suddenly she'd open up in a running monologue that made little sense but was oddly poetic in a medical science sort of way. Other days she'd see me and have a fit, try to kick me with her crushed foot and throw things at me if she could get her hands on a projectile.

Still, every day, her recovery surged forward, and at some point I realized I was watching the day-to-day advancement of a brain healing itself on fast-forward, like watching a baby's life documented on film and played continuously at four or five times regular speed. This was Steph 3.0, and she had that in common with my mother: When my mother was divorced, she picked up right at age sixteen and began her maturity as a single person, then a divorcee, and finally, a woman remarried, all in fast-forward. Steph, with her accident, did an entire reboot of her brain, right from the firmware, and watching her recover on a day-to-day basis was the same as watching a child grow up in hyperreality.

I'd spend some nights at the hospital with her, pulled two chairs together and created a bed of sorts, and I'd listen to my iPod while she slept. When the nurses would come in every three hours for her medications, Steph would insist on logging her pills and dosage in a notebook written in made-up hieroglyphs that only she understood, and I'd help her document every pill and liquid she took while the nurses patiently looked on, before Steph agreed to take anything. This was because, she eventually told me, the other time she was in the hospital, a nurse back on the East Coast very nearly gave her an injection intended for a cancer patient, and so now she was acutely vigilant.

"Very well," I said. "This one is Oxycodone, for pain, fifteen milligrams," and she would make a series of squiggles with her pen and we'd pretend she was in control, as I indicated the next pill: "This one is Tramadol, fifty milligrams," and the next, and the next.

One afternoon, she asked me to take her down to the imaging area, wait with her while she endured another CAT scan of her head to see how the recovery was progressing. We sat and talked in low voices while she waited to be called in, and when she was next, she made herself comfortable on the scanner and the tech invited me into the control room, asked me to sit next to him in a safe, less radioactive place.

"Thanks," I said. "By the way, she has a plate in her head, from a previous accident. Won't that interfere with the imaging?" I asked, curious as to how they were able to see around or through it. It suddenly occurred to me that in all her previous scans and X-rays, I hadn't seen it before.

The scan continued and the fillings in her teeth lit up like a constellation, and her small, proper silver cross lit up like the neon crosses we had seen while camping in the mountains over Twisp the last time, but no plate, no large metallic glow came from her forehead, where she always pointed when she mentioned it to me.

"There's no plate in her head," the tech said, uncomfortably.

"Must be my mistake," I said.

Eventually, she was cognizant enough to carry on conversations and explain to me what she had experienced during those days when she'd stay awake and look at things around her, how her mind would process it. She said she remained in a constant dream logic, that she was wide awake but her mind was making random associations and deep emotional leaps, and I agreed with her because for a very long time there, it was like watching exhalations and fissures of personalities past come to the surface, have their moment, and then make way for the next emanation of buried Stephanie. So inside one hour, you'd see Steph at seven years old calling out for Daddy, then Steph at twenty-two feeling embarrassed for her vulnerability and condition, then Steph at thirty-nine looking at me and hating me for us not working out the way she wanted, and then the cycle would repeat itself, at different ages. As trying as it was for the bedside sitter, I can imagine how exhausting and frightening it was for her, the homunculus inside trying to steer her mind in a manner like it was once capable.

When she was in this state, she said she sometimes saw me as the bastard who left her at the altar and married someone else and had children and a family now. So she hated me and wanted to throw things at me.

She said she even imagined her best friend, Jake, was there, for a month.

"No, that actually happened," I told her.

"You mean Jake was here?" she asked. Jake was her boyfriend in college, before she jumped buses and started dating women. They were able to make better friends than they had been lovers, and Jake, by far, was the best friend Steph ever had. He had flown out after he heard about the accident and was able to get some time off from his work as a physical therapist.

"Yeah, he was here by your bedside for a couple of weeks. He was really helpful. He made charts," I said.

"Charts of what?" she asked.

"Charts of what your recovery might look like. Charts of a brain and its synaptic reconfiguration, which is what the neurologist said was happening to you."

"Oh," she said.

"He also told me about the time you punched him, too," I said.

"I punched him?" she asked, genuinely curious.

"Yeah, when he tried to break up with you back in college," I told her. "He said you brought a rock into the library and set it next to him while he was studying, as a threat."

"I did?"

"Yeah, then later, you punched him in the eye. We actually high-fived, since we were both the victims of your right cross." I giggled, but she looked confused. This had actually happened in front of Steph's mother, who, I think, managed a glimpse of who her daughter really was at that point, and looked stricken.

Now, by recounting these conversations, it might seem that Steph was nearly back to her usual self, but this is far from accurate. Steph believed herself to be at 100 percent recovery when she was really just starting out at about 25 to 30 percent, and it was painful to watch because she felt she was back in command of all her faculties, and she was making decisions where it was clear that she was still very much suffering from a traumatic brain injury.

One afternoon, back at Harborview, where Steph was doing rehabilitative treatment, her parents thought it would be a good idea if they helped her down to the canteen for a coffee or a juice. Steph insisted on using her crutches, and when they were down in the basement level and in the queue, her mother upset her with something and Steph let out a scream with the C-word, aimed at her mother, who flushed and ran out of the room.

I felt a number of things, not least among them a sadness for her mother, but also a bit of responsibility because it had been me and my predilection for British gangster movies that taught Steph how to unleash that particular word, and so I felt guilty, on top of everything. I was exhausted from guilt by this time, but I could still muster it on a moment's notice.

By this point, I had pretty much made it past my resentment of her family, understood the high-stress situation they'd been put in, moving to a foreign city and having only me to depend upon, so of course they'd eventually aim their frustration at the bastard who'd left their daughter.

Even further, I had an overwhelming realization that I was standing between a daughter and a mother who had a second chance at rebuilding their relationship, and that my standing guard and defending a person who was not happy with herself and indeed wanted nothing more—at her very core—than to be with her family, and have her mother's approval, wasn't helping. It made so much more sense now to step away and let these things unfold, rather than try to be some sort of bedside hero for a woman that I had no claim to, who had no claim to me.

That final realization was incredibly liberating, and I was able to visit Steph without the crushing sense of guilt or trauma or responsibility, but instead as a friend, and someone who cared for her, but up to a limit. It gave me boundaries. And it also helped when she started doing really crazy things and I saw that there was nothing I could do anymore to keep her safe, that she would have to navigate the world as she was, and I couldn't stop her from making terrible choices.

She had been moved back to the hospital for a rehab treatment, on a different floor, as a part of her ongoing therapy and was now sharing a room with other patients, and one afternoon I came down to the hospital to see her and she was dressed, sitting upright on her bed and flipping through a magazine. She moved in slow motion, her eyes unfocused and glazed from the medication, and she limped and winced from the pain of all her fractures, so watching her perform simple tasks was like watching her move underwater.

I knocked and walked in, sat down in the chair beside her. I noticed a family in the other part of the room, around the other bed. They were Mexican, and an old man was in the hospital bed, and I caught from their conversation in Spanish that he'd had a heart attack but was recovering. They kept giving Steph dirty looks, I noticed. She said she wanted to walk a little, so we wandered slowly down the hallway to a little nook with couches. She told me the family was mad at her because she complained that the man dribbled on their shared toilet when he relieved himself.

"There's pee on the toilet seat," she said. "He says he lifts the seat, but it's always there."

I felt a compulsion to intervene but decided I didn't want to take that on, as a part of my new boundaries. In the end, the Mexican man was moved to another room and the pee was still appearing on the toilet seat, and Steph realized the droplets on the toilet seat were caused by the cleaners emptying buckets into the toilet. I felt bad for the old man and his family, who were in Seattle from eastern Washington, alone downtown and frightened, and then accused of this humiliation, like he was a barn animal incapable of simple hygiene. But again, this was no longer my fight.

I came back a couple days later and there was a new family in Steph's room, and this time I was getting dirty looks from a young Arab guy. Four generations of people gathered around a woman in a black hijab, covered head to toe and lying on the bed, and the guy, in his thirties, kept looking at me like I'd done something to insult him or his family.

"Let's go sit," Steph said to me, and we walked to the nook.

"I want to see other people," she told me as we sat on the couch, and I nearly burst out laughing.

"I'm sorry; yes, by all means," I said, after everyone at the nurse's station looked my way.

"No, I mean it," she said. "I think we need to split up, and stay friends. I'm seeing someone else already," she told me.

"What?" I said, taken aback. You can't really trust anything someone with a traumatic brain injury is telling you. But this was surprising, and I was concerned about her making these decisions much more than feeling any sort of jealousy. Any at all. I mean, I would have told her I was seeing Sarah, but I didn't think she could process the jealousy and sense of betrayal a person feels when they discover an ex is seeing someone else.

"Steph, what are you doing? You're not in a condition to start a relationship," I said, and I was hoping she wasn't taking that as me being jealous. She wasn't capable of consent.

"I'm seeing that guy whose mother is in the bed next to mine," she told me. "I gave him a blow job yesterday. I cheated on you all the time, by the way. I met people on Craigslist and had sex with them at Lisa's house."

I heard this and, oddly, didn't care in the least. I could see that her intention was to hurt me, somehow, and it did nothing to wound or affect me, not my honor or sense of nostalgia, nothing. Or perhaps it was also, or more so, that I was relieved to hear that Steph wasn't as dependent on me as I'd thought, that she, too, knew that the relationship was doomed. This revelation freed me further from my guilt.

But the idea that she was "seeing" someone right there in the hospital, in her condition, seemed like abuse of a patient, to me. It just didn't seem right. I felt compelled to say something, but I couldn't: I was done. I didn't want to interfere any longer.

Plus, I was in love with Sarah in a way that I had never before felt with anyone, and I had made the transition to full devotional and physical love with her months earlier, so Steph telling me she was giving blowies now and had sex with other people while we were "together" only made me feel sorry for her, made me worry for her much more than anything else, but not like before: She wasn't my responsibility.

During that year, Sarah miraculously understood the complexity around my relationship and sense of obligation with Steph. Sarah was exhausted by the demands of Steph's accident and my responses, and she watched helplessly at the implosion of my health. She made the hard decision to compartmentalize me and our relationship, as a strategy of self-protection, while she navigated her own difficulties and dissolution of the life she had worked so hard to build with her now ex-husband.

It had been him that had left her, she told me, and right out of the blue.

While Sarah is a gentile, their child identifies with the paternal family's line as Jewish, like only a West Coast Seattle liberal could. Their kid had a huge bar mitzvah one Saturday, and it was quite the shindig, with everyone from the karate school attending. Friends and family flew in from all over the country. Though I had been invited, I was incapable of leaving my apartment from depression that afternoon, so I didn't make it. The next morning, Sarah was feeling a bit rough, so she slept in while her husband drove their kid to the airport to catch a flight to Los Angeles to stay with friends, as a birthday present.

When he returned, he woke up Sarah and told her they needed to talk.

She was about to apologize for sleeping in when he leveled his gaze at her and said, flatly, "I don't want to be married to you any longer." She was mid-coffee when she realized the conversation they were having, and she didn't even get through the cup before he loaded his simple travel bag and left for his new rented house, about thirty minutes away and fully furnished. He'd been planning this for months.

Her fifteen-year marriage ended in less time than it took to drink that cup of coffee.

I was able to give Sarah a level of distraction and entertainment, in a way, as I unraveled around her in such large, dramatic, and loud catastrophes with huge emotional tsunamis and explosive, potentially life-threatening ways, but still she had her limits and boundaries. When this had started, Sarah had presented me with an oversize postcard she had purchased during her last trip to Spain, *La Virgen Dolorosa*, from one of the medieval cathedrals in the south. It was an image of the Virgin Mother's anguish, and she had seven swords stabbing her heart.

It was, for me, a perfect image of grief, and it was like a signal directly to the soul of my anguish, how I was metabolizing all the pain and confusion and fear and helplessness. It was more than language, it was more than iconic: It was a subconscious, subcultural chorus of angels. I finally understood my grandmother and father, and how they surrounded themselves with these death images of Jesus and *La Virgen de Guadalupe*, the Virgin Mother. It's how Catholics process grief, sharing it with others in order to process the anguish as a community.

Sarah was a descendant from Lutheran homesteaders, from Idaho, and so she firmed up her top lip, dug up her garden, and made gluten-free casseroles to exhibit her suffering. She spent weeks curled up in bed, her covers pulled up over her head, then went to her doctor, who prescribed lorazapam, trazadone, and other medications to help her endure.

I no longer had health insurance, so I turned to booze, which would give me a good one or two hours of deadened thoughts and tissue, and then come roaring back with blades and horror and keep me from sleeping. And I would bewilder and enthrall Sarah sometimes, with how self-destructive I could become, how utterly beyond redemption I could push myself when the mood took me. Once, we had to attend a funeral together for a former student at the karate school. It was a tragic story, and I won't relay it here, but the funeral services were held in a megachurch in one of those outlying Washington towns full of trees and Starbucks, and I prepared for the funeral with a flask of gin and a due sense of conviction.

The services unfolded with a salesman in a business suit telling us how the girl was now a bride of Jesus, and images of her life in the church were projected onto a screen behind a huge fabricated cross with a cloth draped over it.

This just pissed me off from the start. Where was the body of Christ? Where were the wounds, the blood and the anguish? Where was the depiction of suffering? Where was the echo of compassion in the image of physical suffering? That simple, oversized geometry of a cross hanging center stage was too hygienic, too barren to inspire anything. *You bastards are fucking salesmen,* I kept thinking, *and that's all. Trying to scrub clean the human condition.*

"I want chicken-bone Jesus!" I stage-whispered to Sarah, who was both horrified and stunned. "This is bullshit. They're doing it wrong." If they were still talking about faith, I felt, then they had obviously not suffered enough.

That's the second born, when you have the faith beaten out of you. That's actualization. Toast.

I remember the look on her face in the dark when she went past being disgusted by my antics and instead her clinical analysis kicked in, and she said, "Jesus Christ, Domingo; you really don't care what people think of you, do you?"

"Fuck these people," I said. "I'll never see them again. They're doing it wrong." Then I pulled out my flask and took a long pull of straight gin. At a funeral. In a megachurch.

Take that, Saul of Tarsus.

—◦—

Now, people who know me know that this is just a single part of my personality, and I have other, more endearing parts when I'm not in a self-destructive spiral. On my best days, I could hold up my end of the conversations like we did when we'd take those walks around Greenlake, and I could bring the creativity, passion, and insight to Sarah's work and life that she craved. Perhaps it was because of my particular capacity to suffer that I could withstand and even receive Sarah's anguish as well, could hold her as she grieved for her own suffering. Even though she had family, friends, and a therapist, no one else could receive her grief like I could, in the way she received mine. I threaded through her like a Leonard Cohen song.

What made this possible was that Sarah was able to shut me down and out of her life when she felt I was affecting her badly. There was much of my unraveling she would not watch, and she built a firewall. I was in a free-fall for most of that time, and she knew it, could do nothing some days but watch helplessly as my situation grew worse and worse.

And I would take the cue and focus my spraying elsewhere, because I loved her and respected her. That was the only way our relationship made it through the second act. When we moved into the physical relationship, there was still a solid and obsidian wall that kept me out of Sarah's more personal life, away from her family and her child, but I was all right with that. In fact, I needed it. I wasn't ready to be in a relationship and couldn't shift what was left of my resources—as broken and desiccated as I was—to start another love affair.

But what we had was enough for both of us, for now. And it worked, because neither of us looked down.

———

At some point later on, I developed a curiosity as to how the "newspaper" that I had been working on in eastern Washington was doing, after I'd left, and I thought maybe I'd have a bit of schadenfreude in seeing how far down their design and image had deteriorated without my help. I downloaded the latest edition and was left thoroughly speechless when I read, on their front page, that one of the women who owned the company, wife to Alfred, had died unexpectedly of an aneurysm. Sweet, lovely person that she was, mother of two, and a genuinely good human being, just gone, just like that. Alfred had indeed suffered something similar to what I had cursed him, and I felt completely ashamed and horrible. I sent their family an e-mail, written as sincerely as I could, and hoped I would never hear back.

Back in Texas, my family had taken to calling me in relays; every day or two days, someone would make contact and try to keep me engaged and up to date on a family I had divorced some years ago to make my claim on the American promise, to reinvent myself like my sisters had done in their middle school years, except I had played it out in the long game, and had been trying to make it entirely on my own as a hard man, a rugged individualist of a sort, a macho, macho man. This turned out to be bullshit, and I found myself to be soft, like a bunny. Broken and damaged, wracked with regrets.

My mother's mother died that winter, and in the fog of what I was enduring in Seattle, I missed her funeral, felt horrible about it a year later when I went back and looked at all my notes, all the writing I had done in my little moleskin notebooks I kept with me, most of them surprising me with flashbacks or mentions of things I don't remember doing, people I don't remember meeting. My whole family gathered in Brownsville to bury my maternal grandmother, and even my paternal grandmother, Gramma, made it to the graveside to pay her respects, after years of mutual silence. (Personally, I think Gramma went there to gloat: *See? I told you I'd outlive you.*) And my father, Mingo, in his continued run of surprising his children, had secretly hired a mariachi he knew from his days as a restaurateur and had him sing three of the most ridiculously heartbreaking songs, which had the whole crowd in tears by the time he was through. Well, everyone except for my uncle Abel, who was too incapacitated by his addictions to grieve his mother publicly. Our step-grandfather wouldn't allow him to attend, in the condition he was in, and later, when Dan and Derek drove back to check on him, he was bare-chested and his face was covered in a golden spray paint, from huffing. He kept calling out in shrill, pain-filled agony: *La jefa! La jefa!* That's what the kids called her, my grandmother: the boss lady.

It was a moment that stayed with Derek, and all of us, of course. We all metabolize grief in our way, sure, but when your addictions keep you from properly grieving your mother's passing, that's something else entirely. I felt horrible for Abel. And our other uncle, Johnny, who was in prison during his mother's funeral.

Dan and I were back to talking and we were extraordinarily aware of the triggers that would instantaneously drop us into fighting posture, and we were at a point where we'd be able to stop, stop, stop, then articulate, "When you say this, it makes me want to say that," sort of marriage counseling speak, but it was working, and we were becoming better friends, better brothers.

Derek had disappeared, once again, under his shame.

After his accident, he recovered in my mother's house in Houston until her husband, Robert, had seen enough of his antics and asked him, point-blank, if he was serious about killing himself. Derek had taken to sleeping all day and then watching movies all night, and then doing it all over again after going through all of my mother's pantries. Mom was allowing Derek to do this as a part of his "recovery," but truthfully, Mom had PTSD from receiving that phone call from the hospital in Austin, and she woke up every night at 3:30 a.m., and hearing him downstairs flipping through cable reassured her. Between having this mess of a boy under her roof or not knowing where he was, behaving like a chemical repository in the slums of central Texas, Mom learned to be all right with having him stay downstairs all night, sleep all day while she was at work. Robert, though, he gave it a month or two and then pulled out his pistols, both literally and metaphorically.

The way Derek tells this story, Robert pulled a 9 mm pistol on him and said, "Get out." But that's not true. I know Robert, and he simply told Derek, "If you're intent on killing yourself, take the gun in my closet upstairs and do it, because we're sick of your shit."

Derek instead called Dan and proceeded to do the same thing, except at Dan's house. Ultimately, it seems like this was how Derek manipulated his family, as an addict: *Look at me, I'm helpless! Wouldn't you rather have me living with you, eating your food and drinking your booze, than be frightened of what I might be getting up to?*

It was blackmail, whether he understood he was doing it or not, and it went on for far too long.

In the meantime, I was still struggling, pulling at ends and not making them meet, and my family was trying to help me break the surface and be on my own again. They rooted for me, and it was incredibly touching that they'd suddenly emerged as my only support network, besides Sarah, Amy, and Andy here in Seattle. I had pretty much rendered every other bridge to cinders and was looking at the world through a very tiny hole that showed me very little sunlight.

But still, I tarried on. I didn't know what else to do. I was still waiting to find those final six gears that would get me through this time, awaiting the next level of absurdity the universe had in store for me.

I would still drink a bit too much on some days, but it was nothing like the ferocity of self-destruction I was hell-bent on putting myself through in those first months. That had been almost like another test of macho I had created for myself in my collapse of sense, in that I wanted to destroy myself the same way Steph had, in the same way Derek had done to himself. I wanted to climb on that cross, have those seven swords penetrating my heart. Instead I would come home and collapse on my couch and try to stop my monkey mind from going apeshit, watching whatever series I could find on Netflix and drinking lite beer, and sometimes shooting the Hello Kitty stuffie that Steph's mother had given me with an air pistol I had bought the year before in my war against the rats.

I'd sit there and wait, though I'm not entirely certain for what, maybe to hear from Sarah, who was the only one who could give me something to look forward to, and so I'd keep it cool for her while I shot BB after BB into the heart of the stupid little Kitty, like Elvis would have, as it sat in my bookshelf opposite.

—◆—

Meanwhile, my pieces were in *Epiphany*, a small, underfunded but highly pedigreed little journal out of New York, and I couldn't have been happier. Though I may have told most everyone I know about this, I don't think many people fully understood what it actually meant, and in full transparency, neither could I, really. But I knew it was a really good step.

I was working at the desolation print shop at this time, and instead of pretending to work on nonexistent orders, I decided I would use my time to further pursue the idea of publishing, now that I had a writing credit. There was really little else I could do at the print shop anyhow, since the contention between Phil and his idea of what the shop should be doing was in direct conflict with what Nasir and Zahid wanted out of it, and I had learned by now that I'd been given a task to execute with no authority behind it. They had also hired this Bosnian kid from their mosque when we'd first started this abysmal enterprise, and while he had every level of enthusiasm and optimism, Adnan was a bit too spirited and easily distracted to keep a job in a small, defeated business like this and would instead bring in his laptop to watch soccer games and documentaries on the Bosnian War. I really liked that kid, who had fled to America with his family when he'd been three and was now so entirely and thoroughly American that he wore all the best Reeboks and backward baseball caps and spoke a little bit like Ali G while using a smattering of *inshallahs* and *salaam alaikums*. He was my last good entertainment that passed through those doors, after he squared off, chicken chested, with Phil one afternoon when they locked in a battle of wills over a closed door, and I chuckled as Adnan very nearly cleaned Phil's sixty-five-year-old clock.

I would not have allowed it to happen, as my head was the coolest one nearby and intended to prevail, which is saying something, but I would certainly have liked to see it happen. Old Phil was that much of a prick and deserved it, but Adnan was a young, damaged boy with a civil war background, and it was not right to let him yell at the mean old bastard, so I stepped in, told Adnan to go home and let Phil sputter at the idea that he was about to get his block knocked off by a twenty-three-year-old Bosnian kid. "That's just un-American," I said, and made him even more upset.

By this point, Adnan had decided to quit, and in his place they'd hired this dirty mountain kid who lived in his car, completely illiterate as a result of being "home schooled" by his "Christian mother," and he'd come in some mornings looking like he had pulled his shirt from a pile at the bottom of his backseat. I was taken aback at the poverty. I mean, I grew up around kids taking baths in buckets, but this was something else. This was raw, pioneer poverty, in modern America—well, as much as Snohomish could pass for modern America. I tried to befriend him but felt like it was hopeless, didn't have it in me. He would sit in front of our production computer for an hour in order to write a painful, three-line response to a customer query, and it would be ridiculously broken, pathetically unpunc-tuated, but I just couldn't take that on. Not anymore. No more room for little brothers.

At any rate, most days I had a lot of free time in the afternoons, and I decided to use that for my benefit. I had the idea to develop my own database of agents to get my book published—I mean, I had a credit now, didn't I? The next step was to get an agent, right? Like they do in the mov-ies. So that's what I would do.

I culled a directory of agents in New York City (nothing else felt like it would do) from Google searches, downloaded a tremendous amount of contacts and numbers, and then set about cleaning the data and writ-ing a script using an Excel spreadsheet (I was doing it for other small businesses—why not do it for me?). I wrote a cover letter, updated the information, created a few variable data fields, made PDFs, and then had a production machine send what were, unbeknownst to me at the time, book queries to agents in New York City with an automated script. Then I sat back and waited for the responses.

They were overwhelmingly obstinate, this little club of book publish-ers and industry people, and entirely unwilling to let me in their front doors, it seemed. From my gray perch in Snohomish, it felt like I'd never make it past their gargoyles and security guards or interns, but still I kept on because it was all I had left, and Sarah had said this was going to be my only way out. And I had presented her with the five packages of the six best chapters that she said she'd deliver to all those people, so I was doing my own due diligence.

I just had to keep going.

I'd finally found the bottom gears.

CHAPTER 36

The Way to Say Good-bye

The very last time I saw Steph, she asked me to bring her a key.

She had locked herself out of her house, was waiting back at Harborview for more of her outpatient therapy, and as I drove around to find parking, I saw her quite clearly sitting in one of the glass bridges that connected new constructions to older ones across the city streets. She was staring out the window wearing a sky-blue dress, a large, floppy spring hat, and long white gloves, in winter. I parked, then found her, and it was indeed Steph, dressed like a crazy person. She cried and thanked me, saying she'd accidentally locked herself out of the house up north where she was now living alone, had left her handbag inside. She had to beg a bus driver to allow her on and give her a transfer in order to make it to Harborview, downtown. My throat knotted up, listening to this, but I couldn't give her any more, not any longer.

I drove her home and retrieved her bag after she was done with her outpatient therapy, and Steph showed me a chart she had filled out some weeks earlier where she documented her recovery at 100 percent, even though her handwriting and spelling were entirely distorted and wrong. More artifacts of anguish. But she was now telling me, "Can you believe I thought that? I mean, I'm nowhere near how smart I was," and that hurt to hear, too.

Some days earlier, when her parents were still in town, she had asked me to take her to the house of the two veterinarians who were dog-sitting Cleo, and I picked her up around the corner because I didn't want to see Harold or her mother. I saw Steph from a distance and she was still moving the same way, slowly, as if underwater, and she seemed dust-boned fragile, like a shivering bird in someone's hands. I wasn't able to police my compassion from changing immediately to sorrow and grief. That was my problem with Steph: When I felt anything for her, I would move instantly to sadness and nostalgia and sorrow. And it was like that until she finally declared to me, "I'm seeing someone else," when she sat in my car and put on her seatbelt.

I said, "I know, you're seeing that Arab guy," and she said, "No, I'm seeing someone else. He's white. My parents are much happier about that because when I was with you they didn't want a half-Mexican baby."

Now, I could have been upset or hurt by this, and I think there may have been a tinge of something quite fundamental there, but no: *That's the traumatic brain injury*, I told myself. Harold and her mother might have their issues with me, but I don't believe them to be that reprehensible. So I just nodded my head and said, "That's fine, Steph. I hope you're happy and I wish you all the best. I'm with Sarah. You met her briefly once at the karate school."

"Oh, good," she said.

"And they won't have to call the cops on the baby, like they did with me," I said, because I'm like that. *Cabrón.*

"Oh, that wasn't my mother; that was me. I thought you were coming to hurt her so I called the police department. Can you take me to the store? I need to buy some things for Cleo."

That was news to me, but it made sense, in the end.

At the store, we had a bag of dog food at the cashier when Steph opened her wallet and showed me a clump of hundred dollar bills, something over $1,000.

I immediately pushed her hand down to cover the display of raw cash and asked, "What the hell are you doing with so much fucking money?"

"I need it to impress someone's family," she said.

I had half a mind to say, *Well, why don't you pay me back the money your parents jacked from me first?* but I thought, *Fuck it, let's just get out of this one.* But I was definitely curious about her new boyfriend, felt oddly protective, after all this time.

It turned out, Stephanie 3.0 was doing all sorts of things that Stephanies 1.0 and 2.0 would never have been caught doing, like mingling at poetry readings and watching films in the afternoon at film festivals. And during one such afternoon, she sat directly next to a man in a Prince Valiant haircut who had been updating his blog or Facebook post as the previews had started, and so Steph, having very little regulation from the TBI, proceeded to chastise the guy, and by the end of the movie, they had planned a date to see other films.

In one of the more perfect moments of providence lending a hand, this man turned out to be an autistic software programmer, deeply in the red on the spectrum, and was sitting quite comfortably after selling some sort of search engine plug-in to Amazon back in the '90s, and he was now rather well off. His previous girlfriend, a soul songstress from the Caribbean, had bilked him of something like $200,000 in order to self-produce a vanity album, as Steph told the story, and so Steph felt she was now in charge of protecting him and his interests. It was a perfect match: She wanted someone to push around, and he was willing to be pushed around.

When Steph told me this, I said, "All right, you're safe now. I think it's time for me to go."

"But I want to stay friends," she said.

"I can't do that," I said. "Your voice takes me right back to the grief, puts me right back to that time." She had at least lost the British inflections by this point, but still.

She looked at me a bit sideways, then said, "My God, I really hurt you, didn't I?"

"I helped," I said, and hugged her good-bye when I dropped her off at the corner of her street.

As I drove away, I noticed I'd been playing a song on my car stereo, which was a change because for months, I could not listen to music—any kind of music—at all.

It was Nick Cave and the Bad Seeds reminding me, in the way that only he can, that if you're going to dine with a cannibal, sooner or later, you, too, are going to get eaten.

—◦—

They married on a yacht on Lake Washington, and her parents and extended family flew out from the east, this time for something far better than an extended stay in an ICU, and by all accounts, they seem entirely well and fulfilled and good, an ending that was almost preposterously happy for her. And reports from other people who wander across her Facebook page say that even her relationship with her mother is the best that anyone can imagine, and of course Harold is delighted to see his daughter content, after all this.

Steph made it back home, and her mother has her daughter back.

Thank God, I think every time someone asks me about this, and I mean it: Thank you, God, for giving her that. For giving her family that. They deserve it, after everything.

—◦—

Steph's accident had broken me down, in commiseration, and had reconnected me to my own family in the same way she had reconnected to hers. But I was still in the process of building my life back into something salvageable and worthwhile, as I worked from the final, exhausted reserves that I had left in my soul.

But even Sarah was trying to leave me now. She was the only guiding star left on my compass, the one true north I could count on, and she wanted to leave me. She struggled to withstand my level of exhaustion after so many months of the hospital drama, and she began to see that there would be nothing left over between us if I kept up this level of attention to Steph. And she anguished further at the age difference, which I insisted was not an issue for me. And it wasn't. Isn't.

Still, she thought our affair had run its course, though she really did love me, thoroughly. I worried about it because she exhibited it through compassion and strategy and boundaries—all concepts I'd never really understood.

"You know there's no happily-ever-after for us," she told me one night, and I thought I would lose my mind with panic. I felt like it would really be the end, if she and I were to separate. I wouldn't be able to handle seeing her with someone else. I just couldn't.

I remember lying in my bedroom, darkened and curtained off, my face pressed into the hard mattress, telling her, "You haven't seen what I can do. I've been expending all this energy and focus and grief on Steph and her family, keeping from falling apart, but I can do more, I can do much, much more, Sarah; please don't go yet, not yet, baby," and I very nearly whimpered. I loved her, like I've never loved anyone else.

"You dear, sweet, man," she said back to me. "You knew this wasn't going to extend into our futures. You need to let me go. I need to let you go. We have to go on our ways," she said, and I think I lost that much more life and hope, once again, on that bed in that darkened room.

A few weeks later, I'd caught the attention of an agent, Alice, who has a standing policy of reading nearly everything that comes across her inbox: You just never know in this business.

She had been in my revolving database, had received my e-mail and six-chapter query and had decided, "Yeah, all right; this looks promising. Can you send me the manuscript?"

I was actually at Sarah's when I spoke to Alice for the first time. It was a Sunday, and I was sitting on her bed with Genevieve when my phone lit up with a 212 number. "Holy shit, Sarah!" I said. "It's from New York! I don't owe anybody money in New York! It has to be about the book!"

Indeed, it was Alice, my superagent.

We spoke, and everything in my instincts and guts told me she was the one, though I had every person around me—none of them in the arts or entertainment industry, mind you, all of them repeating wisdoms they'd heard on television and in movies—telling me that I should be suspicious about the first person to express interest, watch out for shysters, et cetera.

Alice completely undermined every sense of caution or suspicion; she was just wonderful and linear and no-bullshit whatsoever, a former lawyer from Philadelphia. I couldn't have imagined a better guide in the industry, and we launched into the business of publishing my first book, together. She believed in it.

It was difficult to place since I had no history in publishing, had never published anything before the few chapters in *Epiphany*, knew no one, had no professional affiliations or contacts, and had no idea what I was doing. But Alice found a way. She contacted my current editor, also gifted with incredible insight, and together they took a risk on what was going to be my first book.

After all this.

When we received word that my publisher had bought the book, Sarah and I celebrated like old times in her kitchen with two bottles of prosecco. She was toasting me, looking at me with delight and pleasure and exquisite happiness when suddenly this shadow crossed her face, and she became serious, frightened almost.

"What's wrong, darling?" I asked. "What just happened?"

"Do you remember how I asked you to fix up those chapters and I said I'd give them to those people?"

"Yeah?"

"They're still upstairs in my office, Domingo. I'm sorry. I never sent them along. I don't know why; I just didn't have it in me."

There was a moment of pause where I had to take in what I was hearing, but then I burst out laughing and hugged her to me and kissed her hard, on the lips.

Sarah had tricked me into doing this, all on my own. She broke the elephant down into parts, gave me a manageable task, and I learned the rest on my own. It made me love her even more profoundly, especially now that I know the business the way I do, and there was nothing really any of those people would have been able to do to help me anyway. Nobody knows nothing, in this business.

And it was Amy who told me, much later, that if I had succeeded in killing myself, she would have published my manuscript at a vanity press with all the typos and mistakes that were in it, because she'd be so mad at me for doing it and she knew it would have made me furious with shame.

And Dougherty, when we would talk two years later, after my insistent barrage of apology e-mails, told me I had frightened him with my ferocity and insanity, that he'd look both ways every time he left his apartment, thinking I was coming after him. But we're friends again, sending stupid text messages and discussing the things we once discussed, before.

I'm not drinking anywhere near what I was drinking back then and have been wrangling with sobriety since April 2013, when I came home from a year-long promotion of my first book, after it was named a finalist for the National Book Award. I've been forced to learn this business from within and with very little room for error, though errors I have made, but thankfully, not like before, and not like I want to die. That first book vaulted me into a serious career as an author, has spoken to some universality for a profound number of people, and changed my life dramatically, and in the end, after all this damage and trouble, I finally managed to get what I wanted, as had Stephanie.

Happy endings. Impossible endings, sure, and yet, there they are.

I just had to learn to hold on to mine.

I tried to carry on in the manner and the mythos of the tortured writer at first—I figured I was allowed at the very least to try it on for size—the Raymonds (Chandler and Carver), Patricia Highsmith and Norman Mailer, Dorothy Parker and Tennessee Williams, but I knew it wasn't something for longevity. Certainly there's no space here to delineate between the alcoholism and the creative imperative, because it's up for debate and actually rather boring, but I will say that my decision came from figuring out finally what it was that I really wanted, above all else: I wanted to be a member of my family again, and I wanted to be with Sarah; that's the only thing that really mattered to me, and she was leaving me because of my drinking and bad health. The choice was clear.

I was in San Antonio late one night with both my brothers after there had been some kerfuffle at a bar, once again, and I was so wound up I'd put my fist through someone's windshield, and then later, when Dan and Derek and some of their friends were dropping me off at my hotel, I had that "road to Damascus" moment where I saw, quite clearly, the pull that my family and especially my brothers have on me, and something deep inside of me named it for the first time and declared it obsolete, and I knew I wanted to come back home to Seattle, back home to Sarah, and get sober, try for sobriety, or at the very least, learn to drink like I want to live, instead of drinking like I want to die.

It separates me from my brothers when I don't drink with them, and it gets awkward really quickly, but I try to maintain my boundaries. My father cried for joy when I told him about my decisions, and he doesn't press me to find out how I am, gives me the room to slip up every few weeks if I break down and have a few drinks at dinner with friends.

But I'm no longer drinking like I don't want to live, because I do want to live, and live with Sarah in my life. "Besides," she said, "success has made you much less of an asshole."

So we're still trying for it.

Like Sarah says, sobriety is not a straight line.

EPILOGUE

It took me more than twenty years, but I came back for him, kept my word after it had long been forgotten by the both of us.

Those years after crushing his head in that fall, Derek wandered lost in that same wilderness that nearly killed him the first time. He, too, had an undiagnosed traumatic brain injury, but it wasn't really obvious to anyone else besides him, when he couldn't concentrate when reading or remember simple nouns in conversation, couldn't perform simple repetitive tasks. Things like that.

I noticed it, those two times I saw him during this period. He would repeat questions asked just hours previously, look at you from a distance in one eye, squint at you with recognition in the other, and it was easy to dismiss it as him having had too much to drink, but there was something else in it, I could tell, and so could Dan.

It's amazing that Derek survived through that time, but survive he did, and it was actually mostly because of Dan, and Dan's insistence and sometimes abusive love and ferocious care. It was all Derek had left, after a while. He had taxed our mother beyond what even she was capable of, and everyone else in the family had noticed, became quietly resentful, because in spite of all the grandchildren and successful daughters and sons she had, Mom continued to focus her worry and care on Derek, only Derek, it felt, and we all just learned to live with it.

He depleted Dan, eventually, too. Broken bones, broken bank account, and a broken heart, Dan said to me once, were what Derek had left him with. Dan had tried to get Derek to independence, there in Texas; Dan forced him, yelled at him, kicked him in the large Texan ass that kept growing larger on Dan's couch, but somehow, Derek's next gear just wouldn't kick in.

Both Dan and I would treat Derek in the same way we treated one another, in our congeries of two, the club of brothers who had room only for one more, and that was Derek, when he'd finally grow up, take his lumps, and be a man.

We kept waiting. Derek kept going the other way.

We couldn't understand him.

Finally, it occurred to me to ask Derek for help. I was in Seattle, I was under some intense deadline stress, not simply with this book, but with a few other projects, and I had the idea to hire him, to bring him here, to Seattle, to coax him out of his comfort zone, which had turned extremely uncomfortable, for everyone.

He was petrified, he told me later. He was frightened of being so far from Texas, from the things he knew, from Mom and Dan.

"You just have to take the step," I said to him, over the phone. "You'll see that it feels right, when you do it."

He was terrified, it turned out, of me. He was frightened to spend so much time with me, scared of my temper and my shifting promises.

"Here's your return ticket," I said to him when he arrived, "to be used whenever you want to go back home. In the meantime, you're to clean the apartment, get me out of the apartment for exercise at least three days a week, and generally keep me from spiraling out of control with stress or anxiety."

In a matter of a week, we both realized that we didn't really know who the other person was. All my suspicions of him were unfounded, and all his fears of me were entirely out of proportion.

Derek immediately was able to see that I'm not the person I am when I'm in Texas, where I suddenly may become the resentful, frustrated twelve-year-old that the family dynamics bring out in me, that I'm not the abusive, angry person that lashed out at him and threatened to kick his ass because Derek was depending far too much on our mother, was too happy to eat and drink on other people's dime, seemingly without shame.

It was shame, it turned out, that was keeping him suffocated, keeping him under, keeping him from moving forward, because he felt so god-damned asphyxiated under all his bad choices and behaviors, his losing the scholarship to UT, and changing the way he did, almost overnight. Shame that he'd medicate with booze and any drugs available for ten years.

Derek was a noncombatant, was very different from Dan and me, I began to realize as he sat on my couch and we started to learn who the other person was, as a grown man. He's a really sweet person, incredibly kindhearted, and he found out that I can be as well, that I'm not only the swaggering asshole he'd meet in Texas when I'd fly down to do events for my book promotions. That we both have a streak of kindness and sentimentality a mile wide; the only difference, really, is that when he gets his feelings hurt, he doesn't immediately turn to lashing out the way Dan and I do, turn to swinging fists when our heart is wounded.

Dan and I were Mingo's sons, it turned out.

Derek was Mom's.

So, twenty years after I left him crying on the sidewalk that night I boarded a bus to Seattle, I invited Derek to fly out to me, stay with me like I promised I would avail to him the morning he made it through his surgery and I wrote him that letter when he was still in the coma. When he arrived here, carrying a red suitcase and a frightened look in his eye, my younger brother began to surface, and our friendship changed, or maybe even started that day, as I was finally able to do my part in helping the only member of our family who hadn't been able to get it together, who needed our mother the most for all of his life, and who had finally broken Dan down in tears and frustration.

When he arrived here in Seattle, I made a spontaneous decision to change our dynamic from "older brother and younger brother," and instead treat him as if he was a cherished friend, make no assumptions, and try a different tactic in how we communicated as family. In other words, instead of the tacit domination that's inherent in the hierarchy of family, I would treat Derek like a friend, with clear and established boundaries and expectations. It started to work immediately. It was as if Mom's umbilical cord finally broke: the distance, the opportunity, the *tabula rasa* with some clean, clear boundaries. He began to individuate, began his life again, completely integrated into the family, all of us rooting for him and treating him the way Sarah treated me for a while: trust, but verify.

After three weeks, he asked if he could stay in Seattle, find work, and try to rebuild himself here. I, of course, agreed, and within a week's time, he was off and running, learning the city through its busing, coming home every day with new stories and wonder. It has been entirely gratifying.

It's been all about family, after all. Derek was the lost sheep, and so was Steph. She was able to reintegrate and complete her family after her accident, which is what she always wanted, truly, under the bravado and fear, and this whole time I thought it was me that had left the orbit, left the family wounded, but it was Derek, really, that was the missing piece. I was trying to get back to the source all this time without even realizing it, and it was only through finally publishing my first book, sort of defining a core within my family, that I was able to do what no one had been able to do previously, and I gave our lost youngest brother a vehicle for redemption, and it's bewildered and amazed everyone.

Everyone except, of course, for Dan, whose feelings are still hurt, and hurt deeply by Derek, and Derek's inability to do there what he's doing here. But this one is not on me. I'm letting Derek take that one on himself, when he's ready, so that the club of three can finally be complete.

Coda

This will likely be the most difficult passage I think I'll ever write, sitting here and thinking about these last two memoirs and the stories I've told— sometimes implicitly, others maybe accidentally, or then without really understanding the consequences of what I was doing when I trudged blindly on, telling my own story, and accidentally braiding other people's life history along with mine. I didn't mean to biograph others, half the time, and I didn't mean to encapsulate their lives with one snapped frame where I just happened through. The thing is, when I met these people described in my books, and I wrote about them, I meant to capture who they were for me, for that time, in order to tell about that specific time. It had nothing to do with them, really; it was entirely, as all artists will tell you, solipsistic. For that moment, or that sequence. What they left, as an impression, on me, and how I report it.

This is what I've figured out about how life works: Shop at Trader Joe's for your basics, and sometimes you should visit the Goodwill, but not on weekends, and then when you're not looking, life is going to slam you in the back with something you weren't expecting—sometimes good, usually bad—but you get up, you just have to get up, dust off, shake the gravel from your palms, see if there's any blood on your knees when you pull away the fabric, and you just continue. You just do. You have to.

Just do that until you can't.

You try to find love in the moments in between, and sometimes you're the guy doing the knocking over to others, and you should *really* try to stop that if you can, but mostly, we're all in this together, trying to get to the same places, so be kind, be kinder, and when you realize you're being a dick, just stop.

It's easy, when you try. Just stop being a dick.

——

I was able to fix most of the damage I did to my family and friends during my implosion of reason and mental health. It took close to two years, but my friendships with Dougherty and others who witnessed my collapse finally circled around, and my friendships are stronger as a result now, held much more gently and closer to the heart. And I treasure, cherish every conversation with each member of my family, won't allow myself to fall into a passive role or take any exchange "for granted," as the saying goes. Trying for fewer endings, more beginnings. I've taught myself how to hold onto and move through those moments now, and appreciate them as much as possible but then let them go like the quiet beats in a poem, like the last time I saw my mother, when I stayed with her overnight for a reading event in Houston, and how she stood outside in the cold morning in front of her house in order to watch me drive my rental back to Houston Hobby, clutching her robe at 5:00 a.m. in that weird Houston morning mist and waving a sad good-bye to her son, whom she trusts now, though she still looks at me in befuddlement and wonder as to who I am, at my core.

I'm reminded of a flight I was taking through the Midwest, flying into Michigan for an event, and my flight came in really late at night, a cloudy, snowing, cold night, and for the first time on a flight, I was actually scared. It was a small plane, smaller than an MD-80, not a Boeing manufacture but, mind you, I've met quite a few Boeing employees and let's just say they don't exactly inspire trust in the product. (I'm joking, of course.) Nevertheless, there I was, flying into a regional airport in Michigan, and when the plane finally broke cloud cover, all the stars of the universe conspired in the most majestic tapestry of light and wonder that I think I'd witnessed only once before, while out in an estuary on the Gulf Coast, with no lights around, and I could actually see the curvature of the earth, how it corresponded with the heavens. It was magical. Far too much to take in. Sublime. But that night, somewhere over Michigan, I was immediately under the Big Dipper, and it pointed directly at the North Star.

Now, this might not be a big deal to most people, but the wonder I felt at that moment, that the two stars in the Dipper were actually pointing at Polaris—and not slightly off to the left or right, like I've always seen from my vantages either in Texas or on the West Coast, informed by the Coriolis effect—this actually brought me to tears.

It wasn't a lie, after all. All those books I'd read, growing up, about how the Big Dipper actually points *directly* at Polaris, they were telling the truth.

I just needed to be in the right place to see it.

The stars, the compass points, were not, in fact, off a little this way or that; the universal compass was not, in fact, broken or drunken: It was true, and right, finally.

It was like what was happening in my life, at the time. Love was its own gravity that was now turning my compass to the true cardinal points. Love was elemental. Love was Polaris, and it was finally lining up, like the books had promised.

⸺⸰⸺

I keep telling people that my next book will be a cookbook, full of recipes, and maybe dick and fart jokes, as a way to break away from memoir.

But how can you, really? Even with fiction, your backstory seeps into your "imaginative" choices; your friends, associates, and coffee handlers inform your memory, your survivor's tale. I can try to come up with characters entirely foreign to the demands of my experiences and I will still see, when I close my eyes and try to come up with an absolute and pure hero, Brenda Brown, when I stung her on the hip and she popped me on the temple, and in that moment, in that zing of contact, she said, in our eye contact, nonverbally, "I know you; look at you. You're so goddamned cute. Give me more."

And I miss her. So, so much. No one will ever meet anyone like her again.

Or Stephanie, broken in her commitment to playground purity and justice and what she determined was right, right above all else, entitled to her ferocity until the universe decided to beat it out of her, then gave her everything she ever wanted, and her family back.

And my older brother, Dan, when he was an absolute protector, twenty-four years old and 165 pounds, firm meat and fresh out of the army and assured of every threat coming at us with a left hook that could knock out Jesus. Just fucking stand behind him and stand your own ground: He was every solution, every right decision, if you trusted him.

All you need to do is follow him, and fight. Fight like him. It's going to be all right. Just get behind him and hold your own.

Then maybe, Derek, struggling just to feel like he's doing something right.

Or Mom, with her epic melancholia, her sad, sad love for her family. Or Dad, bewildered and trying. Sober now, and just needing to know what he needs to do next, to make up for all that time. Sobriety changed him into a father, and he's been our father these last few years in a way we never thought possible.

And God: Sarah.

Sarah, my devoted, my beloved, my love.

Where did you come from?

She wanted to leave, for a while. "You were safer," she told me one morning, "when you were more pathetic."

Fearless Sarah who once skied like a Kennedy, climbed rock faces like a spider, ran a house of interesting broken people until she became broken herself, and let a sliver of light into her perfect world as the cracks started showing, where I was able to slip in and hold her up before she crumbled along with her upper-middle-class existence.

Sarah in the twilight on a weekend morning, her leg pulled over just so, and the wolf I just helped put at bay, with my love and adoration for her, as she sleeps, for now, for a few hours, and I look at her in that morning light, listening to her breathing, listening to her content, listening to her feeling safe—of all things, with me—and it's this bewildering moment that it's me, with her, now, sitting here, my witness to an incomprehensible beauty and the swirl of chaos in both our lives that has put me, here, sitting in her bedroom, as her lover, and her loved, and has me sitting in it still, as I watch her sleep.

What incredible fiction could have imagined that?

That's the magic of memoir, the impossibility of truth. A crystallization of all these lives, told over hundreds of pages, and you, as a reader, can now walk away.

ACKNOWLEDGMENTS

If you thought reading this was exhausting, you should have heard me talking about it for the last three years. For that, I have to express my deepest gratitude to my immediate family: my brothers, Daniel Martinez and Derek Allen Martinez, both of whom are always a fountain of material without the legal complications. My sisters and their husbands: Mary and Mark Guess, Sylvia and Ruben de los Santos, and Margie and Corwin Moczygamba, and all my nieces and nephews, who are forbidden to read these books until they're at least thirty. My mother, Velva Jean Martinez, and her husband, Robert Swanagan. My fantastic father, Domingo Campos Martinez, who's evolved into a wonderful person and is as yet, for you ladies of a certain age, still single. Of course, my grandmother, Virginia Rubio, who is still at the time of this writing, kicking the shit out of life.

And also, in no particular order, cousins and dear friends who helped me through my travels in Texas: Chris Arteaga and his family, Leo and Delia Zuniga, Richard Alaniz and family, Orlene Ezequial, Erwin Ezequial, Tom and Janis, Orlando Castillo, Julie Hinojosa Collier, John Araujo, and Elva Castillo.

And I would not have made it through the darker parts of this story if it wasn't for my friends and their care as well: Amy Niedrich, Philippe Critot, Christopher Dougherty, Andrew McCarty, Bruce Reid, Camille Ball, Eric Lawson, Jana Pagaran, Kim McIver, and Robb Garner. With special recognition for my dear friend, Julia Sanders, who was there more than a few times when I couldn't even ask for help and let me crash on her couch when it was necessary. Thanks, Jules. Won't forget it. And lastly, and of course, Brenda Brown.

The completion of this book did not come without its heroes: Alice Martell, my super agent, Lara Asher, my good friend and editor, along with the support and encouragement of everyone I've met professionally in the last two years: Louise Erdrich, who pointed out the title in one of our exchanges and nudged the scope of the book into focus. Dave Eggers and everyone at 826 Seattle, including Teri Hein and Alicia

Craven, and of course, my Breadloafian friends: Marcy Pomerance, Ted Conover, and Amy Holman—thank you for your calm words and encouragement. There's also Sergio Troncoso, Jennifer Lynne, Jane Hodges, Justin Ordoñez, Stephen Robinson, Brian Miller, Dr. Antonio Zavaleta, and Junot Díaz. And no self-identified Texan author can escape the orbit of Dagoberto Gilb, a strong voice and proponent for Mexican-American literature, and an even better friend.

Special and eternal thanks also go to Salma Hayek and Jose Tamez, even Jerry Weintraub at HBO.

And, finally, for you, Sarah Berry. This is all gravy, darling.

ABOUT THE AUTHOR

Domingo Martinez is the *New York Times* best-selling author of *The Boy Kings of Texas* and was a finalist for the National Book Award in 2012. *The Boy Kings of Texas* is a Gold Medal Winner of the Independent Publishers Book Award and was nominated for a 2013 Pushcart Prize. It has been optioned by HBO for an original series. Martinez's work has appeared in *Epiphany* literary journal, *Huizache* literary magazine, *New Republic*, and *Saveur* magazine, and he is a regular contributor to *This American Life*. He has appeared on NPR's *All Things Considered* and the *Diane Rehm Show* and was the recipient of the Bernard De Voto Fellowship in Nonfiction at the Bread Loaf Writers' Conference in 2013. Martinez is also a widely sought speaker on topics ranging from the contemporary Latino experience in America to the consequences and processes of writing memoir.

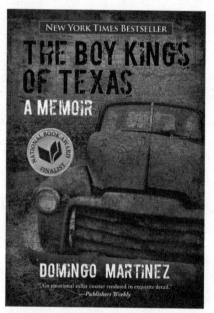